Wires in the Wilderness

Wires in the Wilderness

The Story of the Yukon Telegraph

Bill Miller

VANCOUVER · VICTORIA · CALGARY

Heritage House Publishing Company Ltd.
#108 – 17665 66A Avenue
Surrey, BC V3S 2A7
www.heritagehouse.ca

Library and Archives Canada Cataloguing in Publication
Miller, Bill, 1931-
    Wires in the wilderness: the story of the Yukon Telegraph/Bill Miller.

Includes bibliographical references and index.
ISBN 978-1-894384-58-2

    1. Telegraph—Yukon Territory—History. 2. Yukon Territory—History.
3. Yukon Territory—Biography. 4. Yukon Telegraph Trail (B.C. and Yukon) I. Title.

FC4022.9.Y84M54 2004   971.9'102   C2004-901110-3

Front cover: Lineman Jack Wrathall (NAC PA-95734); telegraph machine, circa
early 1900s, courtesy of the Ricker family of Nanaimo. Back cover: Photos courtesy
of Archie Knill.
Cover and book design by Darlene Nickull.
Edited by Audrey McClellan.

Printed in Canada

Heritage House acknowledges the financial support for its publishing program
from the Government of Canada through the Book Publishing Industry
Development Program (BPIDP), Canada Council for the Arts, and the province
of British Columbia through the British Columbia Arts Council and the Book
Publishing Tax Credit

The Canada Council | Le Conseil des Arts
for the Arts | du Canada

BRITISH
COLUMBIA
ARTS COUNCIL
We acknowledge the support of the Province of British Columbia
through the British Columbia Arts Council

Contents

INTRODUCTION

T he genesis of this book dates to my finding remnants of the old Yukon Telegraph near my home in Atlin, northern British Columbia. This discovery sparked my interest in learning more about this 1,800-mile telegraph line that was built up through the spine of the province 100 years ago to connect the gold fields of the Yukon with southern Canada. I also wanted to become more intimate with the land through which it passed.

All the old-timers in Atlin knew about the telegraph, but few could provide very specific directions as to its location: "it runs along the lake," or "there used to be a trail …," and so forth. People told of coming across wire in the bush, but any trail was long gone, overgrown and forgotten.

Once I had a general idea of the line's route, it was not too difficult to locate sections, to find wire and rotted poles, and to occasionally experience the thrill of coming upon one of the telltale white porcelain insulators. There were places, however, that were so thickly overgrown that the only way to decide where to look for the trail was to pick a space between the larger spruce trees, the ones that would have been alive at the time the telegraph was in operation.

Stimulated by my Atlin success, I headed south into central British Columbia to see what else I could learn about the Yukon Telegraph. At the town and regional historical societies and museums (at Hazelton, Smithers, Prince George, and others), there was great interest in my study. Curators brought out old records and photos, and recounted stories about people who had worked on the telegraph. There were also organizations dedicated to preserving sections of the trail.

Then it was north on the Cassiar Highway to look for remnants of telegraph stations at places where the line ran close by the road, turning west at Dease Lake toward Telegraph Creek. The gravel road to Telegraph Creek, with its 20-degree grades and drop-offs, isn't much less gut-wrenching today than it was when built as a cat trail back in the 1920s. But it was worth it, because to visit Telegraph Creek on the Stikine River is to be transported back to a time of gold rushes and telegraph lines. The local hotel/store/restaurant, the Riversong, in the old Hudson's Bay Company building, is also a museum containing a wealth of information about the telegraph era and Stikine–Cassiar history.

The culmination of my fieldwork was flying into a lake halfway between Atlin and Telegraph Creek near the Nahlin station, and hiking around for a couple of days. I had never before camped in an area where there were so many signs of bears. Their scat was everywhere, evidence of what the linemen who maintained the line through this wilderness lived with all the time. And most of them didn't believe in encumbering themselves with a gun when they went out to "walk the line."

The telegraph through the wilderness was in operation for 35 years, providing communications to the north until replaced by wireless (a different kind of wireless than the one we are acquainted with today). This may not seem like a very long life, but it was long enough for it to acquire an identity, a mythology, and a romantic image. Magazine writers and newspaper reporters painted the picture of dedicated linemen combatting all sorts of problems, from wild animals to horrendous weather, to keep the line open.

Over the years the Yukon Telegraph became "historically significant." It achieved a status that makes it necessary to consider what should be done to preserve this slice of history. Is intellectual preservation (i.e., this book) sufficient, or is some more tangible expression of remembrance warranted? Since it had once been a trail, would that be the most appropriate form of preservation? If a trail is re-established, then what kind of trail? These are questions I hope readers will consider.

Acknowledgements

L ouis LeBourdais wanted to write this book or one much like it, but he never got beyond having a handful of articles published because he died young. John Sutherland also had aspirations of publishing his memoirs of his life trapping and hunting in central British Columbia and as a Yukon Telegraph lineman in the 1930s. The collections of both these men—LeBourdais's in the British Columbia Archives, and Sutherland's (including his many photographs) in the Yukon Archives—were essential sources for this work.

For the use of records and recollections, thanks to the following local museums and archives in central British Columbia: the Hazelton Pioneer Museum, the Bulkley Valley Museum (Smithers), the Stewart Historical Museum, the Fort George Regional Museum (Prince George), and the Quesnel, Vanderhoof, and Burns Lake museums. The attention of the knowledgeable and responsive curators (often volunteers) was greatly appreciated. I am also indebted for their assistance to the staffs of the major repositories: the National Archives of Canada, the British Columbia Archives, and the Yukon Archives.

Diane Solie Smith, Atlin's historian and archivist, was a great inspiration, guide, and critic during the early stage of this project, rewriting and improving sections of my first drafts. I am so sorry that she did not live to share the credit for the finished job. Inspiration also came from Dwight Dodge, the indefatigable force of the Telegraph Trail Preservation Society. My appreciation also goes to all those Atlinites who accompanied me on Telegraph Trail discovery and clearing expeditions. To my hiking companion,

Archie Knill, our foray into the bush will never be forgotten and I thank him for making it possible.

Without the guidance of my wonderful editors at Heritage House, Audrey McClellan and Vivian Sinclair, this book would have been much less readable.

Most especially, I am grateful for the support and tolerance of my life partner and fellow seeker, Nancy Lee Miller.

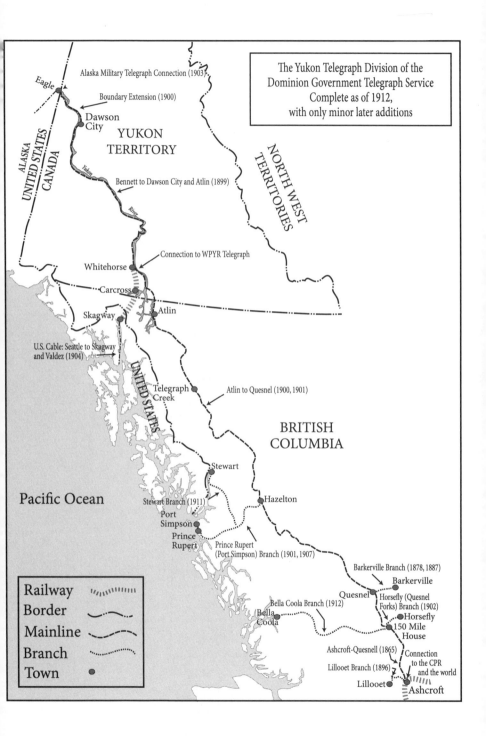

Eagle

Alaska Military Telegraph Connection (1903)

Boundary Extension (1900)

Dawson City

YUKON TERRITORY

NORTH WEST TERRITORIES

The Yukon Telegraph Division of the
Dominion Government Telegraph Service
Complete as of 1912,
with only minor later additions

ALASKA
UNITED STATES
CANADA

Yukon

River

Bennett to Dawson City and Atlin (1899)

Connection to WPYR Telegraph

Whitehorse

Carcross

Skagway

Atlin

U.S. Cable: Seattle to Skagway
and Valdez (1904)

UNITED STATES

Telegraph Creek

Atlin to Quesnel (1900, 1901)

BRITISH COLUMBIA

Stewart

Pacific Ocean

Stewart Branch (1911)

Hazelton

Port Simpson

Prince Rupert

Prince Rupert
(Port Simpson) Branch (1901, 1907)

Barkerville Branch (1878, 1887)

Barkerville

Quesnel

Horsefly (Quesnel
Forks) Branch (1902)

Bella Coola Branch (1912)

Bella Coola

Horsefly

150 Mile House

Ashcroft-Quesnell (1865)

Connection
to the CPR
and the world

Lillooet Branch (1896)

Lillooet

Ashcroft

Railway	⌇⌇⌇⌇⌇
Border	⌇⌇⌇
Mainline	⌇⌇⌇
Branch	⌇⌇⌇
Town	●

CHAPTER 1

Eyes on the Yukon

In 1896, when gold was discovered on Rabbit Creek in the Klondike, Canada was just beginning to recover from a deep recession that had caused 10 percent of the country's population to flee to the United States. The Canadian Pacific Railway, built to unite the country and promote settlement of the west, had as yet done little to populate the thousand miles of prairie between Manitoba and the Rocky Mountains. The newly elected Liberal government of Wilfrid Laurier had pledged to work aggressively to fill this void with farmers, and there were other pressing issues that demanded the attention of Ottawa, not least the unsettled relationship between the Dominion government and British Columbia.

Most of that young province's meagre population of 37,000 whites was clustered in the Vancouver–Victoria area, within 50 miles of the border with the United States.[1] To the north lay the province's vast, sparsely inhabited wilderness,

The Liberals, led by Sir Wilfrid Laurier, formed the national government in 1896 and remained in power until 1911.

13

its rich resources dangling like a tempting lollipop on a long stick, vulnerable to the economic, if not political, domination of the colossus to the south. An anxious federal government was concerned that this gem of the west not be seduced into drifting away from Confederation.

Beyond was the even more remote and unknown Yukon, at the time a district of the North-West Territories. Far away and little valued, the region was not high on the government's agenda. Exploration had been limited to the river valleys; the interior was mostly unmapped and unoccupied. The population consisted of Aboriginal peoples, a few traders and missionaries, and about a thousand transient white prospectors, many of them Americans. Most of the prospectors were working along the Yukon River and its tributaries, such as Fortymile River, on both sides of the border with Alaska. They would jump from strike to strike, from rumour to rumour, seeking the elusive bonanza.

The government's presence in the area was minimal. No taxes were imposed or royalties collected on the gold that was mined, and there were no police or courts. The law of the mining camp prevailed, administered by public meetings called to judge complaints and, when necessary, to decide guilt or innocence. It was a raw form of democracy, a system more acceptable to the American experience than to the Canadian/British tradition of devolved law and authority.[2]

The government in Ottawa had not been completely inattentive to its northern lands. In 1887 Dr. George Dawson of the Geological Survey of Canada led an expedition up the Stikine River in British Columbia to explore the upper Yukon basin. From his observations of the extent of prospecting activity, Dawson concluded that "the prospects for the utilization of this great mining field in the near future appear to me to be very promising."[3] Perhaps because of this prediction, the government began to assert its sovereignty over the region, though it was a slow process.

In 1894 Inspector Charles Constantine of the North West Mounted Police (NWMP) was sent north to assess the need for government authority in the region. He returned the next year with a force of 20 policemen to establish a post opposite the settlement at the mouth of Fortymile River, which was named Fort Constantine. The inspector was soon proud to report to Ottawa from what he labelled "the most northerly military ... post in the British Empire."[4] It may also have been the most isolated.

To return to "civilization" by the most convenient route required a 1,200-mile trip by river steamer down the Yukon River to its mouth, and then an even longer sea voyage to Victoria, Vancouver, or one of the American ports. The entire journey took four weeks; longer in winter when the frozen river was traversed by dogsled, a most uncomfortable and dangerous mode of transportation. During periods when the river was freezing or breaking up, travel was impossible.

Establishing the NWMP presence in the Yukon at that time was fortuitous. Within two years the discovery of significant deposits of gold on Rabbit Creek (later renamed Bonanza Creek) drew a rush of miners from throughout the Yukon and Alaska. And in July 1897, when two gold ships docked—the *Excelsior* in San Francisco and the *Portland* in Seattle—to disgorge their cargoes of miners with bags of Yukon gold, the world soon learned of the fabulous riches to be found there.

The Rush for Gold

The stampede to the Klondike had begun, as hordes of men (and some women) from all parts of Canada and America and from the far lands of Europe and Asia headed north, risking all to seek their fortunes, determined to be in the vanguard to stake claims. Some estimates put the total number as high as 100,000, perhaps 75 percent from the United States, where sections of the economy were still depressed. In Seattle, for example, unemployment continued to be high, and even when a job was available, it paid slave wages.

There were several routes to the gold fields. The most popular were the two trails that started from Dyea and Skagway in the Alaska Panhandle and went through the coastal mountains, via the Chilkoot and White passes, to Bennett City in British Columbia. There the gold seekers built boats for the 550-mile voyage down the Yukon River waterways to the new gold town of Dawson City. Those with more resources could take the longer, but less arduous, sea route to

St. Michael, Alaska, near the mouth of the Yukon River, and then a steamship up the river to Dawson City.

When the magnitude of the stampede became known, the Dominion government recognized that it must expand its control over the Yukon without delay. Although it had not always acted with alacrity concerning the interests of the north, on this occasion Ottawa was quick to respond. By February 1898 the NWMP contingent had increased to 200 men.

The Mounties' task was daunting. Their primary mission was to show the flag and establish the rule of law, to prevent the kind of Wild West anarchy that had been allowed to develop in so many frontier towns in the States. Already Skagway had become a lawless and dangerous boom town to be avoided if at all possible, and the threats of American jingoism and expansionism also justified concern. Many Canadians recalled the California and Oregon examples of America acquiring new land through aggressive settlement. The border with Alaska was still in dispute, and it was feared that the three companies of army soldiers stationed in Alaska, some as close as Circle City, might advance American claims in the Yukon.[5] The American government, spurred on by the "yellow" press, was in the mood to expand and soon embarked on a war with Spain, its first major imperial adventure. There were also reports of a cabal in Alaska, the Order of the Midnight Sun, that harboured plans to "liberate the Yukon from British tyranny."[6]

Initially the NWMP set up posts at entry points along the trails to collect customs duties and to supervise the influx of gold seekers, primarily to ensure that they had enough supplies to survive for a year. In addition, they were assigned tasks that went well beyond their usual responsibilities. They carried the mail and operated the post offices, "were the original recorders of mining claims and of land titles, and they acted as coroners, Indian agents, health officers, tax collectors, jailers, magistrates, guards for the Dawson banks, and later as returning officers at elections."[7]

The police also tried to avert disasters and save lives by controlling passage through dangerous stretches of the Yukon River. At Whitehorse Rapids, for example, they enforced the edict that every boat must employ an experienced pilot through the

From their post at the summit of the Chilkoot Pass, the North West Mounted Police controlled the passage into Canada of gold seekers headed to the Klondike.

rapids. With all these duties, the red-serge line was stretched thin, even with 200 men. Fortunately, help was on the way. To back up the police, Ottawa organized a contingent of 200 regular army soldiers to form the Yukon Field Force. By the fall of 1898, after travelling cross country to Vancouver, by steamship to Wrangel, then up the Stikine River and over the Teslin Trail, the Force had set up camp at Fort Selkirk, 175 miles upriver from Dawson City.

More government officials were sent north, and in June 1898, when the Yukon Territory was separated from the North-West Territories, a nascent form of government was established. It consisted of a commissioner, appointed by Ottawa, who in turn selected a council. This system was not popular with many of the "democratic" American miners.

Communications with the Yukon

As the Dominion government expanded its presence and began to assert its authority, one thing became clear: There had to be

A detachment of the Yukon Field Force guards a gold shipment at Dawson City.

a more efficient method of communication between Ottawa and its officers. The unreliable, slow mail system via Skagway and the Yukon River was unacceptable.

Even communication within the Yukon was a problem. Most of the police detachments were situated along the Yukon River, the route taken by the bulk of the gold seekers. Because the distance between posts was 30 to 50 miles or more, communication with headquarters and the other posts was slow and erratic. A faster and more reliable system was needed—"urgently needed," according to the comptroller of the NWMP, who suggested that a telegraph or telephone line be constructed from the summit of the Chilkoot Pass to Dawson City, a distance of about 600 miles. It should be an inexpensive line, he wrote, a light wire suspended from standing trees that could later be abandoned.[8]

Parliament agreed that a telegraph line should be built and, in anticipation of the project, petitioned the U.S. government to permit access through the Alaska Panhandle.[9] But it took the politicians a while to decide on the details. They had initially given the impression that private enterprise might be involved by granting non-exclusionary charters to two companies that proposed to build lines from Alaska to Dawson City.[10] The Canadian Pacific Railway, whose telegraph system stretched into British Columbia, also expressed interest in operating a line to the north from its station at Ashcroft.[11]

Some government officials endorsed the idea of private capital building the telegraph line. A.G. Blair, the minister of railways and canals, proclaimed, "The government is extremely anxious that the work shall be taken up by private enterprise."[12] Other members of the Laurier government disagreed, and while charters were being granted and proposals considered, the government had already decided that it would build and operate the Yukon Telegraph system. Although they did not admit it publicly, the Liberals realized early on that the line was not likely to be profitable as a commercial enterprise. Its raison d'être was to provide an essential public service for the police and other government officials, and for the people of the Yukon.

After much delay, in March 1899 the minister of public works, J. Israel Tarte, finally submitted a plan to the Privy Council to improve communications with the Klondike. He proposed building a telegraph line between Bennett City, on the Canadian side of the passes through the coastal mountains, and Dawson City. At Bennett City the government line would connect to the telegraph of the White Pass and Yukon Route's railway (WPYR), which was being constructed from Skagway to Whitehorse. At Skagway, messages would be transferred to the first Canadian boat sailing for Vancouver or Victoria, a trip that usually took about four days.

The route of the line north from Bennett City would be along the Yukon River, connecting to the police posts along the way. The estimated cost of the project was $135,750, with construction to be completed by the fall of 1899 before the rivers iced up.

Also included in the plan were improvements to navigation on the Yukon River waterways that would make travel safer and more reliable. The water level would be raised at places where steamers became grounded, and dangerous boulders that threatened boats would be removed. Five locations were listed: Caribou Crossing, where a dam was needed to raise the water level, and the rapids at Six Mile River (between Tagish Lake and Marsh Lake), Thirty Mile River, Five Finger Rapids, and Rink Rapids.

Not included, however, was work to improve passage through the most perilous section of all, the Whitehorse Rapids. The only solution to overcoming the dangers posed by these rapids was to build a dam and lock, at the prohibitive cost of $500,000. Consequently, smaller boats, under the guidance of experienced pilots, would continue to "shoot the rapids"; larger riverboats would dock above, where passengers and cargo would be unloaded for the four-mile portage by tramline to the bottom of the rapids. There they would board a second boat to complete the trip to Dawson City.

The plan also called for an "examination" of an "all-Canadian" telegraph connection through British Columbia that would avoid U.S. territory, precluding further reliance on the Bennett City–Skagway line. On March 13, 1899, the Privy Council gave its approval for the construction of the telegraph line and the improvements to river navigation.[13]

It was the beginning of a project that within six months would reduce the time it took a message to travel between Dawson City and Ottawa from one month to less than one week. And within two more years, after a thousand miles of telegraph wire had been strung through the wilds of British Columbia, the interval would be reduced to minutes.

CHAPTER 2

Bennett City to Dawson City, 1899

J.B. Charleson was assigned to superintend the construction of the telegraph line from Bennett City to Dawson City. He was born in Quebec in 1836 of Scottish parents, and his initials stood for John Baptiste, a name not usually associated with Scottish ancestry.[1] It might suggest a French-Canadian lineage, but this was not the case. As the story was passed down through his family, the midwife at his birth did not think he would survive, so she rushed him to a priest to be baptized. The priest, of course, was French Catholic.[2]

Charleson was not selected to oversee the Yukon Telegraph because of his distinction as a builder of telegraph lines or his knowledge of working conditions in the far north. Rather, he owed his position to the political patronage system in vogue at the time.

A long-time Liberal Party supporter, Charleson had held both elected and appointed offices. When the Liberals, led by fellow Quebecer Wilfrid Laurier, gained national power in 1896, they rewarded his loyalty by appointing him supervisor of construction in the Department of Public Works (DPW). J. Israel Tarte presided over the department, and he assigned his deputy, Aureal Gobeil, to oversee Charleson's direction of the work.

Although he had little construction experience, Charleson was no incompetent political hack. In his 63 years he had accumulated work experiences—as a ship's carpenter, as the operator of a lumber brokering business, and as the owner of a newspaper—that adequately equipped him for his new job.[3] He had shown prowess as an organizer and as an expediter, two skills that would be severely tested.

Notwithstanding, the government was taking a chance with Charleson. Building a telegraph line through an unknown wilderness under adverse conditions was an undertaking fraught with the possibility of failure and embarrassment. The Opposition, always poised to criticize, questioned the government's policies, as did those who argued that private capital should have been employed.

That Tarte assigned direct responsibility through Deputy Minister Gobeil to Charleson seems to prove the importance of the project to the government. Or perhaps it is simply evidence of Tarte's evaluation of the officials of the DPW's Telegraph Service. For whatever reasons, D.H. Keeley, the general superintendent of the service, and Louis Coste, the department's chief engineer, were not involved directly with the construction of the Yukon Telegraph. With the exception of helping to move construction supplies, they seem to have been shut out of the project.

Charleson's instructions were to build a 550-mile[4] telegraph line from Bennett City to Dawson City during the short 1899 construction season. Because there were no roads, it was essential that the area's waterways be used to move the work crew and construction materials. And as the northern climate usually limits travel on the rivers and lakes to less than six months, between break-up in May and freeze-up in October, no time could be wasted. Several factors would determine if communications to Dawson City would be established before winter set in: an early spring start, the timely arrival of materials at the work sites, and the stringing of wire at the average rate of five miles per day.

The progress of the White Pass and Yukon Route's railway (WPYR), under construction at the time from Skagway to Whitehorse, was also essential to the success of the project. The railway's telegraph line had to be completed as far as Bennett City in order for the government's line to be connected to it so that messages could be transmitted to Skagway. At the time the telegraph project was approved, construction of the railway had reached the summit of the White Pass. The most difficult sections, those that required blasting rocky ledges and tunnelling through mountains, had been conquered. All that remained to connect the government's line to Skagway was another 17 miles of track from the summit to Bennett City.[5]

Arrival in Bennett City

The Privy Council's tardiness in granting final approval for the project made an early start problematic. However, with admirable speed and a minimum of red tape, not normally attributes of government undertakings, construction supplies were ordered: 600 miles of No. 8 (5 mm) wire, hundreds of boxes of insulators and side blocks (supports for the insulators), and provisions for the 100-man workforce. When supplies, some of which came from as far away as Great Britain, arrived in Skagway, they were to be shipped by the White Pass railway, or hauled over the Chilkoot Pass, to Bennett City.

On March 29 Charleson arrived in Skagway accompanied by some of his staff: chief engineer J.C. Tache, construction superintendent J.F. Richardson, and his private secretary Joseph E. Gobeil (brother of the deputy minister). Also arriving from the east were about 20 workmen, the nucleus of the construction crew.

To reach Bennett City, Charleson's party had to cross the coastal mountains, much as the gold seekers who preceded them had done. But their passage was made immeasurably easier by the railway, which was now available to take them to the summit. From there, packhorses, obligingly provided by the White Pass's construction superintendent, M.J. Heney, moved their gear the rest of the way. Despite heavy snow, within four days the entire party and its 17 tons of supplies and baggage were in Bennett City.

Although the bulk of the stampeders had passed through the previous year, Bennett continued to give the impression of a town bursting with energy and optimism: the streets alive with humanity and hope, the entrepreneurs still smelling out opportunities, and the hotels and saloons prospering. Most of the gold seekers were

Chief Engineer J.C. Tache on the dock at Skagway prior to going over the pass to Bennett City to begin work on the Yukon Telegraph.

building boats to continue their journey to the Klondike after break-up; others were preparing to travel a shorter route to investigate the promising gold fields around Atlin, British Columbia.

After removing seven feet of snow, the telegraph men started to erect a storage building for the tons of construction materials to follow. The cadre of workers who came north with Charleson was quickly filled out with local hires. There was no shortage of available hands from among the men who had exhausted their stakes and were now forced to work for little more than room and board. The two dollars a day the government was paying offered a way, albeit a very slow way, for some of the unsuccessful gold seekers to accumulate a new stake with which to continue their quests. For others, the job meant a chance to get out of the north, because any man who stayed until the line was completed was promised a free ticket south.

As for the better-paying staff positions, to the prevailing system of patronage was added a considerable dose of nepotism. Deputy Minister Gobeil found a good job for his brother Joseph as Charleson's secretary, and eventually no fewer than seven members of Charleson's extended family were on the payroll. Sons, a daughter, a brother, and even a nephew were employed.

Liberal members of Parliament did not hesitate to recommend political appointees, some with unfortunate results. One young man, sent out to be a timekeeper, refused to work when he was not provided with a private tent and had to be sent back east.[6] Later, when operators and linemen were being hired, Charleson was advised to make no appointments without clearance from the Honourable Hugh Bostock, MP from British Columbia.

The route selected for the telegraph line started from the south end of Lake Bennett and followed the shorelines of lakes and rivers all the way to Dawson City. The plan was for the wire to be strung close to the shore and for the construction camp to be transported on scows as the work progressed.

Waiting for Break-up

Even if the scows had been available when the construction party arrived at Bennett City, it was too early in the season for them to be put to use. The lake ice was still thick and solid. Sleighs had been included in the first shipments of supplies in anticipation of this condition. Rather than wait for the lake to clear, Charleson used the sleighs, pulled by horses, to move construction materials to advanced work sites, avoiding the tedious task of transporting them by pack train over ground covered with melting snow and mud. Sufficient wire had not yet arrived, but once again the White Pass provided assistance, loaning the government 40 miles of its wire, which the sleighs moved north over the ice.

The ice-encased waterways presented another advantage. The improvements to navigation included in the project, to allow for safer and more reliable travel, were best done when the rivers and lakes were frozen and at their lowest levels. Blasting rock impediments and building dams would be more difficult, if not impossible, after break-up, when the streams became torrents of water and ice.

Chief Engineer Tache was placed in charge of the improvements and quickly moved with a crew to Caribou Crossing (the name was

Building the construction scows at Lake Bennett that were used to transport men and materials down the Yukon River.

shortened to Carcross in 1904), a small Native settlement at the north end of Lake Bennett. When water was low during the summer months, steamers were liable to become stranded on sandbars in the channel between Bennett and Nares lakes.

Assessing the situation, Tache wrote to Charleson that the water level at Caribou Crossing could be raised by building a six-foot-high dam to close off a blind slough in the channel. His men were already at work on the dam and were also putting the finishing touches on a large telegraph office. In addition, he reported that he had sent another crew downstream to blast out boulders at Six-Mile River (between Tagish Lake and Marsh Lake). Shortly, he wrote, "the whole of the channel will be clear."[7]

The main body of men waiting at Bennett for break-up was employed building a large telegraph office, a supply depot, and the six scows to be used as a floating base camp. Each scow was 40 feet long by 14 feet wide, with a large, heated, canvas tent on its deck. Two of the six scows would serve as sleeping quarters for the men, one as a dining hall, and one as a commissary, and two would be used to store supplies.[8]

The advantage of using scows was that they could be moved as the work progressed. After the work crew went ashore each day to string wire, the scows would be towed to meet them at day's end. This arrangement greatly simplified the housing and feeding of the men and cut down on the time spent going to and returning from the work sites. A "small steamboat"[9] was acquired at Bennett City to move the scows and transport construction materials and provisions from the supply depot. When the work got beyond the Whitehorse Rapids, Charleson leased the steamer *W.S. Stratton* for the same purpose. This method proved far superior to the alternative of using pack trains and was particularly effective the farther the work progressed from Bennett.[10]

The *W.S. Stratton* transported everything needed for the work (wire, insulators, side blocks, and spikes) except the telegraph poles. The first choice for supports to carry the wire was standing trees, trimmed and topped off. When trees were not available or were not properly spaced along the cutline, workers erected poles, supplied to the job site by a contractor. With an average spacing of 225 feet (or 24 poles to the mile), more than 13,000 trees and poles were required for the entire project.

The work was broken down into specific tasks. Twenty men were assigned to clear the right-of-way, 8 to trim trees, 30 to dig holes and erect poles where needed, and 12 to attach the insulators and wire. Foremen, scowmen, and cooks made up the rest of the 92-man work crew.[11] The workday was 10 hours, six days a week (no work was permitted on Sunday), and the pay was $2.00 a day, later raised to $2.60, with lodging and meals.

Construction Begins

As soon as the ice began to break up on Lake Bennett, the construction scows were on the move. The crew started stringing wire on the east side of the lake and soon crossed the 60th parallel into the Yukon. The first significant water crossing, a span of 650 feet, was at Caribou Crossing, where the line passed to the north side of Nares Lake. To allow clearance for the tall smokestacks of the river steamers, the wire was suspended from 69-foot poles. Because trees of this height were not available, several smaller trees were spliced together and banded with wire.

Work continued along the shores of Nares Lake and Tagish Lake and down Six-Mile River to the settlement of Tagish. In his May 25 progress report to the minister of public works, Charleson

27

listed the project's achievements: the dam at Caribou Crossing was finished, the obstructions in Six-Mile River had been removed, and the telegraph line from Tagish to Skagway was open "over your own wire."[12] This last claim was somewhat disingenuous, since the line between Bennett City and Skagway was owned and operated by the WPYR. Apparently, the White Pass had strung its telegraph line to Bennett before it built the tracks, which did not reach there for another two weeks.

In early June Charleson received a visit from Louis Coste, the DPW's chief engineer, who had played no role in planning and carrying out the Yukon Telegraph project. Charleson viewed his appearance at this late date as an effort by the department's bureaucrats to inspect his work. It was a barely cordial meeting. According to Charleson, Coste, "swelled with his own importance," commented that the work should have been done the year before and at less cost. To which Charleson replied that under "Costly Coste" it would have been a more costly job. This was not the last example of animosity between Charleson and officials of the department.[13]

As the work progressed, telegraph offices were built at intervals, usually at settlements and North West Mounted Police posts. Most were simple one-room cabins barely sufficient for housing two men, an operator and a lineman. The station at Bennett was larger because it was the transfer point for messages going over the railway's wire and was, for the time at least, the headquarters of the Yukon Telegraph.

The carpenters also built a more elaborate structure at Caribou Crossing to provide space for the local post office, the NWMP detachment, and the office of the mining recorder. At Tagish, the small station on the west side of Six-Mile River was connected to the police post on the opposite shore by a "loop line," a wire strung across the stream and then back to the main line.

So far the scows had been able to move freely on the waterways, but when they reached Marsh Lake work came to an abrupt halt. Although the calendar said it was June, usually the beginning of summer, the lake ice was still too thick for the boats to break through. An exasperated Charleson expressed his frustration in his report of June 11: "Everything seems to be paralised [*sic*] here owing to the lowness of the water and the coldness of the season."[14] When the ice finally relinquished its hold, the scows were able to move, and work resumed down the lake.

Moving down the Yukon River

At the foot of Marsh Lake the scows entered the Yukon River, which they would follow the rest of the way to Dawson City. The telegraph line made few deviations from the sinuous course of the river, and the wire was usually strung not more than a mile inland. Nearing Whitehorse, at Miles Canyon and at the rapids below, the first hazardous impediments to the scows' movement were confronted. The narrow canyon between steep basalt cliffs could be safely navigated with the use of cables, held by men on shore, which kept the boats in the middle of the channel. The rapids were more formidable.

Early miners had named this stretch of river the Whitehorse Rapids because the wildly churning waters resembled the flowing, rippling manes of running white horses. Many boats had been wrecked here and lives lost.

The commodious telegraph office at Caribou Crossing (Carcross) also housed a detachment of the NWMP.

The channel is full of projecting rocks, so that the whole surface is broken, foaming and tossing, and there are many strong conflicting currents and eddies. At the end of these rapids, which extend for a quarter of a mile or so, is a narrow gorge in the rocks, through which the whole volume of water is forced. This is said to be only twenty or thirty feet wide ... Through this water plunges at a tremendous velocity—probably thirty miles an hour—forming roaring, foaming, tossing, lashing waves which somehow make the name White Horse seem appropriate.[15]

When the Yukon Telegraph's scows arrived at the start of the rapids, they were unloaded, and an experienced pilot successfully manoeuvred the cumbersome crafts, one at a time, through the turbulent waters. Workers hauled the cargo a few miles beyond the foot of the rapids to the docks at Whitehorse. Here the construction party paused to evaluate the first 100 miles of its work.

With the exception of the delay caused by the late ice on Marsh Lake, no major problems had developed, and, most gratifying, the system of using scows as a base camp had proved a success. The only difficulty was caused by some construction supplies not arriving as scheduled, and as a result Charleson was not pleased with the services of the White Pass railway.

Construction of the railway had made good progress, reaching Bennett City on July 6. This should have greatly simplified the movement of the telegraph's freight, as it no longer had to be hauled partway by pack train or wagon, but such was not the case. According to Charleson, construction materials were not being shipped to Bennett when they were needed, as the railway had agreed. The initially cordial and helpful relationship between the two projects had broken down, deteriorating to such an extent that the WPYR was threatening to sue the government for breach of contract.

The problem resulted from a misunderstanding. The railway was under the impression that it had an exclusive contract to ship the telegraph's freight from Skagway to Bennett. Its representative in Ottawa complained to Deputy Minister Gobeil that Charleson, by sending some supplies over the competing Chilkoot tramline, was not adhering to the contract. Charleson countered that if indeed there was a contract, it was the White Pass that had broken it by its failure to move the government's freight in a timely manner. He charged that there were 90 tons of freight sitting on sidings that the railway was unable, or unwilling, to move. Charleson had anticipated these possible delays and had fortuitously applied the "old adage that it is unsafe to have all your eggs in one basket" by sending some of the supplies over the Chilkoot Pass. He also complained that the railway's freight charges were excessive.[16]

In any event, the railway continued to move most of the telegraph's freight, and the disagreement became moot after the WPYR purchased the tramline and had it dismantled. There was no longer any competition.

At Whitehorse, after pausing for a few days to reload and reorganize, the work crew continued on toward Dawson City, 450 miles downriver. The efficiency of the operation was now greatly improved, and the men were soon stringing wire at the rate of 5 to 10 miles a day, depending upon the difficulty of the terrain and the distance of the cutline from the shore. They needed to move quickly because in less than three months the river would begin to freeze over.

From Whitehorse the line continued on the west side of the river. In an effort to make better time, at places where the Yukon made wide sweeping turns, doubling back upon itself, workers strung the line across the necks of the projections, as at the Jim Boss cut-off above Lake Laberge. By routing the line more than a mile inland, they saved several miles of wire.

Notwithstanding the cut-offs, following the river added many miles to the project compared to going cross-country. For example, from Bennett City the railway and the telegraph line ran parallel on the east side of the lake until they reached Caribou Crossing, where they diverged. The White Pass headed north toward Whitehorse (on about the same course as the later highway), while the telegraph went east, following the wide arc of the lakes and the Yukon River. The railroad's direct route was shorter, 45 miles to the telegraph's 70 miles. Farther along, the disparities were even greater. Below Lake Laberge the river makes another wide swing to the east before reaching Carmacks. The direct route from Whitehorse to Carmacks (followed by the present highway) is 120 miles; the water route is 200 miles.

When Charleson and the engineers planned the location of the telegraph line, they may have considered using the shorter overland route, but it was quickly rejected because one of the initial justifications, if not the primary one, for building the line was to provide communications with the NWMP outposts. Since most of these posts were situated on the river route used by the gold seekers, and now by the steamboats, that was where the line had to be built. In addition, building cross-country would have precluded using the scows. Construction materials and the base camp would have had to be moved by pack train through an unappealing environment of muskegs, swamps, and numerous stream crossings.

Oblivious to these considerations, the Opposition seized on the extra miles of work and wire as fodder for the critical cannons of its newspapers. British Columbia's voice of conservatism, the *Victoria Colonist*, lamented the poor planning of the Liberal bureaucrats, which led to inefficiency and waste resulting from the telegraph line following the winding river when a perfectly good road, 140 miles shorter, was available.[17]

Had the newspaper's report been more objective, it would have explained that this "road" existed only during winter months, when the swamps, muskegs, and creeks that it traversed were frozen. The water route, on the other hand, had the advantage of being available year-round for travel, except during freeze-up and break-up. Even during these periods there was a passable trail system between stations for the maintenance of the telegraph wire.

Where Lake Laberge emptied into the Thirty Mile section of the Yukon River, the line crossed to the east side for about 30 miles, then back to the west before reaching the settlement of Hootalinqua, where the Teslin River (also called the Hootalinqua) joins the Yukon. By July 24 the construction party, using more cut-offs to avoid several wide bends, had reached Big Salmon River. More than 200 miles of wire had been strung; 350 miles remained to reach Dawson City.

If there were no unforeseen delays, supplies arrived as needed, and the wire continued to be strung at the rate of five miles per day, the job just might be completed before the end of September. There was, however, a change in plans that threatened this schedule. Charleson had been given an additional assignment: to build a 75-mile branch line to the new gold town of Atlin.

The Line to Atlin

Atlin, where gold had been discovered the previous year, offered an attractive alternative to many of the stampeders headed to the Klondike. It was closer and easier to get to, and because it was a newer strike, it provided a better chance of staking a lucrative claim. The trickle of men who turned eastward from Bennett City or from the railway station a few miles away at Log Cabin soon became a rush. In August 1898, 1,300 out of 2,000 men working on the White Pass railway laid down their tools, or took them with them, and headed for the Atlin gold fields.[18]

A year later, as the settlement at Atlin grew, it petitioned to be connected to the telegraph. Ottawa agreed and, it seems almost casually, added the job to Charleson's already demanding assignment. A crew, drawn in part from the experienced workers, was quickly assembled at Tagish, where the connection was to be made. Charleson put James Trodden in charge of the work and sent engineer Aurelien Boyer ahead to scout out the land. The plan was to route the line eastward over an old Native trail, then south following Little Atlin Lake and Atlin Lake to the gold town.[19]

The conditions of work on the branch line were different, as pack trains were the primary means of transporting the work camp and construction supplies. No longer dependent upon and tied to the scows, the telegraph builders were free to locate the line farther inland. Nevertheless, along the lake sections the wire was usually strung within a mile of the shore.

The Deadly River

As the Yukon River crew advanced toward Dawson City, it continued to build telegraph stations at critical locations: settlements, river crossings, and police posts. At Canyon City (near Miles Canyon) and farther downriver at Ogilvie, the police shared the telegraph buildings. At most other locations the telegraph offices were built near the police posts, and if they were not on the same side of the river, the police were connected by a loop line.

The Yukon below Whitehorse Rapids was not a dangerous river, but there were a few places that could be perilous. Twenty miles beyond Carmacks lurked the towering rocky protuberances of Five Finger Rapids, followed by Rink Rapids. With great care, experienced boatmen could navigate safely through the fingers. Some telegraph men who attempted passage on their own were not so lucky. Within a week, two lives were lost.

On August 2, according to the *Dawson Daily News*, a Louis Tache, identified as the telegraph's "chief engineer,"[20] drowned at Five Finger Rapids. The tragedy occurred when Tache and three other men attempted to shoot the right channel of the rapids, and his canoe was swamped.

The canoe was upset while plunging over the first rapids before the falls, throwing the occupants into the river. Mr. Tache struck out to swim ashore with one of the men, while the other two wisely clung to the canoe.

The steamer *Merwin* was, at the time, ascending the left channel by means of cable, and the captain, seeing the two men struggling in the rapids, without a moments hesitation slipped the cable and steamed to their assistance.

Tache's companion reached the right bank in safety, and the *Merwin*'s crew made a heroic effort to reach Tache but without avail, and the gallant swimmer sank from exhaustion and was drowned before their eyes …

The two men clinging to the canoe were rescued by several men in a skiff some distance below the rapids.[21]

Five days later Five Finger Rapids claimed another life. Frank Ricord, a construction foreman, drowned under similar circumstances.[22] Actually, Rink Rapids was as dangerous as Five Finger, if not more so. It is described as "a series of haystacks caused by a shallow reef and rocks."[23] In all, four men lost their lives to the river during the course of building the Yukon Telegraph.[24]

Beyond Five Finger and Rink Rapids the going was easier, and soon the wire was strung to connect the Yukon Field Force's encampment at Fort Selkirk. Then the cutline took a sharp turn and went inland about two miles to avoid Victoria Rock, which made following the shoreline impractical, and on September 7 the wire reached the NWMP post at the Selwyn River. With only 130 miles of line remaining to be built, Charleson predicted that the telegraph would be in Dawson City by September 25.[25]

The Workers Revolt

Charleson's optimism was soon tested when disgruntled workers threatened to derail his schedule. The months of hard labour—60-hour workweeks without respite or recreation—had begun to tell on the men. Their discontent boiled over and half the crew went on strike, protesting low pay and poor-quality food. Although earlier their wages had been increased to $2.60 per day, they demanded more.

Charleson, ignoring what were probably legitimate grievances that could have been negotiated, retorted that the strikers only wanted an excuse to quit because as they neared Dawson they saw an opportunity to join the gold rush.[26] He quickly hired replacements from the ready pool of men in Dawson, and the work continued without further interruption.

Some of the now unemployed strikers left the area and headed south; others struck out for the gold fields. Although they had not stayed until the line was completed, those who went south were given travel vouchers as they had been promised when hired. Those who went to Dawson were denied their vouchers by a vindictive Charleson.[27]

The crew continued to string the wire down the west side of the river, which was growing in width and volume. At some point they would have to make a crossing to Dawson on the east side, but because of the considerable span, Charleson was concerned about an overhead wire's vulnerability to the smokestacks of the riverboats, which had already taken down sections of wire at crossings. In August the steamer *Australia* had made a bad landing at Miles Canyon and torn out four pole sections of wire (900 feet). Later, the *Nora* took out seven sections (over 1,500 feet).

Charleson wanted to use underwater cable for the crossing and requested the department order 3,000 feet of cable. This recommendation led to a rather curious communication: Deputy Minister Gobeil wrote directly to Prime Minister Laurier, asking his approval to spend $400 to purchase the cable. The mystery is why Minister Tarte was not involved in the decision, and why the prime minister was consulted on such a minor matter. [28]

In any event, Charleson did not get the cable and was obliged to choose the best location to make the crossing to Dawson with an overhead wire. He and his engineers settled on Ogilvie, an island 48 miles above the town, where the longest span would be 1,600 feet. The *Stratton* was employed to carry the wire across the fast-flowing river and almost capsized in the attempt.[29] The low-lying island was also selected as the site for a telegraph office—an unfortunate decision, as it turned out to be vulnerable to the river's flood waters.

Connected to the Outside World

As the wire approached Dawson, the *Dawson Daily News* sent a reporter to the construction camp to cover the last few days leading up to the great event. He watched as the work advanced, getting closer and closer. When each day's work was finished, a telegraph key was attached to the end of the wire in an attempt to raise the operator at Bennett City. Night after night there was no answer. Then one night, only a few miles from Dawson, the operator sent out the same message, with little hope of a reply.

Accustomed to disappointment he was about to turn away when the little rubber disc upon which his hand had rested, lifted itself up and fell back with a sharp click upon the brass receiver … At last, the dead thing had come alive. Instantly the quickened interest of the little group of telegraph men was concentrated on the instrument and instantly the *News* man, alive to the fact that the hour for which he had waited for so long had arrived, filed his message to the *News* man at Skagway [actually Bennett City]: "The line is connected. Rush your stuff." And in answer, with the speed of the lightning, came the news from … South Africa, and London, and Washington and all the world.[30]

The line to Dawson City was completed at 5:13 a.m. on September 28, 1899, when the wire reached the telegraph office and the words began to flow.[31]

Congratulations poured in. Grandiloquent claims were made for the importance of the event. The *Dawson Daily News* hyperbolized: "From this day we take up our part in the great play of the world."[32] Not to be outdone, F.Z. Congdon, acting commissioner of the Yukon, congratulated the minister of public works on "connecting the golden north with older Canada."[33] The Vancouver and Victoria newspapers were no less ecstatic—at least those with Liberal Party allegiances.

The line to Atlin reached its destination a week later, prompting the *Atlin Claim* to extend muted congratulations. The newspaper, labelled by Charleson a mouthpiece of the Conservative Party, admitted that the government had "made a good showing in completing the work in so short a time."[34]

At the end of each workday a telegraph operator connected his key to the end of the wire to report the day's progress to headquarters.

Charleson, a man with limited construction experience, had pulled off a major coup for the Liberal government and for the Yukon. He and his men had successfully built a 550-mile telegraph line through a distant and little-known land, overcoming many problems, not least the logistics of moving large quantities of construction materials over long distances. The job had been accomplished within the time demanded, the short construction season of 1899. Allowing for the additional cost of the Atlin line, the total cost of $146,937[35] was considered to be on budget, as the original estimate had been $135,750.

Messages could now be transmitted instantly from Dawson and all the in-between stations to Bennett City, and then to Skagway. In Skagway the telegrams were transcribed and put on the first Canadian ship bound for Victoria or Vancouver, a voyage that usually took four days.

Completion of the Yukon Telegraph to Dawson accomplished the government's immediate objective of establishing faster communications with the Yukon. The second stage of the plan was to fulfill the patriotic mission of creating the all-Canadian telegraph system by extending the line from Atlin to connect to the transcontinental line at Quesnel. Work on bridging this 870-mile gap through the harsh terrain of British Columbia would start the next year.

As winter approached, however, it was now time to find out how well the new telegraph line would perform. All that had been accomplished so far was to string a fragile strand of iron wire, not as thick as a child's finger, through 550 miles of wilderness. The line was vulnerable to the environment that hovered around it and to the treacherous weather that would assault it without mercy.

When the din of summer construction had passed, it was left to the telegraph men—the operators and linemen who remained—to deal with any problems that affected the line. As the silence of winter descended upon their isolated cabins, they alone would struggle with the land and the elements to keep the line operating.

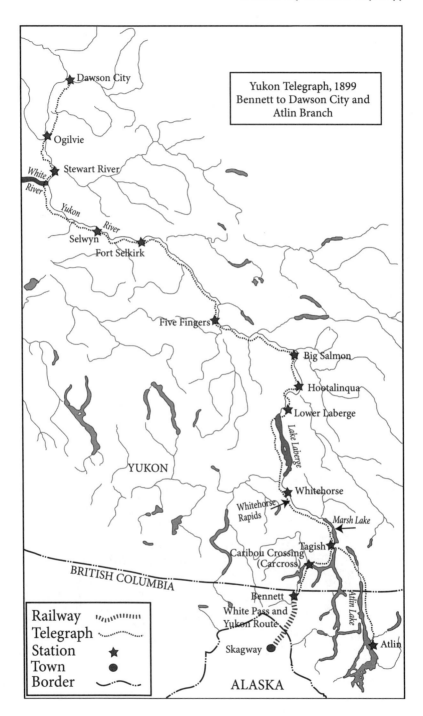

Yukon Telegraph, 1899
Bennett to Dawson City and
Atlin Branch

Dawson City

Ogilvie

White River

Stewart River

Yukon River

Selwyn

Fort Selkirk

Five Fingers

Big Salmon

Hootalinqua

Lower Laberge

Lake Laberge

YUKON

Whitehorse

Whitehorse Rapids

Marsh Lake

Tagish

Caribou Crossing (Carcross)

BRITISH COLUMBIA

Atlin Lake

Bennett

White Pass and Yukon Route

Skagway

Atlin

Railway
Telegraph
Station
Town
Border

ALASKA

CHAPTER 3

The First Winter, 1899–1900

The work of building the telegraph line was completed just in time, as slush ice was beginning to form on the rivers. Freeze-up was sudden and severe, and a hard winter was soon upon the land. Navigation on the Yukon became impossible, and boats and scows unprepared for the early winter were caught in ice jams.[1] The *W.S. Stratton*, which had played such a vital role in the success of the telegraph project, was one of the victims. Less than a month after

The sternwheeler W.S. Stratton *towed the work scows along the Yukon River as the work advanced, and transported construction materials from the supply depot.*

the line was finished, the *Stratton* was crushed by ice and sank near Selwyn as it attempted to make one more trip between Whitehorse and Dawson City.[2] The men on the telegraph line hoped that they were better prepared for their first northern winter.

The Department of Public Works (DPW) had built 14 telegraph stations. At Bennett City, Caribou Crossing, Whitehorse, and Dawson City they were commodious buildings, some sufficient to house other branches of government, such as the police, the postal service, and the gold commissioner's office. At Atlin, a large existing building was renovated for the use of the Telegraph Service. Most of the telegrams would originate from these stations, producing the revenue that the department hoped would offset the cost of operating and maintaining the line.

By contrast, the stations along the Yukon River were crude one-room log affairs, minimally furnished. The government felt that since it had gone to the expense of erecting the buildings, the least the occupants could do was supply the furniture. If the telegraphers wanted tables and chairs, they had best build them themselves.

An operator and a lineman were assigned to each station. The town stations might also employ a second operator, a bookkeeper, and perhaps even a telegram delivery boy. Most of the operators on the Yukon Telegraph during that first winter were experienced men, drawn from the abundant supply of unemployed operators recently displaced by technological developments, such as the ticker tape and the automatic typewriter. In addition to needing the work, they had two other things in common: a thorough knowledge of the Morse code, and a spirit of adventure.

Duties of Operators and Linemen

Operators assigned to offices in the towns kept regular business hours during which they dealt with customers and sent and received telegrams. At the bush stations, where customers were few and far between, the operators' duties were minimal, on some days amounting to no more than a morning call-in to the closest main office and a report of the local weather.

An operator, if he cared to, could "listen in" on all the messages and news reports that passed through his station. He could be

The Telegraph: How it Works[3]

To understand the jobs and responsibilities of the operators and linemen, it is helpful to have a basic knowledge of how a telegraph system functioned in 1899.

The system consisted of three essential parts: a wet cell battery to supply electricity or voltage, a key to complete or break a circuit, and an electromagnet to detect electricity, all joined together by wires. Each cell produced about one volt of electricity. A "battery" was made up of 60 to 100 cells, connected in series, and the building that housed them was called a battery station.

For electricity to flow it requires a complete circuit, as in a household two-wire system, where one wire carries electricity to an appliance and the other returns it to the source. The Yukon Telegraph used only one wire, with the earth serving as the return wire, or ground. A wire connected to one terminal on the battery was carried on poles to the various stations on the line. At the last station a wire was sunk into the ground, which carried the current back to the other terminal on the battery, completing the circuit. The Yukon Telegraph used a No. 8 galvanized iron wire (about 5 millimetres in diameter). It was attached to the poles on insulators mounted on side blocks to avoid unintentional grounding. Grounding occurred when the wire touched the pole or the ground, which would deplete the strength of the telegraph signal.

The key, connected to the line, was manipulated to open and close the electric circuit in a series of longer or shorter interruptions. The resulting pulses of electricity were detected by the electromagnet, also wired into the line, to produce an electric field that moved a piece of metal to make a click. A piece of equipment called a "sounder" then amplified these clicks into the familiar "dots and dashes," which represent letters, numbers, and punctuation that could be read by the Morse operators.

The distance a message could be transmitted on the Yukon Telegraph depended on the amount of voltage supplied by the battery to the wire. The amount most commonly used was about 100 volts, which was not sufficient to carry a message the entire 550 miles between Bennett and Dawson City. Intermediate battery stations, called repeater stations, were required to add voltage to strengthen the signal, and a device called a relay ensured that the augmented transmission was then able to reach its destination. Repeater stations allowed a message to be transmitted over the entire distance without involving operators at the intermediate stations.

Improper care of the cells could enervate the signal. Operators kept the area around their cells dry to prevent voltage being drained off. At the main stations, those containing 100 or more cells, separate battery rooms were provided to further protect against damage. The outlying stations were supplied with just a few cells, only enough to produce sufficient current to boost a severely grounded signal to the next station.

Wet cells at a battery station were connected in series to provide sufficient current to transmit telegraph signals over hundreds of miles of wire.

as knowledgeable about national and foreign affairs as people on the outside who had newspapers available to them. After all, the news reports that appeared in the Dawson City papers had earlier passed over his telegraph wire. In the evenings, when the business transmissions had ended for the day, operators could spend time "chatting," or two men might play a game of telegraph checkers, with any number of kibitzers.

A proficient operator could use his key like a musical instrument, at times so rapidly that if the person on the other end were any less skilled, he could not read the transmission. Each operator developed an individual style, or "signature," and was further identified by the call letters of his station. For example, HN stood for the station at Hootalinqua, FN for the one at Five Fingers.

Because it was both costly and time-consuming to replace operators and linemen, especially those assigned to the remote stations, they had to agree to work for three years, after which they were eligible for a two-month paid leave. An operator's pay was $110 a month, plus food and lodging.

The skill required of operators may have warranted higher pay, but their job was not the most important or physically demanding. For $20 a month less, the linemen had the daunting and sometimes dangerous task of keeping the line in operation. They were on call 24 hours a day, every day. When an interruption occurred, their responsibility was to fix it as quickly as possible. More often than not during the winter months, the cause was a storm that had uprooted trees and dropped them onto the wire. The wind might be blowing a gale, the temperature dropping to minus 40° Celsius, and the snow piling up, but it was the lineman's job to go out from his warm cabin to correct the problem. Until he did, the line either north or south of his station was cut off.

Within a short time the DPW came to realize that the operators in the bush cabins were being underused. The skills of an expert Morse operator were less essential than a second hand to keep the line operating. Thereafter the operators were also expected to patrol and repair the line, and the bush cabins were considered little more than maintenance stations. The department also began to hire married men, a shrewd move on its part, as the services of two workers were had for the price of one. The women likely did not do much maintenance work, but most of them probably picked up enough Morse to mind the telegraph key when their husbands were out on the line, and of course they did more than their share of the drudge work around the station.

At the town stations, where men could buy their own provisions, they were given an allowance of $30 per month. Those at the remote locations were periodically supplied in bulk. The men could also arrange to have special orders sent in and frequently requested bottles of their favourite libation: overproof rum. They claimed they needed something warm and comforting to combat the chill when called out in foul weather to repair a break, of which there were many that first winter.

Most stations were located along the Yukon River, where they could be supplied by boat during the summer. In winter the cabins were accessible by dogsleds, which travelled over the ice, and by a growing network of trails cleared by the telegraph men and the police. Frozen winter roads over the muskegs and swamps also ran near some of the cabins.

Keeping the Line Open

Some critics claimed that the haste with which the telegraph line had been built would severely undermine its ability to function effectively during the winter months. For the most part the line ran through a narrow clearing in dense woodland, and the wire, barely 12 feet above the ground, was vulnerable to the taller trees that loomed around it. A fallen tree did not need to break the wire, but only had to lean on it to cause grounding sufficient to decrease the strength of the signal so that it would not reach the next station. The wire might also be broken by a storm or an avalanche or, as the operator at Tagish reported, by "contraction," when a tightly strung section of wire shrank, as metal tends to do in cold weather. Overall, though, trees falling against the wire, either grounding or breaking it, caused most of the interruptions.

The men at each cabin were responsible for maintaining the line halfway to the adjacent cabins in each direction. They made regular

Table I

Provisions for Two Men for a Month[4]

Bacon 60 lbs.	Eggs (powder) I can
Ham 13 lbs.	Sugar 15 lbs.
Sausage Meat I can	Pepper 1/4 lb.
Beef 5 cans	Salt 2 lbs.
Tongue 5 cans	Baking Powder I lb.
Salmon I can	Yeast Cakes I pkg.
Sardines 5 cans	Syrup 1/2 gal.
Cheese 2 lbs.	Pearline 2 pkgs.
Flour 35 lbs.	Marmalade I lb.
Barley I lb.	Cream 5 tins
Wheat (bulk) I can	Milk 10 cans
Oats 10 lbs.	Bulk Tea 3 lbs.
Rice 5 lbs.	Coffee 5 lbs.
Macaroni 2 lbs.	Raisins I lb.
Potatoes I ctn.	Currants 2 lbs.
Beans (bulk) I can	Apricots 3 lbs.
Brown Beans 10 lbs.	Dry Apples 5 lbs.
Peas (dried) 10 lbs.	Peaches 5 cans
Sweet Peas 5 cans	Prunes 3 lbs.
Corn 5 cans	Pears 5 cans
Tomatoes 5 cans	Lamp Wick I ea.
Beets 2 cans	Coal Oil 2 gals.
Cabbage I can	Matches (boxes) 3 ea.
Lard 5 lbs.	Soap (bars) 3 ea.
Butter 10 lbs.	

inspections to remove potential problems, but their efforts were never enough to completely avoid the effects of grounding. When grounding noticeably weakened the signal, the line was said to be "heavy." When the signal was no longer strong enough to reach the next station, it was time for the lineman to "walk the line" to find and correct the problem.

In the meantime, there was an emergency procedure the operator could use to keep the messages flowing. First, he "would ground his end of the wire, cutting it off at that point. He would [then] receive the messages as they came to him and copy them. Then, hooking into his batteries, he would transmit to the next cabin, where the operator would do likewise if the current was still too weak. They called that method 'repeating.'"[5]

Should an actual break occur, the operator would attempt to call up the neighbouring stations. Whichever one did not answer indicated the direction of the interruption. But he could not be more specific about the exact location of the break along the 30 to 40 miles of wire between the two stations. The problem might be five miles from his cabin, or it could be much farther.

It was now the job of the linemen from the two stations to find and correct the problem. They started walking toward each other, not knowing how far they would have to go, hoping that they would find the break quickly so that they could make the repair and return to their warm cabins. But sometimes, when darkness fell before the break was found, or when they were too far from their cabins, they had to stay overnight in one of the intermediate refuge cabins. Spaced no more than 10 miles apart along the telegraph line, and often built by the linemen themselves, these cabins were modest in size (8 by 10 feet at most) and minimally equipped with a stove, bunk, and food, along with wire and other materials to make repairs. When a lineman was caught out in a blizzard, one of these cabins could literally save his life.

A lineman out working on the wire was expected to keep in touch with his home station. At intervals the wire had been brought down to ground level so that a telegraph key could be attached. However, not all the linemen had acquired the minimal knowledge of Morse code needed to use the key to contact the station. Within a few years a new electrical device overcame this problem: a field phone that could be attached to the wire to transmit and receive voice messages.

About the time construction of the Bennett to Dawson telegraph was winding down in 1899, the question arose as to what role the North West Mounted Police would play in maintaining the line. The ears of top police officials perked up when they heard that "Mr. Charleson has said the police will do it."[6] Apparently these were the instructions given to the telegraph men. In one instance, when the line went down near Upper Laberge, the operator asked the local constable to find the break and repair it. Farther south, around Tagish, the police launch was employed to make repairs.[7] Although it does not appear that the DPW intended to foist complete responsibility for making repairs onto the police, it does seem that the department expected considerable assistance. After all, was it not in the police's interest to keep the line operating?

The police were willing to assist by providing transport, but not by actually making repairs except in the most pressing situations. Superintendent A. Bowen Perry agreed that, for a price, the Mounties would provide drivers and dogsleds to assist the linemen. The drivers were to be paid three dollars a day, less their regular regimental pay (perhaps half that amount); each dog was provided for 50 cents a day.[8]

In Skagway, the police also conveyed telegrams between the White Pass telegraph office and the ships going to or arriving from Vancouver or Victoria.[9] Messages received at the office were transcribed and placed in a bag addressed to the manager of the Canadian Pacific Railway Telegraph Office in Vancouver or Victoria. When boats arrived from the south, a constable would routinely collect the telegrams and take them to the White Pass office, where they would be transmitted to the government's station at Bennett City.

The new telegraph service was expensive. A 10-word message from Dawson to Vancouver was pricey at $4.50, a day's pay for many men. Because of the cost, few personal telegrams were sent. Nevertheless, a successful miner might splurge $20, or more than the value of an ounce of gold, on a telegram to connect with the folks back home. The best customers were businesses, newspapers, and government agencies, which rode free. Perhaps because of the novelty, during the first months the line was kept buzzing as 120 messages went each way between Bennett and Dawson every day.[10] M.W. Crean, the newly appointed superintendent of the Yukon Telegraph, reported that net revenue between September 28 and November 30 totalled $12,660.[11]

From the standpoint of volume, the most voracious consumers were the newspapers, which daily received thousands of words of news reports. The editor of the *Yukon Sun*, Henry J. Woodside, a self-proclaimed 20-year adherent of the Liberal Party, asked the government to establish a special lower rate for his newspaper. In his petition he pointed out that his courageous support of the government's unpopular actions in Dawson had been costly and had made him a pariah, especially among the Americans. He had "suffered severely" for his loyalty, and he needed help.[12] The justice of his plea was recognized and answered. When the tariffs were established, they included a special rate for news reports of one dollar per 100 words, transmitted during the evening hours. Unjustly, as Woodside saw it, the rate also applied to his competitors, the other Dawson newspapers.

For all the interest in and publicity about the building of the telegraph, it was not the north's first means of communication over wires. Telephones were already in limited use. At the height of the rush in 1898 a telephone wire was strung from Dyea to the summit of the Chilkoot Pass,[13] and wires from Dawson connected some of the mining camps. At Atlin, at least a year before the telegraph arrived, a telephone line was operating over the five miles between the town and the mining camp at Discovery City. After the telegraph was built, these and the later telephone lines served to complement and extend its range. They were the tributaries that fed into the main stream.

Interruptions of Service

Although the telegraph was generally welcomed as a great improvement to communications, there were those who reserved judgement. The Yukon Telegraph had to prove that its service would be fast and reliable. Unfortunately, no sooner had the last congratulatory messages been received than the line went down. Within days of the first transmissions from Dawson there was a major break above Selkirk that resulted in a considerable backup of messages. These "interruptions" (as they were euphemistically called) were a recurring theme during the early years.

It seemed at times that the line was down as much as it was in operation. One interruption might be corrected within hours, the next could last for several days, or even a week. Although no complete record is available, a journal kept at the Bennett station during the winter of 1899–1900 gives an idea of the extent of the problem:

> September 28 [the line's first day of operation]—Line to Dawson open but "very heavy" owing to large number of trees fallen on it causing ground.
> December 21—Line down due to slide four miles north of Bennett causing backup of 125 messages at both Bennett and Dawson.
> January 18–26—Down White Horse to Dawson.
> March 17—Not had Atlin for some time.[14]

Other stations reported comparable numbers of breaks, including one from a snow slide on New Year's Eve that carried away three sections of wire north of Bennett. Superintendent Crean noted interruptions during December on the northern part of the line: on the 13th there were breaks between Stewart River and Selwyn, on the 16th and 19th between Five Fingers and Selkirk, and on the 20th between Ogilvie and Dawson.[15]

The WPYR telegraph, on which the government's line depended to relay its messages, also had difficulty staying in operation. The railway's pass through the coastal mountains was regularly subjected to vicious wind and heavy snow.

If the Yukon Telegraph was going to attract customers, it had to overcome the problem of frequent interruptions. The editor of the *Dawson Daily News* warned that the government must make every effort to keep the line open by providing sufficient linemen to make timely repairs. "Should the confidence of the public ... be shaken in the efficiency of the line ... [it would prove] disastrous to the financial end of the undertaking."[16]

The slower but less costly postal service was making improvements, becoming more reliable and much faster. During the summer it now took only a few days by river steamer for a letter from Dawson to reach Bennett, where it could be put aboard the railway to Skagway. When the river began to freeze up, the post was at a disadvantage, but after the impassable morass of muskeg, beaver ponds, and stream crossings froze solid, a winter road, a mode of travel unique to the north, could be levelled out for use by horse-drawn sleighs and dogsleds.

The Canadian Development Company, which held the mail contract, built a winter road between Dawson and Bennett for its sleighs, which also carried passengers. The company advertised that it would employ no fewer than 18 couriers and 36 post keepers and cooks at its roadhouses, which were spaced about 25 miles apart. "The Arctic Express," as the service was called, would commence as soon as the land was frozen and sufficient snow had accumulated for the sleighs. The company claimed that the trip from Dawson to Bennett, which presently took eight days, would shortly be reduced even more.[17] Still, travel over the winter road was not without some risks and delays. There were equipment breakdowns, and storms and frigid temperatures could make travel impossible. The mail did not always get through on schedule.

There was also a winter mail service to and from Atlin, a 42-mile trail over frozen land and lake to Log Cabin, a station on the White Pass railway. Although it was a much shorter distance than that between Bennett and Dawson, there were times when even its service was suspended. At one point during the winter the *Atlin Claim* reported that, owing to heavy snowstorms, there had been no mail delivery for a week, leaving the telegraph the town's only source of news.[18]

Murder on the Line

Keeping the line operating was the key to success, and when a break occurred, the effort a lineman was willing to put out determined how long the interruption would last. There was no boss to drive him out into the storm, no one to decide if he should wait a while until the weather abated, no one to help him over the trail.

For the most part it was solitary work, especially for the men in the cabins along the Yukon River. For these men, cut off from family and friends, Christmas could be an especially lonely time. But most of them were kept so busy they had little time to dwell on their melancholy. The holiday respite from work enjoyed by residents of the towns did not apply to them. When the line went down they were bound to forsake the comforts of their cabins to repair the break.

Lawrence "Ole" Olsen, the lineman at Five Fingers, was one of those called out a few days before the holidays.[19] Working his way north looking for the problem, he reached the NWMP post at Hootchikoo, where Corporal Patrick Ryan invited him to stop for Christmas dinner on his way back.

Continuing north, Olsen finally located and fixed the break and started back to his station. On December 24 he reached the Minto Road House, 14 miles north of Hootchikoo. There he met Fred Clayson, a merchant from Skagway, and Linn (or Lynn) Relfe, described as hardly more than a boy, lately employed as a cashier in a Dawson City hotel. Both men were also heading south. The three stayed overnight at Minto and set out early the next morning on the river trail toward Corporal Ryan's cabin. Olsen probably assured the others that they would be welcome to share the Christmas meal.

Six miles from Minto, a short distance off the trail, was the camp of George O'Brien and Thomas Graves. Both men had criminal records. Most recently they had been charged with stealing from caches of provisions along the river. O'Brien in particular was a habitual criminal who had served six years in an English prison for attempted murder. He had arrived in the Yukon the year before, intending to organize a gang to rob travellers between Bennett and Dawson, but at this point the gang comprised only O'Brien and Graves. Their camp was situated so that they could see the river trail and anyone who travelled on it. The trio from Minto never made it past this point.

Meanwhile, at Hootchikoo, Corporal Ryan had prepared the Christmas feast and awaited Olsen. He was surprised and disappointed, but not alarmed, when Olsen did not show up, reckoning he had been delayed working on the line or had decided to stay elsewhere. Besides, Olsen was an experienced backwoodsman who could take care of himself.

It was several days later, when Constable Bacon arrived from Five Fingers looking for Olsen, that the alarm was sounded. Initially

Ryan thought Olsen had been injured; only later did he suspect that something more sinister had happened to him. Ryan set off on his dogsled on the trail to Minto. He found O'Brien's camp, deserted but containing a quantity of supplies. A subsequent police investigation and search of the area suggested a scenario of what probably happened on that fateful Christmas Day.

O'Brien and his partner intercepted the travellers, most likely only intending to rob them; Clayson was reputed to be carrying a large amount of cash. Nevertheless, for whatever reason, the three men were shot dead and their bodies pushed under the river ice.

Although two weeks had passed since the crime, the new telegraph made it possible for the police to alert their detachments along the river to watch for the two suspected murderers. Supplied with descriptions, the police at Tagish post, not far from the border, identified and detained O'Brien. Had it not been for the speed of the telegraph, he might have passed through the area and into Alaska without notice.

There was ample evidence that Clayson, Relfe, and Olsen had been murdered at the O'Brien camp, but the bodies had not been found, so murder charges could not be laid. Fortunately, the authorities were able to hold O'Brien on other violations, and when the bodies emerged from the ice after break-up, he was charged with murder. With the bodies and a preponderance of physical evidence, a jury convicted O'Brien and sentenced him to death. He was hanged in Dawson City on August 23, 1901.

As to the fate of O'Brien's partner, Thomas Graves, one

Mug shot of George O'Brien taken at the time he was serving a seven-year jail term in Great Britain for attempted murder.

53

report placed him outside the country, but he was never found—or maybe he was. A fourth body emerged from the Yukon River that spring, one that fit the general description of the missing Graves.

During the history of the Yukon Telegraph, other men died on the job by drowning in swollen streams, from exposure to fierce weather, due to unattended illness, or as the result of an accident. At least one was killed by a grizzly, and one lineman's death was viewed by some as a suicide. But Ole Olsen was the only telegraph man who was ever murdered in cold blood.

Christmas in Atlin

A happier Christmas was observed in Atlin that year. Hulet Wells, a young adventurer, was in Atlin after completing an arduous 11-month journey over the Ashcroft and Teslin trails.[20] After working at several mining jobs, he was selected as the town's first schoolmaster, mainly because he was the only candidate who had a teaching certificate.

According to Wells, Atlin was a lively town that winter. The miners were in from their claims and spending the fruits of their labours with abandon. On Christmas Day, Wells played in an icy football (soccer) game on Atlin Lake, and there were social gatherings and dances. At one event he notes the attendance of "Annabel the telegrapher."[21] Annabel's identity remains a mystery, for although women served as operators elsewhere on government lines, there is no evidence that a female was employed this far north by the Yukon Telegraph. Perhaps the busy town was in need of a part-time relief operator, as the area's gold fields were thriving and the telegraph was in great demand.

Wells also met Guy Lawrence, whom he described as a "pink-cheeked, curly-haired, English boy who seemed to be known and liked by everyone."[22] Within a few years Lawrence would take a job with the Yukon Telegraph, the beginning of a career that was to span more than 40 years.[23]

The new telegraph's performance during its first winter in the often inhospitable Yukon environment was moderately successful. Although there were many service interruptions, repairs were usually made promptly, weather permitting. Most importantly,

YUKON WINTER

F. H. Anderson

Silence and frost! A landscape still
As depths of deepest sea.
Steel-bright stars and a moon as chill
As moon of ice would be.

Silence such as you feel and see
In presence of the dead;
Silence that leaves the soul not free
From something like to dread.

And cold! Like that of Arctic caves
Which ope on frozen seas,
Where never hint of sunlight braves
The deep eternal freeze.

Like spellbound specters silent stand
The spruce trees draped in white,
As they by some magician's wand
Were frozen with affright.

No faintest zephyr stirs the air —
The winds far south have fled,
Leaving the landscape whitely fair
And pulseless as the dead.

The solemn solitudes are bare
Of aught that moves with breath,
Unless it be a hungry hare
That slowly starves to death.

From out the north pale flashes rise
And dim, mysterious haze,
Auroral fires quoth the wise —
The phantoms of a blaze.

Dawn comes to warn pale Arctic Night
That from his southern bed
The Day god cometh in his might
Upon her skirts to tread.

With shud'ring steps toward the north
She drags her shining throng.
Dawn follows, and the sun comes forth,
But not to tarry long.

For in this grewsome time of cold
Short is the sunlight's sway,
And cold its gleam as is the gold
That lures men's minds away.

Weird land! upon my soul is grav'd
Thy beauty pale and cold.
And comes the wish I had not crav'd
Thy dearly purchas'd gold.

In far off lands are weeping eyes
For those whom thou wilt keep —
From thy cold bosom ne'er to rise —
In an eternal sleep.

Dominion Creek, Yukon Territory,
January 2, 1899.[24]

The conditions the linemen encountered during their Yukon winter are captured in the words of an earlier gold seeker.

the system of maintenance cabins spaced every 30 to 40 miles worked reasonably well.

The linemen stationed at these cabins were frequently called out to work under the most horrendous weather conditions of storm, snow, and minus 40° Celsius temperatures. They established a standard, an *esprit de corps* that was to continue through the life of the telegraph line.

Without diminishing the extent of the hardships and dangers experienced by the linemen on this initial section of the telegraph, they were only a warm-up for what was to follow. During the next two years the government would complete the second stage of construction, the all-Canadian line through the wilderness of British Columbia between Atlin and Quesnel. The telegraph stations along this section were even more isolated, some located more than 100 miles from the nearest settlements. It could take a man a week just to get to his cabin. No river steamboats passed the lineman's door, and few dogsled mushers travelled the winter trails. They would have to survive on the provisions the government supplied them by pack train once a year.

Although this new line would be built through a little-known land, the area was not a complete blank on the map. Natives had moved through it for centuries, and white men had explored and created a few trails to gain their objectives. In the 1860s they had started to build a telegraph line, soon followed by gold seekers headed for the strikes in the Cassiar, and later by stampeders struggling to get to the Klondike.

CHAPTER 4

Routes through the Wilderness

W hen Father Nobili, the first French priest to minister to the Carrier and Babine peoples in the central interior of British Columbia, left the region in 1847, no one came to replace him for 20 years. Into this spiritual vacuum appeared pseudo-priests, one a Babine man named Peni. Peni, who was prone to having seizures, on one occasion had a vision and declared himself a prophet. Thereafter he began to make predictions, some with uncanny accuracy. One of his most startling prognostications was that telegraphic communications would be introduced into the region. And so it was, many years later.[1]

After Samuel Morse successfully demonstrated his telegraph system in 1844, government and business interests were quick to recognize the importance of his groundbreaking invention. Within a few years, thousands of miles of wire had been strung between the major cities of Europe and North America. It remained only to connect the two continents by a cable under the Atlantic Ocean to complete the worldwide communications network.[2]

The Collins Overland Telegraph

When initial attempts to lay an Atlantic cable failed, the Western Union Company, whose telegraph lines by the 1860s spanned the United States, embarked upon an imaginative alternative plan: to string a line westward through Canada and Alaska and by cable across the Bering Strait to connect to a Russian line in Siberia. This was the idea of Perry McDonough Collins, and so the project became known as the Collins Overland Telegraph.

In the summer of 1864 work began. From California the line was built north into British Columbia, proceeding the following year on the Cariboo Road, which had been built in the early 1860s to provide access to the Cariboo gold fields. Previously miners had been obliged to struggle through an almost inaccessible wilderness, "studded with mountains closely packed together ... scores of miles of steep, densely forested inclines, rocky gorges and precipices, with only occasional flimsy rope-and-pole bridges, left by Aboriginals, to show that humans had ever passed that way before."[3]

The Royal Engineers had been sent from Great Britain to oversee the daunting and prodigious undertaking. Starting from Yale on the Fraser River, which could be reached by boat, the engineers built a road through the treacherous Fraser Canyon, blasting ledges from the sheer rock walls to provide a bed for the roadway. They bridged deep chasms between ledges with

The Cariboo Road at Hells Gate along the Fraser River, showing the telegraph line that was built in 1865 by the Collins Overland Telegraph.

cribbing filled with tons of rock. At one place the road overhung the rushing torrent below; at another it was perched hundreds of feet up on the dizzying edge of a cliff.[4] The building of the Cariboo Road, with its attendant roadhouses, made travel to the gold fields immeasurably easier.

It also simplified the task of the telegraph builders, whose work progressed steadily. By September 1865, barely six months after work started in B.C., 450 miles of wire had been strung to Quesnel, where the work crew was disbanded for the winter.

In 1866 the crew continued stringing wire to Hazelton and the Native village of Kispiox seven miles up the Skeena River, and a further 50 miles beyond. During the year, in preparation for continuing the line north, exploration parties scouted the wilderness area between Hazelton and Telegraph Creek for the best route. However, when work ended for the year, two months had already passed since Cyrus Field and the *Great Eastern* had successfully laid an Atlantic cable, rendering the Collins Overland project redundant. Thus ended, in the words of Peter C. Newman, "one of the greatest adventures—and most magnificent failures—in commercial history."[5] It was certainly an adventure, and from a financial standpoint a $3-million failure.

A few years later Western Union abandoned the line between Quesnel and Hazelton (Kispiox). It continued to operate the line south of Quesnel until 1871, when it leased this section to the colonial government. In July of the same year, when British Columbia became a province, the Canadian government took over the lease as part of the terms of union, and in 1880 purchased all Western Union properties in British Columbia for the bargain price of $24,000.

Not long after the Quesnel–Kispiox section was abandoned, William F. Butler, an English travel writer, passed through the area on his epic trip through northern Canada. After crossing the Nacharole River, he "reached a broadly cut trail which bore curious traces of past civilization. Old telegraph poles stood at intervals along the forest-cleared opening, and rusted wire hung in loose festoons down from their tops ... [which] told of the wreck of a great enterprise"[6]

This cairn on the banks of the Fraser River at Quesnel, unveiled August 19, 1932, commemorates the Collins Overland Telegraph.

But the enterprise was not completely dead, for 30 years later this ambitious project—at least, the part that would have connected southern Canada to the Yukon and Alaska—would become a part of the Yukon Telegraph.

Trails Through the Wilderness

With the demise of the Collins Overland project, Telegraph Creek, which was to have served as a major supply depot, returned to being a small, quiet, Native village. But not for long. When gold was discovered around Dease Lake in the Cassiar region in 1872, and two years later at McDame Creek, hundreds of miners journeyed up the Stikine River to Telegraph Creek and over trails to the gold fields. Herds of cattle and horses were driven north from ranches in southern British Columbia on the Cariboo Road to Quesnel and then along the route of the earlier telegraph line to Hazelton.

Beyond Hazelton, several routes were available to the drovers. One, referred to as the "Telegraph Trail," most likely derived its name from the scouting work of the Collins Overland explorers. A map prepared by Franklin Pope, the chief of explorations, titled "Sketch Map shewing the proposed route of the Western Union

Telegraph between Fort Fraser and the Stikeen River," indicates the probable route the line would have taken had the work been continued north of Hazelton.[7]

The line on the map followed the Kispiox River to its junction with the Skeena, then up that river to its headwaters and across the low divide into the watershed of the Stikine River. From there to Telegraph Creek the map supplies few details, although the line seems to follow the Klappan River part of the way.[8] Deficient as it was in details, Pope's route made sense in that it followed the river valleys and avoided the troublesome highlands, especially the Skeena Mountains. Another telegraph exploration party, which scouted out the passes to the west, may also have provided direction for some of the gold seekers.

In addition to the information gleaned from the telegraph explorers, there were accounts of a "cattle trail," which generally followed the Skeena except for a shortcut through a pass at Groundhog Mountain.

As so often happened with gold rushes, after the best claims in the Cassiar region were staked, interest waned, and the unsuccessful moved on. By 1880 activity around Telegraph Creek had died down and the village once again reverted to its normal somnolence—that is, until the next gold strike, this one in 1896 in the Klondike. It produced a rush of stampeders headed north, some through central British Columbia.

There were any number of ways to get to the gold fields, but most required passing through U.S. territory. Two routes that did not were the Ashcroft Trail and the Stikine–Teslin Route. Both are germane to the subject of this book because they were followed, at least part of the way, by the Yukon Telegraph. A description of the terrain through which they passed will provide an idea of the conditions the telegraph builders faced.

The Ashcroft Trail

The Ashcroft Trail derived its name from the south-central B.C. town where the Canadian Pacific Railway had its northernmost station in the province, the drop-off point for those headed to the Klondike. It was by far the longest land route to the gold fields, save for the

Edmonton Trail, which was sheer madness. The Ashcroft Trail ran over 880 miles of wagon roads and bush trails from Ashcroft to Glenora on the Stikine River (12 miles below Telegraph Creek), where it joined the Teslin Trail. From there it was a further 160 miles to Teslin Lake and 530 miles by water to Dawson City—a total of about 1,570 miles.

The great distance and difficulty of this trail took a heavy toll on those unfortunates who chose it as the road to their riches. Few of those who started from Ashcroft in 1898 made it all the way. One who did, Walter Hamilton, reported that he knew of only six men who had reached Dawson City.

From Ashcroft to Quesnel (220 miles), wagons and stagecoaches were available to carry travellers over the Cariboo Road, although most gold seekers, having limited means, chose to haul their own outfits. Those who could afford them purchased pack animals; others, out of necessity or foolhardiness, attempted to carry their supplies on their backs.

The wagon road/trail north of Quesnel to Hazelton (330 miles) generally followed the abandoned Collins telegraph line. The country it passed through was sparsely peopled, with a few white settlers among a sprinkling of Native villages and ranches. It was a rolling, open terrain that provided ample grazing for pack animals.

Between Hazelton and Telegraph Creek lay 330 miles of wilderness. Although the Cassiar stampeders had travelled through the area, the precise locations of their trails were lost to memory. There were plenty of anecdotes, but no reliable map was available to guide the Klondikers who started on this trail in the spring and summer of 1898. Consequently, those who travelled this way were tragically underprepared for the difficulties they would encounter.

This lack of information did not deter the trail's boosters. Like the other routes to the Klondike, the Ashcroft Trail had its seducers, the businessmen and their political allies, who extolled the advantages of their trail in order to induce the gold seekers to come their way. One outspoken promoter of the Ashcroft Trail was James Reid, the federal senator from Quesnel, who testified in April

1898 before a Senate committee studying the most feasible route for a road and railway to the Klondike.

Reid, who also happened to be a Quesnel outfitter, took full advantage of his position to misinform the committee and the citizenry. He testified, "From Quesnelle Mouth up to Telegraph Creek there is a pack trail in existence on the old telegraph line built in 1864–65 that has been kept open more or less ever since." He said that pack trains and cattle had been moved over the trail and "there is excellent feed for any number of horses or cattle that may come along." Furthermore, the British Columbia government was currently improving the trail, bridging smaller streams, putting ferries on the larger ones, and "creating a road up to Telegraph Creek."[9]

Gold seekers who relied upon Mr. Reid's information were justifiably unhappy with him when they found that not only was there not sufficient grass for their animals, but there were also no bridges or ferries, and certainly nothing that resembled a road.

The publicity and propaganda emanating from the supporters of the trail succeeded in enlisting 1,500 or so ambitious and adventurous argonauts who were undeterred by its formidable distance. Those who started north in 1898 were perhaps motivated by patriotism, it being the "All-Canadian" route, untainted by passing through U.S. territory. It may have found favour with the less fortunate because it was called the "poor man's trail." When it was christened the "prairie trail," it may have appealed to mid-westerners who preferred flat, grassy terrain. Later, after they had travelled a way, it was more accurately described and disparaged as the "long trail," and then it became the "racing with wolves trail."

Encounters with the Trail

The Ashcroft Trail attracted an inordinate number of literate travellers who recorded their experiences. Men whose accounts were published include Hulet Wells, Walter Hamilton, and Norman Lee. But the foremost chronicler was the American novelist and short-story writer Hamlin Garland, who was not out for gold but to experience the wilderness "before it became civilised." During his journey he observed his fellow trekkers and took copious notes for his book *The Trail of the Goldseekers*.[10]

In April 1898, Garland and his boyhood chum Burton Babcock arrived in Ashcroft, which he described as a dusty cowtown of lodging houses and saloons, swarming with "the rudest and crudest type of men ... thoughtless and profane teamsters and cow-boys, who drank thirstily and ate like wolves." Most of the local business types extolled the trail. A few of the more thoughtful townspeople quietly warned of the difficulties that lay ahead, but in the excitement and euphoria of the moment, no one was listening.

Hamlin Garland on the Ashcroft Trail, making notes for his book The Trail of the Goldseekers.

Garland recorded that he reached Quesnel in mid-May, then continued on the old road/trail to Hazelton, along the way finding the rusted and twisted wire of the earlier telegraph. He described the trail cut by the telegraph men as a "white man's road," lacking "grace and charm," cutting "uselessly over hills and plung[ing] senselessly into ravines." The few sections created by Native people were more aesthetically pleasing. They followed the natural terrain on an "easy and graceful grade which it was a joy to follow"; they were longer but less laborious.

When Garland and Babcock reached the village of Hazelton, they were able to resupply and make final preparations for the remainder of their journey to Telegraph Creek through the 330 miles of wilderness. Or was it 400? Or only 200? Nobody was certain, and as Garland wrote: "No one knew its condition. In fact, it had not been travelled in seventeen years, except by the Indians on foot with their packs of furs. As I now reread all the advance literature of this 'prairie route,' I perceived how skilfully every detail with regard to the last half of the trail had been slurred over. We had been led into a sort of a sack, and the string was tied behind us."[11]

At Kispiox, Garland and Babcock crossed the mighty Skeena River with the help of Natives. "The horses were obliged to swim nearly half a mile, and some of them would not have reached the other shore had it not been for the Indians, who held their heads out of water from the sterns of the canoes."[12]

Beyond, the terrain and weather began to change. The rain was incessant, and as the men were drawn ever deeper into the oppressive dripping forest, grazing areas for the horses became less frequent. They "plunged into bottomless mudholes, slid down slippery slopes of slate, and leaped innumerable fallen logs of fir." There was reputed to be a road crew ahead improving the trail, but Garland and Babcock enjoyed little evidence of their work.

Mile after mile they followed the Skeena River valley, the trail so poorly marked that they were never sure of their location. Comparing their map with the maps of other parties, "all drew by guess," they figured they were way off the Telegraph Trail and on to the old trail to Dease Lake, which went more to the north. If true, this would add many days to their trip, raising concerns about their dwindling food supply. From then on, every time Garland and Babcock came to a grassy area they were torn between staying for a day, to let the horses eat and rest, and moving on to conserve their grub.

Into their camp one night strode a lone trekker, thin and weak-looking, "a little man with a curly red beard [who] was exceedingly chipper and jocular for one in his condition." Out of food, he had been living on squirrels, groundhogs, and other small game. The outfits in the area chipped in from their own meagre larders to enable the little tramper to keep going. To Garland, he was the more extreme type of gold seeker: "insanely persistent, blind to all danger, deaf to all warning, and doomed to failure at the start."[13]

By July 3 the horses were so weak and sick that they could no longer be ridden. Garland and his partner were forced to cross innumerable little rivulets on foot, wading in water up to their ankles, wet and covered with mud all day. And they were down to 10 days of food. They met other parties that were also low on food, some completely out, staving off starvation only by the charity of other outfits and an occasional grouse. "I could no longer deceive myself. Our journey had become a grim race with the wolf."

Finally one morning they topped a rise and looked down upon the glistening waters of the Stikine River. Two days later they reached its banks opposite Telegraph Creek, out of food, "ragged and worn and weary." Garland's 880-mile trek of drudgery had taken 79 days.

Summing up his experience of the Ashcroft Trail, the "All-Canadian—poor man's—prairie route," Garland emphatically concluded that it was a great disappointment. It went through a "barren, monotonous, silent, gloomy and rainy country," an "absurd and foolish" way to reach the gold fields. It should be "given back to the Indians."[14]

Of the four men who wrote about their experience of the Ashcroft Trail, Garland was the only one to put his words to paper

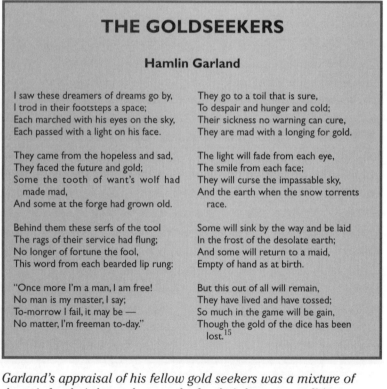

THE GOLDSEEKERS

Hamlin Garland

I saw these dreamers of dreams go by,
I trod in their footsteps a space;
Each marched with his eyes on the sky,
Each passed with a light on his face.

They came from the hopeless and sad,
They faced the future and gold;
Some the tooth of want's wolf had
  made mad,
And some at the forge had grown old.

Behind them these serfs of the tool
The rags of their service had flung;
No longer of fortune the fool,
This word from each bearded lip rung:

"Once more I'm a man, I am free!
No man is my master, I say;
To-morrow I fail, it may be —
No matter, I'm freeman to-day."

They go to a toil that is sure,
To despair and hunger and cold;
Their sickness no warning can cure,
They are mad with a longing for gold.

The light will fade from each eye,
The smile from each face;
They will curse the impassable sky,
And the earth when the snow torrents
  race.

Some will sink by the way and be laid
In the frost of the desolate earth;
And some will return to a maid,
Empty of hand as at birth.

But this out of all will remain,
They have lived and have tossed;
So much in the game will be gain,
Though the gold of the dice has been
  lost.[15]

Garland's appraisal of his fellow gold seekers was a mixture of despair for their lot and sympathy for their human condition, as expressed in one of his poems interspersed with the book's text.

with any immediacy, publishing *The Trail of the Goldseekers* in 1899. The others' accounts were all published decades later: Hulet Wells' in 1960; Norman Lee's also in 1960, but compiled from diaries after his death in 1939; and Walter Hamilton's a short time after his death in 1964.[16]

The 20-year-old Wells (mentioned in the previous chapter) started his trip, accompanied by his father, from Mission, a small town only seven miles off the Cariboo Road. The depression years of the mid-1890s had hit the area hard. There were few jobs and limited prospects for an ambitious young man.

The first part of their trip was uneventful, although north of Kispiox they did meet up with Norman Lee, his bunch of rambunctious cowboys, and the 200 bovines that they were driving to the Klondike. As there are few ordeals more repellent than following a herd of cattle on a trail, they quickly passed Lee's group and entered the Skeena wilderness. His observations were about the same as Hamlin Garland's: "not enough feed for the horses," "rain fell almost every day and made a bad trail almost impassable." They lost the trail; they lost horses.[17]

Entering Glenora in September, Hulet and the elder Wells presented a pretty sight, "bearded, dirty and ragged." The hardships of the trail had taken a toll, and Hulet's father admitted defeat and headed home to his family on the last boat going down the Stikine River before freeze-up. The son remained to have other adventures after wintering over in Glenora, where he became friendly with Walter Hamilton.

Hamilton, 26, had come from Ontario with two companions to seek his fortune. Like the others, they followed the Cariboo Road until they ran out of road, then continued beyond Quesnel on the old telegraph line. Along the way they met many other groups, including some big parties organized in eastern states—one from New York, another from Ohio.

At the Mud (Chilako) River, an outfit from Boston had erected a wooden grave marker with a curious inscription: "Sacred to the memory of ____. May he rest in hell. He claimed to be a guide, but he was a liar." It seems that the subject of the epitaph had represented himself as an experienced guide and was well paid for his services. When he got the party hopelessly lost, however, he was exposed as a fraud. They threatened to lynch him, but he escaped their wrath, and the frustrated group had to settle for the mock epitaph as a measure of grim satisfaction.[18] This was not the first example of guides, fraudulently or merely out of ignorance, making claims they could not live up to. In truth, there were few white men competent to direct parties through the area.

At Kispiox, before entering the big Skeena swamp, Hamilton also met and passed Norman Lee and his herd of cattle. "Long green moss, hanging from the trees, and devil's club with prickly leaves added to the gloom and discomfort." The thorny prickles made the horses feverish and weak; they became hungry for want of grass and were forced to eat leaves. The exhausted and starving animals floundered in the muskeg, and when Hamilton and his partners could not get them out, they were unloaded and mercifully shot.

Farther on, at Groundhog Mountain, he came upon Hulet Wells cutting wood. He noticed a short, pithy doggerel written on a fresh blaze:

> There is a land of pure delight,
> Where grass grows belly high,
> Where horses don't sink out of sight,
> We'll reach it by-and-by.

Trivial verse? Not to Walter Hamilton, who still, decades later, felt that these words "best express for me the spirit of those who completed the trails of '98 to the Klondike, or died in the attempt."[19]

Klondike Cattle Drive

Norman Lee's encounter with the trail was somewhat different from the experiences of Garland, Wells, and Hamilton. As a 35-year-old rancher in the Upper Chilcotin, Lee was struggling to survive in a depressed beef market when he heard about the fabulous gold strike in the Klondike. He figured he had nothing to lose by gambling on a cattle drive of 1,300 miles to his bonanza at Dawson City.

The tent section of Glenora on the shore of the Stikine River. This was the staging point for travel over the Teslin Trail.

After a winter of preparations he set out on May 17, 1898, with 200 head of cattle from his ranch at Hanceville, 40 miles west of present-day Williams Lake. His party headed north, following the Blackwater River part of the way, and joined the old Telegraph Trail 50 miles north of Quesnel. They were now on "the main road to the golden north," somewhat surprised to see so many "pilgrims" on the trail. Lee observed all sorts of humanity, many "evidently prepared for war, as hardly a man passed but was hung all over with six shooters and bowie knives." Contrary to Garland's aesthetic sensibility, as a cattleman Lee liked the trail. It was eight feet wide and in places "straight as an arrow for miles."[20]

When they arrived at the Mud River, a narrow and deep stream, they encountered an Indian charging a handsome fee to ferry travellers and their outfits across. By chance, Lee followed a trail downstream and, much to the delight of his pocketbook, discovered a shallow place where his horses and cattle could ford the river. Later, he learned the real reason for the higher water upstream. The Indian had built a dam to back up and deepen the stream. When it was discovered, the trickster was quickly put out of business.

Walter Hamilton, after his journey over the Ashcroft and Teslin trails, worked in the Klondike gold fields. He is shown here at a mine, operating a winch.

Driving a herd of cattle through the wilderness added complexities to Lee's trip. His were not the only livestock on the trail. Other ranchers had started about the same time, driving herds of 75 to 200 head. The competition for forage became intense, with some aggressive drovers forging ahead to be first to the best feeding grounds. Throughout the drive, finding sufficient food for the animals was a constant problem.

Completing the first leg of the trip at Hazelton, Lee was impressed by the Native totem poles, and by their burying grounds overlooking the village. "Little buildings, like summer houses, were placed over the graves, many very neatly built, with doors and windows. In these buildings were placed all manner of things belonging to the deceased. The most splendid of the lot was furnished complete with a carpet, table, chairs, washbasin etc., two new umbrellas, and a whole assortment of new shawls, blankets and all manner of nameless lady's properties, not to mention a full sized portrait of the tenant in a massive frame ... Even the poorest of the graves had one or two large trunks apparently filled with the deceased's property."[21]

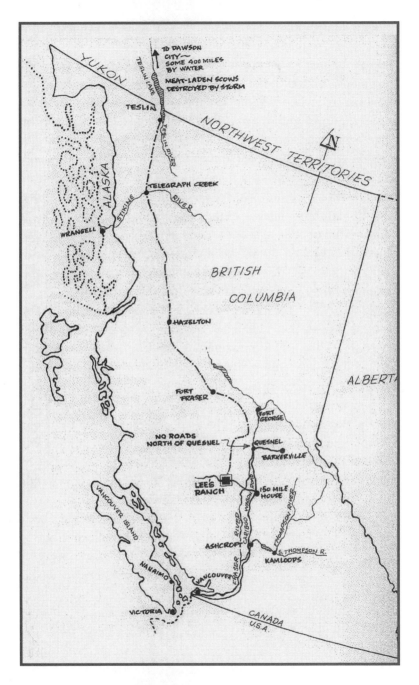

*Map of the route of Norman Lee's cattle drive over the Ashcroft and
Teslin trails.*[22]

In Hazelton he met a man who said he had worked on a government road party cutting a trail 180 miles north to the "Summit." Since government reports had led Lee to believe that the distance from Hazelton to Telegraph Creek was only 200 miles, he figured that when they reached this summit it should be an easy drop right down to the Stikine River. Such, of course, was not the case, and it soon became apparent that little work had been done to improve the trail, whose course in places seemed incomprehensibly erratic. Evidently, when the road crew left Hazelton it was closely followed by a horde of gold seekers, impatiently urging the men on. Although often unsure of the best route, the crew members were allowed no time to scout ahead, and if they went wrong, "the idiots behind them" did not allow them to retrace their steps to make corrections. This resulted in some sections that twisted and turned for no apparent reason.

On August 15 Lee's party reached the summit of Groundhog Mountain, where they rested and were happy to feast on the local inhabitants—the rodents for whom the mountain was named. Beyond was no easy drop down to the river, as it took three more weeks for them to reach the Stikine, where they successfully swam the herd across. Lee described Telegraph Creek as "dead." Many of the earlier stampeders had given up and returned south. Those who were continuing to the gold fields were already on their way to Teslin Lake, most hauling their outfits on cut-down wagons to fit the narrow trail. Others were pushing "man-killing" barrows or moving their outfits in relays on their backs.

Lee did not have the luxury of choice. He could not turn back or winter over. The cattle demanded that he press on immediately to Teslin Lake and down the Yukon River to Dawson City. And time was growing short; winter was setting in and the waterways would soon freeze up.

Overcoming all obstacles, the cowboys drove the herd over the narrow trail to Teslin Lake. There the cattle were slaughtered and their carcasses loaded on two scows for the voyage to Dawson. It was already mid-October when the party set sail down the long lake. They never made it to the foot of the lake, much less to the Yukon River or Dawson. Within days the wind churned up waves that forced the boats ashore. The scows began to break up and most of the meat was ruined. There was nothing to do but give up the "gamble" and return to the ranch. After an often-harrowing trip, Lee made it back to his Chilcotin home, completely broke and further in debt.

Ironically, amidst the accumulated mail that awaited his return was a bill for supplies from senator/outfitter James Reid, the vociferous extoller of the virtues of the Ashcroft Trail. The bill was couched in the form of a poem:

Equally adept as a rhymester, Lee replied:

Prologue
    I do not aim, like Reid by name, at Poet's fame,
    And if I was as poor a poet
    I'd take good care I didn't show it.
Epilogue
    To[o] bad to wait, to such a date,
    For such a sum, to see it come.

It breaks my heart, with gold to part,
Dear Mr. Reid. I have more need
Of gold than you, for it is true,
At Teslin Lake, I struck a fake
Which cleaned me out, and made me doubt
If I should ever more again
Be even with my fellow men.[23]

Hamlin Garland, Hulet Wells, Walter Hamilton, and Norman Lee were in general agreement about the Ashcroft Trail. They had been misinformed. It was a rotten trail, a poorly marked trail, and little effort had been made to improve it. There were seemingly endless quagmires of swamp and mud, and long stretches lacking adequate forage for their animals. The cost in lost horses and mules was horrific, and the human cost was also high. All four reached Glenora exhausted, bedraggled, and out of food. But unlike many of their fellow trekkers, none of them had been defeated by the trail. One way or another, they all continued on.

There seems to have been some confusion about the exact route of the trail, as each gave slightly different descriptions. Garland reported possibly being on the Dease Lake trail to the north; Wells was somewhere south when he crossed the Iskut River; and all but Garland mentioned crossing the pass at Groundhog Mountain.

In any event, when surveyors came along two years later to lay out the route for the Yukon Telegraph, they were indebted to the gold seekers of '98. Their accounts of the trail and the country were invaluable, and by their numbers alone they had cut a path through the wilderness that had not existed before. How closely the telegraph builders would follow this path remained to be determined.

CHAPTER 5

The Stikine–Teslin Route

The telegraph builders also used a portion of the Teslin Trail, which was the land part of the Stikine–Teslin Route. The development of this trail was the result of complaints from Canadian gold seekers headed to the Klondike and from West Coast business interests.

The most popular routes to the gold fields passed through U.S. territory, mainly over the Chilkoot and White passes from Skagway. This resulted in the incongruous situation of Canadian citizens travelling from one part of their country to another being penalized for purchasing their supplies in Canada, because when they passed through U.S. territory they were charged customs duties of up to 30 percent. This could be a crushing assessment for men and women with limited funds. Those who attempted to move their Canadian outfits under bond (a guarantee that goods would not be used or sold while passing through U.S. territory) were preyed upon by officials who imposed "inspection fees" that often equalled the duty charges. Consequently, fully 90 percent of the Canadians heading for the Klondike were acquiring their provisions and mining equipment from American companies, much to the displeasure of West Coast merchants and political leaders who wanted the gold seekers to buy their outfits in Canada.[1]

The Canadian stampeders and business interests demanded that the government establish a route to the Yukon that passed entirely through Canadian territory—a route that would not only avoid the onerous duties charged by the Americans, but would also encourage the gold seekers to spend their money in Vancouver or Victoria.

The All-Canadian Route

The Laurier government determined that it would support the development of the Stikine–Teslin Route, a combination of river and land travel through B.C. and the Yukon, as the all-Canadian way for stampeders to get to the Klondike. Starting at Wrangell, near the mouth of the Stikine River, the route went upriver 140 miles to the settlement at Glenora,[2] then overland 160 miles to Teslin Lake and the headwaters of the Yukon River, concluding with a 530-mile voyage downriver to Dawson City.

Although Wrangell and the first 30 miles of the Stikine were in U.S. territory, the Washington Treaty of 1871 allowed for free navigation of the river by British (including Canadian) ships. The Canadian government interpreted the treaty to mean that goods could be offloaded at Wrangell and transshipped without the imposition of customs duties.[3]

The route pleased the merchants and entrepreneurs of the Canadian west coast; now the job was to entice the gold seekers to come their way. Compliant newspapers were enlisted to make exaggerated claims: The river was "easily navigable for six months of the year"; the land travel, "passing through an exceptionally easy country," required "but a short portage before a chain of waters leading to the upper Yukon."[4]

Most seductive was the plan announced by Ottawa to upgrade the 160-mile "short portage" between Glenora and Teslin Lake with a first-class wagon road, and then with a railway. This created the impression that when the railway was completed, travellers between Wrangell and Dawson City would encounter few hardships.

The government and the fifth estate were not the only apostles spreading the word about the virtues of the route. There was no shortage of enthusiastic advocates providing glowing descriptions. Even before Ottawa decided to build the railway, *The Chicago Record's Book for Gold Seekers*, which claimed to evaluate the several routes to the Klondike, reported that the government was about to improve the existing trail from Telegraph Creek to Teslin Lake to make it "the best and easiest route to the Yukon."[5] The *British Columbia Mining Record* promised that "the country from Telegraph Creek to Teslin is flat and easily travelled, and pack trains can be hired at the former place at relatively reasonable rates."[6]

With assurances of such an easy journey it is not surprising that as many as 6,000 gold seekers chose the Stikine–Teslin Route. They would soon learn that, either through ignorance or avarice, the writers of these laudatory descriptions had subverted reality. The "devil was in the details," which were largely omitted.

Determined to reach the gold fields before all the good claims were staked, most of those who chose the route started over the frozen river in the winter and early spring of 1898. Those who could not get to Glenora before the ice began to run out were doomed to be stranded on the shore, forced to wait for the riverboats to begin operations before continuing their journeys.

Many of the gold seekers were cheechakos (greenhorns), totally unprepared for living and surviving in a northern environment. George Kirkendale, part of a group heading up the Stikine in early 1898, commented on the inexperience of some of the other parties. On Cottonwood Island, a staging point near the mouth of the river, he found among the 800 souls camped there "the greatest assortment of people you can imagine: Old men, young men, women and children, all starting up the Stikine trail with every kind of conveyance, and with horses, mules, dogs, goats, sheep, cattle, anything that could pull a sleigh. None of these animals except dogs were any use in the deep snow until the trail was well packed, but everyone was full of excitement and confidence."[7]

Travellers on the ice were constantly aware of the powerful river flowing beneath them—they could hear it—and of the dangers. There were instances of men venturing to the edge of ice to fetch water who misstepped and slid off into the current and under the ice shelf, never to be seen alive again. Horses with their loads broke through the ice; the lucky ones were hauled out.

Those gold seekers struggling upriver, whether over the ice or, after break-up, by boat, kept going because they believed that

An unusual pole cabin at Glenora.

A cheechako at the Glenora camp preparing to head out for the Klondike on the Teslin Trail.

once they reached Glenora the travails of their journey would be eased. The portage to Teslin Lake would be over the fine wagon road promised by the government. They were to be sorely disappointed.

Almost at the same time as the announcement in January 1898 of the plan for the railway, the government granted a contract to Mackenzie, Mann and Company, premier railway builders, to "build a wagon road in six weeks, and have a railroad in operation by September 1st." As compensation, for each mile of track laid the company would be granted 25,000 acres of Crown land. The company could potentially gain 3.75 million acres from the deal.[8]

The government signed the contract with Mackenzie and Mann between sessions of Parliament. This impetuous action, Prime Minister Laurier later argued, was necessary to forestall plans for a competing railway through U.S. territory, the White Pass and Yukon Route line. The government believed it was imperative to have a railway to the Canadian Yukon that was not controlled by the Americans.[9] No doubt the Liberals assumed that their patriotic motive and sense of urgency would be shared by the entire Parliament.

Unfortunately, the haste with which the project had been advanced made it vulnerable to some embarrassing questions: Why had tenders not been taken? And why was the land grant to Mackenzie and Mann so overly generous? The government could count on its majority in the Commons to approve the contract, but the Senate, controlled by Conservative Party members, refused to pass the bill authorizing the project.

The railroad was dead, but what about the wagon road? Although a subsequent agreement was made with Mackenzie and Mann to continue clearing the trail, and some government crews were also put to work, their accomplishments were too little and too late to ease the way of the stampeders of '98.

The new reality of a trail without a road did not, however, stop the city newspapers from continuing to publish favourable reports of the Stikine–Teslin Route, and with the founding of the *Glenora News* it gained a full-time champion. Editor W.F. Thompson proclaimed the raison d'être of his newspaper was "to advance the interests of the All-Canadian route to the Klondike ... for the merchants of Canada." Glenora, he announced, would grow to be "the metropolis of the Cassiar."[10] Beginning with the first issue on June 9, he promoted the trail with persistence and imagination, grasping at every favourable experience, reporting every rumour of the imminent construction of the road to Teslin Lake.

The *News* saw itself as being engaged in a relentless struggle with the hired guns of Skagway, who could be found everywhere on the streets of Glenora attempting to lure gullible prospectors to the Sin City of the north. All that these liars "should receive [from] ... our good citizens, is a cold bath in the river and a swim to Wrangel."[11]

To counter the enticements of Skagway, Thompson presented the "facts," the true accounts of people who had actually travelled over the competing trails. First up was Henry Woodside, who was in Glenora accompanying the 200 soldiers of the Yukon Field Force on their way to the Yukon. Woodside, who would later become editor of the *Yukon Sun* in Dawson City, recounted the litany of horrors endured during his earlier crossing of the Chilkoot Pass, starting with the lawlessness of Skagway and ending with the scarcity of trees remaining at Bennett City with which to build boats and the

Two stampeders on the Teslin Trail with their one-wheel "man killer" wheelbarrow, necessitated by the narrowness of the trail.

dangers of the rapids on the Yukon River. He cautioned anyone in Glenora who was thinking of rerouting to Skagway not to do it. Regardless of the fact that work on the road had been halted, Woodside continued to argue that the Teslin Trail was still the best way and "that a wagon road will be completed from Glenora to Teslin Lake at an early date."[12]

The actual conditions faced by the gold seekers starting from Glenora could not have been more at odds with the descriptions provided by the newspapers. What they found was a wet and overgrown trail too narrow for their wagons. Many of the wider sleighs and wagons, so laboriously brought over the ice, had to be abandoned or resized.

The journey over the portage proved to be arduous and time-consuming, taking much longer than anticipated. Consider the experience of the John Smith party, which started on April 4 from Telegraph Creek, where the ground was frozen and covered with snow. Smith recorded in his diary that the trail climbed steeply, the footing becoming very rocky in some places, and in others was composed of slippery mud over ice. The party was slowed by heavy overgrowth that had to be cut back, and when the trail became even narrower, the width of their sleighs had to be further reduced to 21 inches. Eventually they reached the abandoned Hudson's Bay Company post at the Shesley River.

From Shesley they traversed a difficult hill, crossed a flat and swampy area, and, after slogging through 12 inches of icy water, reached the Nahlin River. It had taken the party 22 days to attain this juncture, only 90 miles from Telegraph Creek.[13] (This section of the Teslin Trail would be used by the Yukon Telegraph.)

The Yukon Field Force Arrives

Gold seekers who got to Glenora intending to buy horses or mules to haul their supplies were out of luck after June 1898. All available pack animals had been commandeered by the Yukon Field Force (YFF), which was on its way over the Teslin Trail to support the police in the Yukon.

When tens of thousands of gold seekers threatened to overwhelm the North West Mounted Police's efforts to maintain law and order, the government dispatched this force of 200 regular soldiers to back them up. The police were the first line of defence against frontier-style lawlessness; the YFF was the reserve, to be used only if needed.

Its presence in the Yukon would also discourage any challenge to Canadian sovereignty. Ever since the United States had purchased Alaska from Russia in 1867, British Columbia had been bordered on two sides by its formidable and sometimes aggressive neighbour. Now, with Americans flooding the Klondike (by some estimates comprising 75 percent of the stampeders), the sense of being surrounded was intensified. The government's apprehension was not allayed by U.S. newspaper reports that repeatedly referred to the Klondike as being located in Alaska (a misconception that continues to this day). It was not likely that disgruntled Americans chafing at restrictive Canadian laws and mining regulations would attempt a coup, but the possibility could not be ruled out.[14]

The YFF, under the command of Colonel T.D.B. Evans, was drawn from active units and comprised nearly one-quarter of the country's standing army. Accompanying the troops, and sharing the difficulties of the journey, were six women: four nurses (members of the Victoria Order of Nurses, or VON, organized just a year earlier to bring nursing services to outlying areas[15]); Mrs. Starnes, who was travelling to Dawson City to join her husband, NWMP inspector Cortlandt Starnes; and Faith Fenton, a *Toronto Globe* reporter.[16]

Starting from Ottawa, the soldiers travelled cross-country by train to Vancouver, where they boarded steamers for the trip to Wrangell, arriving on May 16. It was in Wrangell, while changing boats, that Colonel Evans faced and overcame the first emergency of his Yukon expedition. The problem arose when Miss Fenton descended the ship's gangplank "in a travelling dress so short as to indecently expose her ankles! ... The horrified bachelor colonel quickly deputed the only married woman, Mrs. Starnes, to have a quick chat with the young reporter," resulting in a "strip of black sateen" being sewn around the bottom of Miss Fenton's dress. "Colonel Evans's 'brutal and licentious soldiery' had been saved from temptation!"[17]

The group of four members of the Victoria Order of Nurses and Toronto Globe *reporter Faith Fenton, who accompanied the Yukon Field Force on the Teslin Trail.*

Early in June, the YFF and its 60 tons of supplies reached Glenora. A month later, with loads of 200 pounds for each mule and 50 pounds for each trooper, they were ready to start on the trail to Teslin Lake, which they soon learned was a trail in name only. Several herds of cattle had already passed through, so it was more like a quagmire, and the journey turned out to be "a true feat of endurance." George Jacques, a member of the Field Force, recounted his experience: "The day's march was usually about fifteen miles, clambering over fallen trees and boulders that barred our path, hacking our way through bush, sinking into swampy ground and all the while fighting off swarms of mosquitoes and flies."[18]

The nurses found their services in demand. In addition to attending to the illnesses and injuries of the soldiers, they were sought out by miners and packers. "[Word of their] kindness and willingness to help has spread up and down the trail, so that the sick man's first thought is to reach them," reported Faith Fenton.[19]

Soldiers of the Yukon Field Force hiking on the Teslin Trail from Glenora to Teslin Lake, where they boarded boats to take them to their post at Fort Selkirk.

One of the nurses, Georgina Powell, wrote graphically of the rigours of the trail:

> From mountains to swamp and bog—bogs into whose cold, damp, mossy depths we would sink to our knees, and under which the ice still remains; where we trampled down bushes and shrubs to make footing for ourselves, and where the mules stick many times, often as many as twenty down at once ...
>
> Through deep forest we went, where the trail was narrow and the branches of trees threatened our eyes or tore our [mosquito] veils disastrously, through tracts of burnt and blackened country, in some places the ashes still hot from recent burnings, and the dust rising in choking

clouds under our feet; through forests of wind-fallen, upturned trees, whose gnarled roots and tangled branches made insecure and often painful footing; over sharp and jagged rocks, where slipping would be dangerous, we went trampling, leaping, springing and climbing, a strain that only the most sinewy women could bear.[20]

Upon reaching Teslin Lake, the soldiers built boats for the 360-mile voyage to Fort Selkirk, the camp built by an advance party 170 miles upriver from Dawson City.

Travelling on the trail a few months later were 17-year-old Guy Lawrence and his father, from England. Assured by the London newspapers that the Teslin Trail was almost completed, the two had landed in Wrangell from the same boat that transported the Yukon Field Force.[21] Continuing upriver, they arrived in Glenora about the time word was received that plans for a railway had been cancelled. Disappointed but not deterred, they continued to push on to Teslin Lake.

Their transport consisted of a jury-built wagon, described by Lawrence as "a small platform built over [an] axle," pulled by a balky horse. They had to relay their supplies in 400-pound loads, requiring several trips to move the entire outfit ahead. It was a slow and laborious procedure. By October, with the weather changing, they had made only 36 miles and decided to build a cabin to wait out the winter.

Continuing their trek the following February, they came to a lone cabin in the wilderness. Seeing no footprints in the snow or smoke coming from the chimney, they decided that the place must be deserted and looked forward to a warm respite from sleeping rough in the cold. As Lawrence recalled the experience:

Boldly opening the door, my father bade me bring the sleeping bags in. I brought them in, and soon found that after the brilliant sunshine outside it was next to impossible to see in the dark cabin. However in the far corner I could distinguish two bunks—one above the other. I threw my sleeping bag on the top one. It fell off. I threw it up again, and the same thing happened. Reaching up with my hand I felt for the obstruction.

I touched a man's face, frozen solid. In the lower bunk I could just distinguish another face. Both men, of course, were dead. They had died of scurvy, neither one able to help the other.

We did not stay there that night.[22]

The Stampede Ends

Back at Glenora, even the optimism of *News* editor Thompson began to weaken when official word came from Ottawa that no road would be built to Teslin Lake in 1898. Stirring the conspiracy-plot pot, he headlined an article "It's a Damn Shame, There's Some Crooked Work Being Done Somewhere, Depend Upon It." The "four thousand poor suckers" who had come to Glenora on the promise of a road were out of luck.[23]

Thompson's reactions were typical of the emotional roller coaster experienced by so many of the gold seekers who had gambled on Glenora and the Teslin Trail. At one moment he would be despondent, feeling deserted and deceived, at the next, buoyed by the latest good news. For example, when he received word that the Cassiar Central Railway between Glenora and Dease Lake would soon be started, he wrote that, contrary to the skeptics, the *News* "intends to camp right here until the cows of prosperity come home. We have paper enough to last for five years, after which date we can print the *News* on birch bark, if necessary."[24]

But it soon became apparent, even to Thompson, that the gold rush was ending; opportunity had passed. The businesses of Glenora were moving on, and with them, reluctantly, went the publisher of the *News*, which ceased publication with the issue of September 16.

George Kirkendale, who had stayed in Glenora during the summer to work on the railway warehouses, had had a grandstand view of the passing human story. He summed it all up:

> Of all the mad, senseless, unreasoning and hopeless rushes I doubt if the world has ever seen the equal. Day

after day crowds of men of all classes and conditions, hauling their sleighs, struggling, cursing, and sweating, thrashing their horses, mules and dogs, all filled with the mad, hopeless idea that if they could get as far as Telegraph Creek they would be in good shape for the Klondike ... Some gave up on the river, sold their outfits, and went back. Many threw away parts of their outfits to lighten their loads. Thousands arrived at Glenora and Telegraph Creek and started over the Teslin trail, but by this time it was April or May, and the snow was beginning to go off the trail leaving pools of water and swamps through which it was almost impossible to transport their outfits. You could buy food and outfits at Telegraph for less than half what they would cost in Victoria. Hundreds stopped at Glenora until the river steamers started to run in the spring, and then went home poorer and wiser.[25]

By the end of the year the great stampede for gold had ceased to rumble through the Stikine. The tents at Glenora were being taken down and some of the buildings moved to Telegraph Creek. However, within two years there was renewed activity around Telegraph Creek. Another outfit was passing through, but this one would leave a more permanent impression. Riverboats were arriving laden with construction materials to build the Dominion Government's Yukon Telegraph. A depot was being set up just north of town, and soon the workmen would begin to arrive.

CHAPTER 6

The "All-Canadian" Line: Quesnel to Atlin, 1900

The Bennett to Dawson telegraph line significantly reduced the time required for messages to travel between central Canada and the Yukon, but it was only a temporary solution. For one thing, it still took about a week for a telegram to reach its destination; for another, the need to transcribe transmissions at Skagway was an awkward and time-consuming procedure. The sea leg was also subject to misadventure, as ships were delayed by unfavourable weather and messages were misplaced.

And then there was Skagway. Despite the death of the infamous Soapy Smith the year before, the town was still plagued by other hoodlums who preyed upon the gullible stampeders. One of the Smith-inspired scams was the phoney telegraph office, where customers were guaranteed that they could send a wire anywhere in the world for five dollars. Before leaving for the passes, many gold seekers sent messages to their families, and within two or three hours they would receive a reply—always collect.[1]

But the most compelling shortcoming, as far as the Dominion government was concerned, was that messages had to pass through American territory, where they were vulnerable to obstruction should disagreements arise between the two nations over such issues as the disputed boundary between Alaska and Canada.

Although both sides denied it, they were deploying troops to provide support for their claims. Canada, with some justification, maintained that the 200-man Yukon Field Force was helping the NWMP keep order in the gold fields. The American government countered—one might say overreacted—by sending a force of 500 soldiers to establish posts in Alaska along the Yukon River. Some of the units were stationed provocatively close to the Canadian border, at Fort Egbert and Eagle City,[2] whereas the YFF was no closer to the border than Dawson City and Fort Selkirk.

The presence of troops, combined with America's aggressive expansionist policy, displayed in the Spanish–American War, further induced the Laurier government to establish telegraph communications with the Yukon that were not threatened by U.S. interference. It would build the all-Canadian line even if it had to push it through 900 difficult miles of British Columbia wilderness. The question was, who should build it?

Public or Private?

Although it seemed this question had been settled when the government decided to build the Dawson City line, capitalist interests were not easily discouraged. Groups of speculators, some politically connected, argued that they should be allowed to build and operate the new telegraph. Considerable confusion had been created when Parliament earlier granted charters to two companies to build the line to Dawson City. Although the government insisted that these charters were non-exclusionary, the impression remained that private enterprise had not been ruled out.

One of the charter recipients, the Northern Commercial Telegraph Company, composed mostly of British speculators and Canadian directors, lobbied long and hard. They proposed that the line from Bennett City to Dawson City be turned over to them to operate and that they be allowed to build the Atlin–Quesnel section.[3] A second group of British investors, the Canadian, British Columbia, and Dawson City Telegraph Company, also proposed to take over construction.[4] The company preferred to lay an underwater cable along the coast, but was prepared to build the land line if required.

Although he was opposed to private involvement, Minister of Public Works J. Israel Tarte, in a burst of self-deceiving optimism, divined from the private speculators' "strenuous efforts to get possession of the line ... very convincing evidence that the telegraph lines in the Yukon will be a remunerative business."[5]

The Canadian Pacific Railway (CPR), which operated an extensive telegraph system across the country, was also interested in taking over the government project. Its proposal elicited from Tarte a most adamant expression of his opposition to private ownership. In a letter to Prime Minister Laurier, he pointed out that in many countries the telegraph system was operated by the government, but that the U.S. and, to some degree, Canada were exceptions. And furthermore: "I do not know of anything that would be more detrimental to the public interest than such a policy [of private ownership], whose effect would be to isolate from the outside world the 660 miles of telegraph constructed by Government [between Atlin and Dawson] and place the same at the tender mercy of private speculators."[6]

Tarte's warning was contrary to what he was telling the private investors. In response to one proposal to build the telegraph he wrote, "[If] sufficient guarantee for the completion of the line was given to us, we would very seriously consider the matter."[7] In fact, he never seriously considered construction by private contractors as an alternative, but the duplicitous Tarte continued to string along the speculators. Perhaps he was only keeping all options open should the project be sidelined for some unforeseen reason, or maybe he did not want to offend influential investors. Tarte's seeming to approve of private proposals, however, gave the companies grounds to claim compensation. And claim they did. The Canadian, British Columbia, and Dawson City Company petitioned for relief and continued to press its case for a number of years.[8]

Ottawa Vacillates

Although the government was committed to build and operate the connecting link through British Columbia, Laurier and his advisors had reservations about the actual need for the line. Their major concern was that a sea cable would be laid along the coast from Seattle or Vancouver to Skagway in the near future. This would render the Quesnel–Atlin project redundant. It might also prove to be more reliable and less costly to maintain than a land line, resulting in lower rates. The patriotic argument that an all-Canadian telegraph was necessary for "the public interest" was not sufficient to justify the cost or negate the criticism of the Conservative Opposition.

A report in September 1899 concluded that, due to lack of funding, "the chances of [the cable's] success are too remote to have any influence on the construction of a land telegraph line … "[9]

Still, Ottawa vacillated. No telegraph line of this length had ever been built in Canada through such a harsh and forbidding landscape. But time was running out. If the Department of Public Works did not soon place orders for construction materials, work could not start in the early spring and the project would be seriously delayed. Construction materials and provisions not only had to be procured, but they also had to be transported thousands of miles to the supply depots by ship and rail, and in the north by sleigh over frozen lakes.

Finally the decision was made. On December 22, 1899, Tarte authorized J.B. Charleson to start the wheels of supply rolling to complete the gap between Quesnel in the south and Atlin in the north, a distance estimated to be about 900 miles.[10]

An Unrealistic Schedule

Although Charleson's initial appointment to superintend construction of the Bennett–Dawson City line was due more to his political connections then to his facility as an engineer, he was now an experienced builder who had proved his ability as an organizer and expediter, and his staff, on whom he depended to do the engineering and to supervise construction, had also honed their skills. They were recognized for their outstanding accomplishment of completing the earlier work within the allotted time and under budget.

But as the saying goes, "No good deed will go unpunished." To the functionaries in Ottawa, the earlier achievement meant only that they were free to make even more outrageous demands upon the telegraph builders. It all seemed so easy, so obvious. If 550 miles of telegraph line could be built in one season, they reasoned, then surely, with a little greater effort and efficiency, and by using two crews, 900 miles in one season was not out of the question.[11] Success would beget success. In this instance, the reward for success was a near-impossible schedule: to complete the Quesnel–Atlin section during the limited 1900 construction season.

Basing expectations on the performance of building the Bennett–Dawson line was inappropriate and illogical. For one thing, the working conditions were quite different. The earlier line had been built along lakes and rivers using a floating base camp. The scows, used to house and feed the workers, greatly facilitated the work, allowing for the rapid rate of five miles per day. And the support ship, *W.S. Stratton*, could move the construction materials and provisions from the depots to the work sites relatively easily.

In comparison, the connecting line was to be built through a much more isolated and inhospitable terrain, bereft of easy supply routes or established trails. For most of the distance, the crews would have to hack their way through virgin country, crossing innumerable streams, muskegs, and swamps. Everything, all the construction materials, all the provisions for the men, had to be moved by pack trains. And as the work progressed, the supply lines would get longer and longer, eventually extending to more than 100 miles. Even moving the work camps ahead was an added arduous daily chore of loading and unloading, breaking down and setting up tents. The men were also more vulnerable to the frequent rains and constant wetness, and to the irritating, ever-present mosquitoes and black flies.

Charleson apparently accepted the demanding schedule without objection, although he warned that any delay in supplying construction materials would threaten the completion date. And there were to be delays, caused by supplies not being sent to the proper depots and not being available when needed.

A more realistic estimate of the progress that could be expected through this terrain and under these conditions would have allowed two years to complete the project. But the government, Tarte in particular, foolishly insisted on the unreasonable schedule. No consideration was given to the extreme differences in the two routes. As George Fleming, later the superintendent of the Dawson–Whitehorse division of the Yukon Telegraph, put it in 1917: "While many difficulties had been encountered in the construction of the Bennett–Dawson line, they were trivial as compared to those met between Quesnel and Atlin, where it was necessary to transport all the material, camp equipment and supplies by pack horse across swamps, over mountain summits and through dense forests where no trails existed."[12]

The amazing thing is that, if not for a few miscalculations and supply foul-ups, the impossible might have been accomplished.

Choosing the Route

The key to completing the job in 1900 was the use of two crews, one working south from Atlin, the other north from Quesnel. The plan was for them to meet about midpoint, somewhere south of Telegraph Creek. Supplies were to be sent to Atlin and Quesnel and also stockpiled at two intermediate depots accessible by river steamers, at Hazelton on the Skeena River and at Telegraph Creek on the Stikine River.

The exact route of the line would be determined in the field by the surveyors, who were sent ahead of the work crews. Because of the demanding schedule, they were instructed to limit the amount of wire to be strung by laying out a straight cutline wherever possible. If mileage could be saved, they were to deviate from the river valleys and go into the higher elevations.

The goal of stringing the wire in a straight line was appropriate for both the northern and southern sections. In the south, from Quesnel to Hazelton, the line would follow the abandoned Collins Overland Telegraph along an existing road/trail. Some straightening would be required, but there was no need to deviate significantly from this established route. In the north, from Atlin to Telegraph Creek, although the line would pass through wilderness, it was possible to survey a reasonably direct line to connect to the Teslin Trail, then to build south 90 miles to Telegraph Creek.[13]

The central section, the 330 miles of wilderness between Hazelton and Telegraph Creek, was where decisions had to be made between alternative routes. There were several possibilities: the Ashcroft Trail(s) used by the gold seekers of `98, the route sketched by Pope in 1866 that followed the Skeena River, and the deviation called the "cattle trail"[14] through the Groundhog Pass. There was also a route through the river valleys to the west that had been scouted by other Collins explorers, referred to as the Burns–Leech route.[15]

The Yukon Telegraph surveyors, seeking the shortest way, included some portions of these earlier routes and then went their own way. From Hazelton they followed the Kispiox and Skeena rivers and then the cattle trail until it turned north toward Groundhog Mountain, choosing instead to continue in a northwesterly direction up the valleys of the Nass River and its tributary, Muskaboo Creek, to its headwaters above treeline in the Nass Mountains. Whereas the other trails generally stayed in the river valleys to avoid the problems of the higher elevations (with the exception of the shortcut over Groundhog), the telegraph trailblazers went over one of the region's highest mountain crossings, which at 5,000 feet was certain to be vulnerable to prodigious snowfalls and avalanches.

Emerging into the valley of the Bell-Irving River, the surveyors turned northward to parallel the Iskut River (the route of the later Cassiar Highway). Not content to follow the lower waterways north and approach Telegraph Creek from the east, they again went cross-country over the Tahltan Highlands through Raspberry Pass to gain the valley of Mess Creek, then up the Stikine River to Telegraph Creek.

A cursory look at a topographic map suggests that several other routes might have been chosen that would have avoided the higher elevations, with little increase in mileage. For example, Pope described a route following the Skeena River that provided a relatively easy crossing into the watershed of the Stikine via the Klappan River. A similar crossing could have been made by following the Nass River and its tributaries.

However, the urgency of the project did not allow the surveyors the luxury of exploring for the best route. Unlike the Collins Overland Telegraph 35 years earlier, which had employed several exploration parties well ahead of construction, the Yukon Telegraph surveyors apparently did no preliminary fieldwork. This was a serious error on the part of Charleson and DPW officials. Their failure to authorize a survey in 1899 might be explained by the fact that no firm decision had been made to build the line, but there was no excuse for not sending survey parties into this crucial middle section well before the two work crews arrived in the area seeking to link up. While they were engaged stringing wire from Atlin toward Telegraph Creek, and from Quesnel toward Hazelton, there was ample time to explore the intervening section to select and cut a survey line between Hazelton and Telegraph Creek.

Without this through-survey line, an absurd situation developed in which the two crews proceeded independently, each forging ahead in a direction they hoped would link them up with the other party. The lack of a survey line would have embarrassing consequences for Charleson and the DPW.

On the positive side of the ledger, the DPW should be credited for placing orders for construction materials before the project gained final approval. Otherwise, work could not have begun as early as it did in the spring of 1900. The Seybold Company of Great Britain was contracted to supply the No. 8 galvanized iron wire; the white porcelain insulators came from St. John's Potteries in Quebec; and the wooden side blocks, used to attach the insulators to the poles, were provided by Firstbrook Brothers of Toronto.[16]

As soon as materials became available they were shipped to the several depots. In the south they went by rail to Ashcroft and then by wagon or pack train to the base camp in Quesnel. Other loads went up the Skeena on Hudson's Bay Company steamers to Hazelton, where they were packed south to meet the crew working from Quesnel. In the north they went by boat to Skagway and then via the White Pass railway to Log Cabin or Bennett City. As the lakes were frozen solid and the land covered with snow, horse-drawn sleighs, brought north expressly for the job, hauled the loads the rest of the way to Atlin. The last five miles were across the ice on beautiful Atlin Lake. Supplies were also ferried up the Stikine River to be cached at Telegraph Creek for the crew working south from Atlin.

Horse-drawn sleighs cross frozen Atlin Lake loaded with construction materials and provisions for the work crew building the Yukon Telegraph south from Atlin.

From Atlin to the South

In early March, engineer Aurelien Boyer arrived in Atlin with a party of 24 men and "47 tons of oats, and 40 tons of hay, 14 tons of building materials, hardware, and 30 tons of provisions ... "[17] He soon set off with a survey crew to blaze a line to Telegraph Creek. Packers followed, moving the construction materials, which were cached along the trail.[18] They wanted to get the materials into the bush while the trail was still frozen and snow-covered.

One of the problems of travelling in the spring is that when the temperature rises during the day, the snow becomes soft and heavy. Travel is best done during the early hours, when the surface is still firm from overnight freezing. Later in the spring, the trails turn to mud and become even more difficult.

Charleson, his staff, and a party of workmen from the east arrived in Atlin on March 19. He quickly selected a building at the northwest corner of Second and Pearl streets to serve as a telegraph office. Renovations were soon underway, including the addition of a third storey. To accommodate the men and to store supplies, he rented two additional buildings, and piles of coiled wire, barrels of insulators, kegs of spikes, and all the other items needed to build a telegraph line were strewn around the downtown area. The *Atlin Claim* reported that the men were pleased to be in Atlin, calling it "the prettiest place they have yet seen."[19]

Although the construction activity promised to provide a shot in the arm for Atlin's economy, not everyone was pleased. The *Claim*, venting its dislike of the Liberal government, particularly of the Quebecer Wilfrid Laurier, was incensed that so many easterners had been sent to do work that should have been given to British Columbians. The newspaper claimed that it was never the intention of Confederation "that this fair province should have to bear [the] expense of helping Eastern Canadians—from Quebec principally— to finding shelter."[20] In response, an advertisement appeared in the next issue, soliciting for 50 men, "Canadians preferred," to work on the telegraph, for two dollars a day and board.[21] There followed a letter from "Justice," complaining that the wages were insufficient for men who, unlike those whose transport had been provided from the east, had paid their own way. "Proper wages should be offered to local men."[22]

In a move intended to create a positive image in the community, Charleson donated a sum of money and a cooking range to the newly established St. Andrew's Hospital. His generosity was equally motivated by a desire to ensure good treatment in the future for any of his men who might require medical attention.[23]

On March 28, work began in earnest. The 100-man work crew, under J.Y. Rochester, was divided into teams with specific tasks: to clear the 20-foot right-of-way, to trim trees and/or cut and erect poles, to attach the insulators, and to string the wire. A crew of carpenters was assigned to build the telegraph cabins that were to be spaced every 40 miles or so along the line.

Starting south, the crew followed the shore of Atlin Lake 20 miles to the mouth of Pike River, where they constructed the first telegraph station. The route then turned inland along the river in a generally east-southeasterly direction. At the end of each day an operator would connect a key to the wire to report the day's progress back to Atlin. Within three weeks, 50 miles of wire had been strung. Except for the pace of the work, all was going smoothly and the crew was well on its way to Telegraph Creek.

Not long after, however, progress was disrupted by a labour dispute. Some of the men expressed dissatisfaction with the way they were being treated, complaining about the catering

Construction party at lunch wearing mosquito netting to ward off the bothersome beasts.

arrangements and the high prices charged by the commissariat. As reported by the *Atlin Claim*, when one of the men ventured to raise these issues with a foreman, he was summarily dismissed. Requests to have him reinstated were denied by the foreman and then by the construction boss, Rochester, who disingenuously declared that there was no provision in DPW regulations allowing for reinstating a fired employee. In support of their fellow worker, 21 men walked off the job and headed back to Atlin.[24]

Their departure did not seem to overly concern Charleson. With an abundant labour force of failed gold miners available nearby, the grievances of discontented workers could be ignored. Not so easy to ignore was the growing evidence that building the Atlin–Quesnel section was turning out to be a much more difficult and time-consuming task than Ottawa had envisioned.

For the first 63 miles out of Atlin, the terrain was not particularly difficult, although it was heavily wooded and boggy in places. But at the Nakina River, the steep sides of the river's canyon made it impossible for the pack animals to carry loads safely down the steep trail. The men had to erect a 1,700-foot aerial tramway to move the heavy boxes and barrels across the canyon. Once free of their heavy loads, the animals were able to descend to the river, which they crossed on a 70-foot-long bridge. Beyond, the trail climbed steadily to Nakina Pass, where the crew encountered nine-foot snowdrifts—in the middle of May.[25]

All the construction materials and provisions had to be transported by pack animals, except for meat, which was provided by a herd of cattle driven along with the construction party. After two months the hard work was taking a toll on the horses and mules, and 40 to 50 replacements were ordered. They would be ferried from the coast up the Stikine River to meet the work crew at Telegraph Creek.

On June 12, Charleson reported that the work had reached the junction with the Teslin Trail at the Nahlin River. The crew now turned south, following the well-trod trail, and reached Telegraph Creek on July 18. The first major objective had been achieved, but the construction schedule was in a shambles.

It had taken 16 weeks to string 220 miles of wire, less than 2.5 miles per workday—about half the projected rate of progress. The weather, the many stream crossings, and at times the shortage of materials and animals all played a part in hindering the work. But the overriding factor was the ruggedness of the terrain, which, according to Charleson, was "the hardest possible country to conceive."[26]

After almost four months in the wilderness, the men were looking forward to a little relaxation when they reached Telegraph Creek—a dance hall or saloon, or perhaps a gambling parlour. They were sorely disappointed. Two years earlier, at the height of the Klondike stampede, the town had been flourishing, a lively place with its share of entertainments. But by July 1900 the rush was over and Telegraph Creek had reverted to a quiet Native village. There was a church, a police post, the Hudson's Bay Company store, and some outfitters' buildings, but little more. There wasn't much for the men to do.

For those who were tired of the hardships and deprivations of working in the wilderness, there were riverboats to take them down the Stikine to Wrangell and civilization. For those who chose

A Native spirit or burial house near Telegraph Creek. These houses were usually furnished with many of the deceased's possessions.

to stay, there was more work to be done on the other side of the river. The wire was strung across at a point about two miles above the town, and the crew continued south, looking to connect with the men from Quesnel.

From Quesnel to the North

The crew from the south faced a more formidable task. Because no thorough survey had been made, the exact distances were unknown. A report prepared shortly before the work began could only say that the distance between Hazelton and Telegraph Creek was "over 300 miles, many people put it down as four hundred."[27]

The first job of the southern crew, under the direction of James Trodden, was to build a telegraph office, including a battery room, at the far north end of Quesnel. Charleson selected this location because he considered the wooden town a tinderbox. Initially, this office was used only to communicate with the work party, to monitor the progress of the work. It was not connected to the line that went south to the railway's telegraph at Ashcroft. There was no need, Charleson wrote, for the public to know "all our movements."[28] He wanted to avoid broadcasting information about problems the project might encounter, which the Opposition could use for political ends. Charleson's paranoia about the "many ears" that might be listening was one reason he limited his own use of the telegraph, sending his detailed reports to Ottawa by mail.

The crew started stringing wire from Quesnel at the end of March, about the same time the other crew started from Atlin. Their route was along the east bank of the Fraser River, which they crossed at a point where it was 1,200 feet wide, using two wires so that if one later broke, the other would still be available. The old trail/road they were following went northwest to Blackwater, about 52 miles from Quesnel, then continued to Fraser Lake. In his May 13 report, Charleson stated that 75 miles of telegraph had been built with no major difficulties.[29] But there were some frustrations.

There was a lack of communication between the DPW's Telegraph Service office and Charleson as to where supplies should be shipped. Most shipments went by rail to Ashcroft or Vancouver, from where they were forwarded, on Charleson's directions, to one of the depots. On more than one occasion, however, his instructions were either misunderstood or arbitrarily changed, resulting in shortages at the work sites. He repeatedly warned Ottawa that if the wire was not available when required, "it will be impossible to get our work completed on time ... "[30]

Upon reaching Hazelton, the crew paused briefly, then headed up the Kispiox River and by the end of the summer was 100 miles beyond Hazelton. The northern crew reported that it was 100 miles south of Telegraph Creek, so it seemed that no more than 130 miles separated the two parties. Confidence was growing that the line could be completed before winter halted work. A letter from one of the foremen of the southern crew claimed that on September 9 they were only 80 miles from the other crew and were progressing at the rate of 2.5 miles per day. "We should join hands with them ... by October 1."[31]

Buoyed with optimism, Charleson went to Vancouver to take part in the "momentous ceremony ... and receive the first message."[32] He waited in vain for word that the line had been completed, eventually going to Ashcroft to get a closer report. When Rochester claimed that his crew was 160 miles northwest of Hazelton, and Trodden reported that he was 157 miles northwest of the same place, it did not require Sherlock Holmes to deduce that something was amiss. Using some form of new math, Charleson concluded that there was no more than a 30-mile gap between the two work parties. Surely they would link up in a few more days. But it was not to be.

There had been too many obstacles to overcome, and now the weather was beginning to change. The cold was killing the forage, and already in places there were four feet of snow. The starving pack animals were dying at the rate of five a day. On the southern end, the crew had run out of wire, and it was impossible to get more in to the job site. The work was finished for the year.

Of critical concern to Charleson was getting the men out of the bush and down the rivers before freeze-up. Each crew had to retrace its steps more than 100 miles—Rochester's back to Telegraph Creek on the Stikine, Trodden's to Hazelton on the Skeena. Fortunately, both crews were able to catch steamers before the boats stopped running for the year.[33]

A Pall of Failure

Not long after the work stopped, rumours of an "overlap" began, reports that the two work parties had passed each other, in one story by as much as 175 miles. Although there had been an irresponsible lack of proper planning, it was unlikely that the engineers and surveyors could have made such a horrendous error. And they had not. The distance between the two crews was not an overlap; it was a gap. But this did not stop the newspapers from reporting the story of an overlap, requiring the government to refute the rumour when questioned on the floor of Parliament.[34]

Although the Liberals were able to rebut the overlap rumours, they could not escape the embarrassment of not knowing the extent of the gap. Charleson at first reported that it was 30 miles. As more information was made available, it became 50 miles. Thereafter the number increased until it seemed that no one in the DPW was certain of the actual distance.

Charleson had to answer for why the line had not been finished in the allotted time. The unrealistic schedule imposed by Ottawa was ignored, as were the extra assignments added to his workload during the summer. In 1899 the government had taken over the telegraph line between Ashcroft and Quesnel, previously operated by the telegraph department of the Canadian Pacific Railway. It was in bad shape; the wire and many of the poles needed to be replaced. The CPR estimated it could rebuild the section for $20,000 to $25,000; Charleson thought he could do it for half that amount, and he got the job. He was also directed to extend the Bennett–Dawson line 95 miles from Dawson City to the border to connect to the U.S. military telegraph line.[35]

In his defence, Charleson maintained that the DPW had supplied inaccurate distances, which he used as the basis for ordering the wire and other supplies. He claimed that he had been told the distance between Quesnel and Atlin was 844 miles, whereas his crews had strung a total of 1,040 miles of wire.[36] Assuming that he was not including in his calculation any of the added work, and that the correct distance (as measured later) between Atlin and Quesnel is 870 miles, it is difficult to credit his charge.

The failure to complete the Yukon Telegraph in 1900 cast a pall of failure over the project and embarrassed the government when it was challenged to provide explanations. This was unjust, but the situation could have been avoided if Ottawa had not broadcast such an unrealistic completion date. By any standard, the stringing of 800 or 1,000 miles of telegraph line through an environment as inhospitable as that of northern British Columbia was an admirable achievement.

Working from early spring over snow-covered frozen trails, which then turned to horrid gluey mud, the crews persevered until the last possible day in the fall, when heavy snows put a halt to the work. From March through October the men had lived in difficult, primitive conditions, subject to the whims of the weather and the agonies inflicted by ubiquitous, merciless insects. (The lives of the men and the hardships they overcame are, unfortunately, not recorded. There is no "people's history." Of the hundreds of men who worked on the project, from the axemen and wire stringers to the wranglers and foremen, not a single voice has been located to relate their experiences. The history of building the Yukon Telegraph relies exclusively on the records of the government, mainly the communications of its top officials and construction bosses. The newspapers that followed the project relied for their facts on the reports provided by these same sources, interpreting the data as dictated by their political proclivities.)

As for Charleson, if ever a man had been set up for a fall, it was him. Acclaimed for his achievements in 1899, a year later he was demeaned for his failure to repeat the performance. And he faced other problems, including misgivings about the completeness of the project's financial accounts and about how some of the money had been spent. These concerns first arose soon after the Dawson line was completed and reached a crescendo after the finish of work in 1900.

The Opposition Attacks

In the spring of 1901 the Opposition raised questions in House of Commons debates about the propriety of certain financial arrangements and costs. There were suggestions of shady dealings by Charleson, much to the embarrassment of Minister Tarte, who had to respond to the barbs. He was hard-pressed to rationalize some of the superintendent's practices and expenditures.

From the beginning, the Bennett to Dawson project was tainted by the appearance of favouritism and profiteering well beyond the usual rewards of patronage. Most damning was the charge that immediately after J.B. Charleson was assigned to superintend the work, his son, William George Charleson, went into the hardware business. Subsequently, it was claimed, no less than $90,000 worth of supplies was purchased by the father from the son's store, in some instances at retail prices.

The Opposition also questioned the generous personal allowances permitted staff members going north. They charged clothing (shirts, trousers, gloves, and Stetson hats) and many other items to the projects, all purchased at William Charleson's store. Skepticism about the legitimacy of some of these charges increased when it was learned that they included payments for haircuts, shaves, and tobacco. Tarte tried to fob off these excesses as mere "trifles" of no significance; and anyway, he taunted, they were the results of "bad habits [learned] under the former [Conservative] government." Replying with indignation, the Opposition challenged anyone to find "that under the Conservative regime the officer of any department established his son in business, went immediately to his son to purchase all his supplies, approved the accounts himself and paid for them."[37]

Also questioned were the salaries of some staff members, particularly Charleson's secretary, Joseph Gobeil, the brother of Deputy Minister Aureal Gobeil. Credulity was stretched when it was learned that Gobeil, previously a two-dollar-a-day temporary employee of the department, was hired as Charleson's secretary at the munificent salary of $2,000, not far below what his boss was being paid. It was hard to believe that a mere secretary could demand such a salary.

Another questionable practice involved the arrangement made to provide telegraph poles. Initially Charleson had signed a contract with the Victoria Trading Company to supply the poles at three dollars each. After the delivery of 330 poles for the section between Bennett City and Caribou Crossing, Charleson voided the contract in favour of one with J.Y. Rochester, at the time a government employee, who offered to provide the poles at a cost of two dollars each.

Rochester had originally been employed in the dual capacities of construction foreman and bookkeeper. The latter assignment included maintaining the project's financial accounts. Upon being granted the pole contract he promptly and properly resigned both his government positions. However, Tarte claimed that because there was no one else qualified to do the accounting job, Rochester had generously agreed to continue keeping the books, at no charge. Thereafter, from March to October 1899, Rochester operated both as the project's bookkeeper and as a private contractor, who was reputed to have supplied 6,000 poles worth $12,000. The poles were actually cut by a subcontractor for an undisclosed price, which Rochester, backed by the government, refused to divulge, saying it was privileged business information.

The Opposition forces in the Commons protested that such an arrangement put Charleson and Rochester "too much in each other's hands." Rochester, by the award of this lucrative contract, was indebted to his benefactor Charleson. As keeper of the books, how better to reciprocate than with favourable evaluations of J.B.'s expenditures? It was also repeatedly pointed out to Minister Tarte that bookkeeper Rochester had a personal financial interest in the entries for which he was responsible, particularly those relating to the payment for poles. Tarte was forced to concede that this relationship might have been "imprudent"; he himself would not have made such an arrangement. He settled, however, for the mildest rebuke, admitting that Charleson "may have made some mistakes."[38]

These charges and innuendoes were particularly embarrassing to Tarte, who had established a reputation as "an uncompromising enemy of robbery and corruption" and had previously exposed the chicanery of more than one political malfeasant.[39]

Another hindrance to divining the truth was the continued unavailability of Charleson's accounts. The usual procedure was for departments to submit their accounts to the auditor general's office, which, after evaluation, forwarded them to the Commons' Public Accounts Committee for approval. The committee usually began meeting in February to review the accounts of the previous year. It would routinely interview officers of the various departments, and when areas of concern arose it might call other individuals to answer questions. Committee members were especially interested in meeting with Charleson to review his accounts, many of which had not been made available either to the auditor general's office or to the committee.

During the course of construction, Charleson had been sent money to pay on-the-job expenses: wages for the workers, bills for materials and provisions, charges for transportation, costs of lodgings in towns, etc. Some of the funds were deposited in banks, from which he drew cheques, but many payments were made in cash. These payments should have been recorded in a cashbook, which was to be transmitted periodically to Ottawa along with vouchers and other records. Charleson was less than diligent in following these procedures.

The auditor general repeatedly asked him to submit vouchers to document how he was spending the money. Apparently not satisfied with the records received up to that point, in December 1900 the auditor general explicitly requested an accounting of over $90,000 in time for his annual report.[40] The Public Accounts Committee also called for back records. Some of the accounts requested were for monies spent more than a year earlier on the Bennett–Dawson job, for which complete records were still not available. They requested that all of Charleson's vouchers and papers relating to a particular $48,000 allotment be produced.[41]

Whatever records were assembled, they did not satisfy the auditor general, eliciting further requests, specifically for the cashbooks, which set off a flurry of activity. Charleson maintained that the books had been sent to Ottawa, but they could not immediately be located, nor was it clear who had them. First Charleson claimed that a Mr. Hayter had received them, then that a "man from Montreal" was involved, finally that they were in a box in Charleson's Ottawa office. If they were not there, Charleson said, then Mr. Hayter had them. But there should be no problem because a "Mr. Reid, of the Auditor General's Department, checked and initialled all the entries in that book and gave me a certificate which is locked up in my tin box in the house and if you ask my son, he will get it."[42]

The mystery continued, for Deputy Minister Gobeil reported that, having "opened every box, drawer, etc. [we] have found no cash book."[43] Charleson, who was in Vancouver at the time, gave a perplexing interview to the *Vancouver Province* in which he feigned ignorance of the Public Accounts Committee's interest in his cashbooks.

"What cash books?" asked Mr. Charleson, in obvious surprise.

He knew nothing whatever about the proceedings of the committee at Ottawa, and to say that he was angry when the situation was explained, would be to put it mildly.

"Disappeared!" he echoed, when told of the vanished records. "Why that is quite impossible. Every book in connection with the work in the north was deposited in the department in Ottawa with Mr. Hayter. The cash book was with the other records ... "

He called Mr. Rochester, who was standing close by, and asked to whom the books and records were handed over.

"To Mr. Hayter," responded Mr. Rochester, promptly, "and I took a receipt for every one."[44]

It is not clear how the matter was resolved, other than to observe that Charleson remained in his position and Rochester continued to be employed as a construction superintendent. The Public Accounts Committee did recommend that thereafter a DPW accountant be assigned to Charleson. For several years, members of the Public Accounts Committee attempted to quiz Charleson in person about some of these matters and repeatedly requested his presence to answer their concerns, but he was too adroit for them. He always managed to be leaving Ottawa just before the committee met, claiming that it was essential that he return to his construction duties.

Although he avoided the opportunity to answer his critics before the committee, Charleson aggressively claimed he was innocent of any wrongdoing. He was indignant and incensed at the suggestion of impropriety, vowing that in the future he would "make no payment except Hardy [the accountant assigned to him by the department] is present or somebody else to take receipts. I want no imputations to be cast on me ... Whoever comes will take charge of all vouchers and make all payments as I am not in with anybody and have nothing to conceal or keep back."[45] Charleson felt that he had been maligned, and his bitterness was evident in some of his later dealings with officials in Ottawa.

He was correct in insisting that he needed to return to the west to complete the project, although perhaps not as early as he did. There was more work to be done to close the gap and complete the all-Canadian telegraph line. As he calculated that there could be no more than 100 miles of wire left to string, the work should not take long—a month, two at the most.

CHAPTER 7

Completion of the "All-Canadian" Telegraph, 1901

Before heading out of the bush in October 1900, the last job for both the northern and southern construction crews had been to build a cabin at the end of the wire on each side of the gap. Two men were assigned to spend the winter in each of these cabin stations.

When it was first estimated that the gap was only 30 miles, J.B. Charleson proposed running relays of dogsleds to carry messages between the two stations.[1] This would have reduced the time for a telegram to reach the south to one day. However, the distance between the two stations was much greater than expected, and when the scheme was tried, it yielded dire results: Dogs died of exhaustion, and one driver suffered frostbite. The idea was quickly abandoned.[2]

Charleson was forced to revise his estimate of the size of the gap. In his report of November 22, 1900, to Deputy Minister Gobeil, he admits that it is more likely 50 to 60 miles.[3] On the map prepared by Aurelien Boyer to accompany this report, the gap scales out to be at least 75 miles.[4]

One explanation for Charleson's inability to determine the distance is that the reports submitted to him by the construction

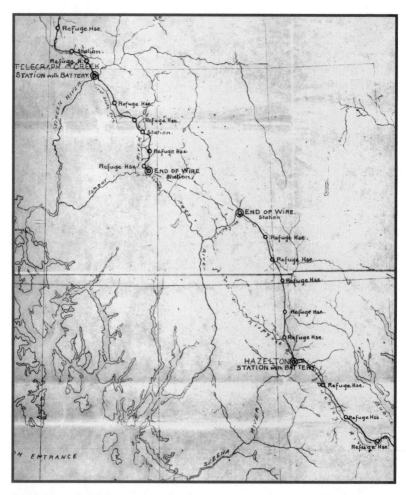

Map prepared by engineer Aurelien Boyer showing work done on the telegraph line during 1900, the location of cabins (refuges), and the gap that remained to complete the line.

supervisors were inaccurate. For example, the final location of the north end of the wire, as shown by Boyer, was actually at the Ningunsaw River, about 100 miles from Telegraph Creek, whereas construction superintendent Rochester reported that his crew was within 160 miles of Hazelton, or 170 miles from Telegraph Creek. At the southern end, James Trodden's claims were equally inaccurate, overestimated by at least 50 miles. In a report to Gobeil, in which he explains why he initially stated that the gap was only 30 miles,

Charleson ignores Rochester's culpability and places the blame entirely on Trodden, concluding that "either through ignorance or through design [he] had misled me and the consequence was that I misled you."[5]

Finding a scapegoat may have deflected some of the criticism from Charleson, but it did not excuse his failure to have a cutline surveyed through the unmapped area. A survey would not have eliminated the gap, but it would have avoided the embarrassment of having to admit ignorance of the actual amount of work remaining to complete the line.

Exploring the Gap

To finally settle the question of the extent of the gap, and to establish the route to complete the line, engineer Boyer led a party to explore the terrain between the two ends. Starting from Wrangell on March 1, 1901, the party travelled up the Stikine River ice to Glenora, which Boyer described as "entirely covered" with mounds of snow, the deepest old-timers could remember. Following the wire south to the station at Ningunsaw, they found the men who had wintered there lonely but in good health. Continuing south through the gap, the party crossed several previously unnamed (by white men) streams, which they proceeded to christen, naming one the Simon River, after an old Indian man who lived nearby, and another the Edward River, after King Edward VII.[6]

As the days grew warmer, travel in the deep snow became more difficult. To take advantage of the overnight freeze that temporarily hardened the trail, the men would start as early as 3:00 a.m., stopping by noon when the footing softened and they sank into the heavy snow. After crossing the pass through the windswept Nass Mountains, they reached the south end of the wire 12 days after starting from Glenora. Boyer reported that the gap was 100 miles, over terrain that was rough but posed no special difficulties to finishing the line.

The party continued another 100 miles or so to Hazelton, then down the Skeena River to its mouth, where Charleson met them. The men were exhausted by their ordeal, especially Boyer, who had to be placed in hospital to recover. Charleson, upon receiving

Boyer's report, grudgingly admitted that the gap "is a little longer than what we thought it was," maybe as much as 104 miles.[7]

The inconsistencies between Charleson's and his construction supervisors' reports about the size of the gap were grounds for questioning their competence, but from a practical standpoint it did not seem important at the time to determine the exact length of the gap. Be it 50 miles or 100 miles or a bit more, the work could easily be completed by the end of the summer of 1901.

During the hiatus between construction seasons, other problems demanded Charleson's attention. As noted, he was called upon to answer questions and criticisms relating to his financial accounts and expenditure of funds. He was also faulted when it was revealed that although the project had not been completed, it was already over budget.

Keeping track of the money sent to him and maintaining accurate accounts, especially the cashbooks, seems to have been a bother and a nuisance for Charleson. From his perspective, however, there was an even bigger headache: actually getting the money he needed to pay the project's expenses. He was repeatedly forced to ask Ottawa to send funds, often to cover cheques he had already issued. This problem was to become even more acute when the work resumed in 1901.

Branch Line along the Skeena

Charleson's plan was to start the two crews from where they had stopped the year before. While he was anxious to get the men into the field as soon as possible in the early spring, they were delayed because of the heavy accumulation of snow. The trails were blocked and forage for the pack animals would not be available until much later than usual.

There was one project that could be started earlier: a branch line between Hazelton and Port Simpson, a fishing village on the coast. Advantageously situated at the mouth of the Portland Canal, Port Simpson was an old (1831) Hudson's Bay Company trading post that at one time had attracted as many as 2,000 Tsimshian people to live and trade in the area. It was accessible to the coastal fishing fleet and to a number of nearby canneries.

Taking advantage of the milder climate at the coast, the work would start from the Port Simpson end, then follow the inland waterway, called Work Channel, 40 miles to the Skeena River before continuing up the river to connect to the main line at Hazelton, a total distance of 200 miles. The work crew started in March, reached the Skeena opposite Port Essington, then proceeded up the rugged north side of the river.[8] It was a difficult and inhospitable terrain through which to string a telegraph line. In places the mountains plunged steeply down to the river's edge, making it impossible to build a trail along the line. And there were huge trees to be removed, some measuring 3.5 feet in diameter, a size that the men were not accustomed to handling. One newspaper claimed that it was "the hardest country ever travelled over by a Canadian."[9] By the beginning of May the work had progressed 120 miles to the "Canyon of the Skeena."[10]

If there was any advantage to building along a river, it was that boats rather than packhorses could be used to move supplies to the work sites. The Port Simpson, or as it became known, Skeena branch, was completed on June 14.[11] Port Simpson was now connected to the rest of the country and beyond.

As the work progressed on the branch line, Charleson continued to chafe at the mistreatment and indignities he felt he had been subjected to by Ottawa: the investigation of his financial accounts, the charges of nepotism, the insinuations against his probity, and now the criticism for exceeding the project's budget. His department bosses had warned him not to overspend the funds allocated to him, but when the Port Simpson branch was completed, he could not refrain from loosing a few comments about the failings of the pusillanimous bureaucrats in the Department of Public Works:

Mr. Kingston [a government official] wrote me a letter saying that the cheques that were issued [by me] for payments in June on the Port-Simpson Line could not be honoured by the Auditor General because there [was] no money voted to be used before the first of July. This seems very strange that I built and completed the line before the

13th of June and that I could not pay the men until July. I wonder if the people in the Department think that the men out here labour simply for patriotism's sake and not for cash.

How was I to pay these men and accounts if I was not to issue cheques ... When a man leaves he wants his pay ... There is no use to try to get him to receipt a paysheet which can be sent down to Ottawa and trust that he will get paid. They will not do it.[12]

The Port Simpson branch was considered a part of the Yukon Telegraph system. It served the fishing villages, canning companies, and mining enterprises along the coast north of the Skeena River, and until 1904 (when a cable was laid between Seattle and Alaska) it handled messages from some of the American settlements along the coast, such as Ketchikan.

The line had been roughly built, leaving much finishing work to be done by the linemen who remained to keep it operating. Although spared the extremes of weather, they experienced conditions as demanding and dangerous as any faced by their counterparts on the main line, with the added vagaries of working on a tidal river of awe-inspiring and capricious power.

When the line was opened in 1901, the first operator at Port Simpson was a Mr. Callaghan, who, although experienced and popular, had a problem with the spirits. He was soon banished to an interior station where temptation was less likely to call, certainly less frequently than it might in a hard-drinking fishing village. Fortunately, living in Port Simpson at the time was 21-year-old Martha Washington O'Neill, who had pursued an interest in telegraphy. Although inexperienced, she was a satisfactory operator, and when Superintendent John T. Phelan learned that she was available, he offered her the job of replacing Callaghan.

Many women were employed as telegraph operators at the time, but they usually worked in the cities and towns and on the railways, in more settled and cultured environs. Port Simpson was different. It was at the edge of nowhere, a rough seaport town accessible only by boat or after a long wilderness trek.

As well, the station there was not an easy assignment. It was a battery station with all the added responsibilities of maintaining the wet cells. Only expediency, blind faith, or the Divinity can explain what motivated Phelan to put such a young and inexperienced person, male or female, in charge of Port Simpson. And it was a truly audacious act on Martha O'Neill's part to assume responsibility for the station, a statement of her character and confidence. As she recalled in her memoir:

What a time I had learning the "tricks" of electricity. I am sure I died many times within myself. Sometimes when things went wrong with the batteries or wires, my hair fairly stood on end, as there was no one I could appeal to for advice so I had to learn by experience. What a line that was. My battery consisted of 130 wet cells, the only one on the line west of [the] Hazelton office, 180 miles by the crow. Sometimes the glass batteries would crack in extreme cold or thunderstorms and bluestone water [the conducting agent] ran all over the office.[13]

On one occasion, after searching for half an hour to find the cause of the line not working, she "discovered the cow had caught her foot in the ground wire [and] pulled it out of the muddy spring near the house."[14] O'Neill also reported some of the difficulties encountered by the linemen at the intermediate stations.

[They] ... had a difficult time, especially in winter as the wire was strung along steep precipices, on trees, across mountain portages and deep ravines, in perhaps seven or eight feet of snow and no trail to guide them. They also ran the rapids in the ice floes and contended with many other hardships. In summer they risked the dangers during high water on the river and suffered from the mosquitoes. I remember the boys at Graveyard Point had to vacate their station at night and sleep on an island to escape the pests. This line work was carried out at a salary of seventy-five dollars a month and an annual supply of provisions.

The men often complained of the mouldy bacon, wormy dried fruit, and weavily flour supplied to them by the wholesale[rs] in Vancouver, who deserved to be shot for their graft ... These men were our "empire builders" and since I have heard them remark that they wouldn't do that work at the present time for seven hundred a month.

I had charge of the fifty odd miles of wire from my station to the head of Work Channel and a launch and two linemen at my disposal. During the winter after a storm, it was not unusual to report from 50 to 100 breaks or grounds. Consequently the wire was down most of the snow period. Beyond my section, two men were stationed every forty miles and covered their beats 20 miles each side of their cabins.[15]

The 121-Mile Gap

As the work was winding down on the Port Simpson branch, a crew of 40 men went down the Skeena, around to Wrangell, and up the Stikine River to Telegraph Creek, where they prepared to start work on the gap from the north. The remainder of the crew, when they reached Hazelton, continued to the end of the wire to start working from the south.[16] J.Y. Rochester was again the construction boss of the northern crew, but in the south, the disgraced James Trodden had been replaced by J.B.'s brother, Alexander Charleson.

Initially it was thought that closing the gap would be a simple undertaking; the two crews would string the 100 miles of wire in short order. Certainly the job could take no longer than a month. But in the wilderness of British Columbia, the unanticipated always seemed to happen. Work did not commence until July because of the heavy snow cover and the lack of feed for the pack animals, and then it went slowly, especially through the Nass Mountains, where all the poles had to be cut below and hauled up to the areas above treeline. In addition, spring floods had knocked out many of the bridges built the year before. Problems like these never deterred the always-optimistic Charleson, who announced that the gap would probably be closed by August 1.[17] One would think that,

Linemen along the Skeena branch used boats to maintain the telegraph because the terrain was too steep for a trail.

A crew building a bridge over the Ningunsaw River, one of many built along the route of the telegraph. Although the engineers tried to anticipate the height of the annual spring floods, most of the bridges were washed out within a few years.

considering his past record as a soothsayer, Charleson would have learned not to offer gratuitous predictions.

A month after Charleson's predicted completion date, with the leaves beginning to show signs of approaching winter, barely 66 miles of wire had been strung, 36 by Rochester's crew, 30 by Alex Charleson's. And due to a supply foul-up, the southern crew was out of wire. However, the men continued to work clearing the right-of-way, preparing it for the northern crew to finish. J.B. made his final promise: the gap would be closed by September 15.[18]

On September 24 the two crews met at a point 145 miles north of Hazelton, and the much-anticipated splice was made. The southern crew had strung about 41 miles of the wire, the northern crew 80 miles. The size of the gap had finally been determined—121 miles.

What had started out as a short and simple operation to finish the previous year's work turned out to be a much more difficult and time-consuming task than anyone had imagined. In fact, it had taken so long that the workmen were once again in a race to get out of the bush before winter set in. Both crews headed toward Hazelton, their progress hindered by early snowstorms that slowed their travel and covered the forage. Only 23 pack animals survived to reach Second Cabin, with 40 miles still to go. These remaining animals were so played out and starving that they were mercifully shot, at a place forever after known as "Boneyard Camp."[19] All the workmen managed to get to Hazelton safely, barely two weeks earlier than they had the previous year.

No Golden Strand

It was finally finished. The all-Canadian Yukon Telegraph, stretching 1,800 miles to link Dawson City with Ashcroft and the rest of the country and the world, was open for business. The citizens of Vancouver showed their appreciation by planning a dinner to honour Charleson,[20] and the messages of congratulations began to flow. But most were muted in their enthusiasm. Prime Minister Laurier telegraphed Charleson: "I thank you very much for the good news and offer you my sincere congratulations on your success."[21] Hardly an inspiring or memorable message. Nothing about a "magnificent achievement" or "service to the country" or "overcoming obstacles," accolades that were warranted and would have been welcomed by Charleson and the other men who had given so much to the project. As one writer later put it: "No golden strand was used on the last pole to tie in this 1,800-mile stretch of No. 8 galvanised wire that linked Alaska and the Yukon with the rest of Canada and the United States. No silk-hatted, frock-coated statesmen were on hand to witness the notable event. Indeed, there was no ceremony at all except the drawing of corks from two bottles of brandy carried against sickness in the saddlebags of the head packer."[22] The only witnesses were a bunch of grubby workmen standing around, wondering when they were going to get out of the bush and back to civilization.

Perhaps because people had expected it to be finished the year before, its tardy completion was anticlimactic. Any emotional response or expression of Canadian pride had been deflated. Or it might have been that the sense of adventure and romance inspired by the Klondike stampede, the original purpose for the telegraph line, had faded as mining passed into the big-business phase. The Klondike's time had passed and the bloom was off—only four years · after the historic docking of the gold ships in San Francisco and Seattle. The government's and the public's attention had passed to other matters, to more immediate and important concerns. For Americans it was the War against Spain, while Canadian soldiers were becoming more deeply and tragically involved in the Anglo–Boer War.

The government's perception of the line had also begun to change. Initially viewed as a great national undertaking, a vital public service deserving Ottawa's continued subsidy, it was now considered something of a liability that no longer warranted much attention or support. The Yukon Telegraph was expected to be financially accountable.

Minister Tarte was still convinced of the line's fiscal viability and potential. In January 1901 he reported that the Bennett–Dawson–Atlin section had earned a total of $107,000, or $50,000 over costs. He expected the entire line to pay "fairly well," going so far as to suggest that rates could be lowered and the line would still break even.[23]

Tarte's chimerical assessment was not reflected in Ottawa's support for the workers who were charged with operating and maintaining the telegraph. The government did little more than provide minimal living and working conditions for the operators and linemen. They were left to their own devices to equip their home cabins and build additional refuge cabins. The most telling expression of the government's attitude toward them was Ottawa's demand, within a year, that they accept a reduction in their wages.

.

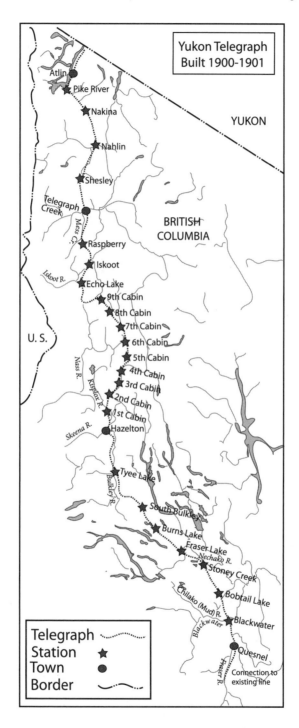

Yukon Telegraph
Built 1900-1901

YUKON

BRITISH COLUMBIA

U.S.

Atlin
Pike River
Nakina
Nahlin
Shesley
Telegraph Creek
Raspberry
Iskoot
Echo Lake
9th Cabin
8th Cabin
7th Cabin
6th Cabin
5th Cabin
4th Cabin
3rd Cabin
2nd Cabin
1st Cabin
Hazelton
Tyee Lake
South Bulkley
Burns Lake
Fraser Lake
Stoney Creek
Bobtail Lake
Blackwater
Quesnel
Connection to existing line

Mess Cr.
Iskoot R.
Nass R.
Kispiox R.
Skeena R.
Bulkley R.
Nechako R.
Chilako (Mud) R.
Blackwater
Fraser R.

Telegraph
Station
Town
Border

CHAPTER 8

The Early Years: Discontent and Description

The Yukon Telegraph was a division of the Dominion Government Telegraph Service within the Department of Public Works. The service operated lines throughout Canada, providing communications to areas that were not covered by the railway telegraph systems or were unattractive to private investment. These areas were usually in the less populated parts of the country: the Maritime provinces, the lower St. Lawrence, northern Alberta, and the North-West Territories. In British Columbia, in addition to the Yukon Telegraph, the government operated lines in the southern part of the province and on Vancouver Island.

In 1904 the Dominion Service was the third-largest system in the country, behind only the Great North Western Telegraph Company and Canadian Pacific Telegraph. Its 6,270 miles of wire made up 17 percent of the national total. The Yukon Division, with over 2,200 miles of line, was the largest in the government system.[1]

From the Bay of Fundy to the far northwest, the government lines were all money-losers. The Yukon Telegraph was no exception, but generally it performed better than most of the other lines. It was by far the most costly to operate, but it also produced the most revenue.

D.H. Keeley was the general superintendent of the Dominion Service from the time the Yukon Telegraph was built until his retirement in 1921. However, during construction and until about 1905, Keeley's authority was circumvented by the officials in charge of the Yukon Telegraph. Charleson, for example, reported directly to the deputy minister of public works.

Description of the Yukon Telegraph

The Yukon Telegraph was headed by a superintendent. It was divided into a northern district (Atlin to Dawson City) and a southern district (Ashcroft to Atlin), each with a district superintendent. The southern district included several branch lines: to Barkerville, Lillooet, Port Simpson, and Quesnel Forks. The northern district also included the section north of Dawson City that connected to the U.S. military telegraph system in Alaska.

When the White Pass and Yukon Route completed its telegraph line to Caribou Crossing and to Whitehorse in 1900, the Yukon Telegraph line from Bennett to Caribou Crossing was abandoned, although the section from Tagish to Caribou Crossing was retained as an alternative connection to the White Pass telegraph. The large telegraph station/depot erected at Bennett just two years earlier was no longer needed.

In September 1901, the distance of the main line from Ashcroft to Boundary was calculated to be 1,850 miles. Initially there were 37 stations. The major battery stations were located at Dawson (400 wet cells), Selkirk (175), Bennett (250), Atlin (100), Telegraph Creek (100), Hazelton (150), Quesnel (150), and Port Simpson (100). Repeaters were fitted at the Ashcroft, Hazelton, and Atlin stations.[2] Including the branches and extensions, the total length of the line in 1902 was 2,279 miles.

The Barkerville branch, extending 61 miles from Quesnel, was built between 1878 and 1887 to serve the Cariboo gold fields. Between Ashcroft, Quesnel, and Barkerville, a distance of 277 miles, there were two wires: One carried long-distance messages, the other only local traffic.

The branch from Ashcroft to Lillooet, 62 miles in length, was built in 1896. The Canadian Pacific Railway temporarily operated both the Lillooet and Barkerville branches until they were reacquired by the government in May 1901.

Table 2

Yukon Division of the Dominion Telegraph

A list of the Yukon Division's sections and branches, with mileage and costs of construction, was made available by the DPW in 1902.[3]

Costs of Construction	Miles	Cost $	Cost/ Mile $
Atlin–Dawson City	637	174,500	274
Dawson City–Boundary	95	18,600	195
Quesnel–Atlin*	944	500,495	530
Port Simpson–Hazelton (Branch)	200	64,600	323
Total	**1,876**	**758,195**	**404**
Other Division Sections			
Ashcroft to Quesnel	216		
Quesnel to Barkerville	61		
Ashcroft to Lillooet	62		
150 Mile House to Quesnel Forks	64		
Total Miles	2,279		

* Closing the 121-mile gap cost $700/mile

The Quesnel Forks branch, also called the Horsefly branch, was built from 150 Mile House to the mining area by a private contractor, J.C. Shields of Ashcroft, who completed the 64-mile section on November 1, 1902.

The Port Simpson line was extended in 1902 to service the canneries at Aberdeen, and when the Grand Trunk Pacific Railway (GTP) announced plans to establish its terminus at Prince Rupert, an additional 40 miles of line was built to include that fledgling, but potentially important, community.

On some of the branch lines, at places where there was not sufficient business to justify a telegraph station with an operator, telephone offices were established. The operators of these offices were not paid a regular salary; rather, they received a portion of the rate charged for messages sent from their stations, usually 50 percent. There were telephone offices on the Lillooet branch at Cache Creek, Bonaparte, and Pavilion, and on the Barkerville line at LaFontaine.[4]

Economies on the Backs of the Workers

As mentioned in the previous chapter, not long after the line was completed, Ottawa's perception began to change. It no longer saw the Yukon Telegraph as a vital public service, necessary to protect Canadian sovereignty, but as a financial liability. When M.W. Crean was appointed superintendent of the Yukon Division in November 1901, it marked the transition from the construction phase to the operational—and accountability—phase. Crean was instructed to carry out economies.

When telegraphers were hired, they had to sign on for a minimum of three years, after which they were eligible for a two-month paid furlough. Pay varied little for veterans and rookies. It was generally $100 or $110 a month for an operator and $80 or $90 for a lineman, with lodging and provisions provided. There were no annual raises or cost-of-living adjustments. (During the 35 years of the main line's operation, workers' monthly salaries increased only marginally, perhaps $10 or $20 a month.) Although they were required to commit to the job for three years, the government made no similar promise to maintain their conditions of work, namely wages.

The government soon found that the initial cost it set for telegrams was considered very high. A message from Dawson City to Ashcroft was pricey: $4.50 for 10 words and $.30 for each additional word, with more charges added beyond Ashcroft.[5] These rates were widely criticized, leading to Ottawa's decision to reduce tariffs by one-third on June 1, 1902. At about the same time, the operators and linemen were told that their wages would be cut by 33 percent. In other words, the savings to the customers, which were mostly commercial accounts, were to come out of the pockets of the lowest-paid workers.

Superintendent Crean was directed to further cut costs by reducing the number of operators at Dawson, Ashcroft, and Hazelton. He did not seem overly concerned about the reduction in pay, but he strongly objected to the cuts in staff. In his appeal to the department to retain the operators, he has provided a look at how these stations functioned. He argued that the Dawson office could not be worked with less than the three operators presently employed, since the office was open from 8:00 a.m. until 2:00 a.m., or whenever the last Associated Press report was received from Vancouver. Two operators were required, each averaging 10 hours per day, and a third person was needed to keep the books and make out returns for the $7,000 of business the office was doing each month. At Ashcroft the conditions were the same, and three operators were fully occupied. At Hazelton, two operators were needed because the repeaters required constant attention from 8:00 a.m. until 2:00 a.m., or whenever Dawson shut down.[6] Crean's appeal must have been heeded because there was no reduction in the number of operators, but the reductions in pay, which affected all the men, were put into effect.

The operators and linemen up and down the line felt betrayed. Many wanted to show their displeasure by stopping work at once, but others wanted to hold off a strike until they could discuss their concerns directly with the department in Ottawa. Getting no satisfaction from Crean, who was only carrying out orders, they made repeated remonstrances to Minister Tarte, who had approved the reductions and was the only official who could rescind them.

When the newspapers began to report the dispute, other grievances came to public attention. Men complained that they had not been paid on time, some claiming they were owed a year's back wages. And there were reports that stations were not being supplied with adequate food.

A.S. Congdon, editor of the *Yukon Sun*, transmitted this information to Tarte, requesting that he address the matter.[7] Tarte's reply exposed his insensitivity toward government workers who were peacefully expressing legitimate grievances. His answer reads more like a treatise on Social Darwinism or a Conservative Party election plank: "We are in a free country. Men have a perfect right not to work for the government, if they find that their wages are not sufficient. On the other hand, my Department shall not be bull dosed as long as I am at the head of it by the threats of the employees. Any organised [sic] resistance amongst the men of our Yukon lines will be met with all the energy that I will be able to command."[8]

Tarte chose to confront the men as if they were making unreasonable demands rather then resisting a sizeable pay cut. He also, more ominously, informed the comptroller of the North West Mounted Police of the situation, alerting him to the possible need for protection from "hot heads [who] talk of destroying our Yukon line."[9]

For several weeks in July and August, the men, particularly those in the Dawson office, engaged in what can best be described as a job action or a part-time strike. They refused to work, but would go back periodically, whenever they were given assurances that their concerns would be addressed. The operators were not in the strongest position because supervisors could perform their jobs. It was the linemen who controlled the fate of the strike, at least in the short run. There is no indication that anyone openly advocated cutting the line, but the linemen could be dilatory in making repairs.

For a while there were no serious breaks, and supervisors filling in for the operators were able to keep the line operating. But eventually there was an interruption, much to the relief of District Supervisor Klegg, who had been trying to do the job of three men to keep the Dawson office operating. In a clear conflict of interest, he was reported to have expressed his thanks for the break so that he could get some rest.

On balance, the men's opposition to the cuts had been moderate. They had not attempted to organize a union, nor had they engaged in any destructive acts. On the contrary, they were merely resisting an extreme wage reduction, a response that hardly warranted their being called "hot heads." The government's actions, however, deserve to be questioned. It does not appear that it had any intention of negotiating with its employees, and, although it promised not to, it began to send out replacement workers. In September, six new men arrived and replaced strikers on the northern section.[10]

The dispute resulted from Ottawa's desire to have the Yukon line pay its own way, something it was unable to do in 1902 and was never able to do while it operated. In the short time since the Yukon Telegraph had begun operating, its original purpose had been forgotten. This observation was succinctly expressed by the *Dawson Daily News*:

> The argument put forward that the line has not paid for itself cannot be used in justification. Public works of this character are not supposed to pay for themselves. If they do so, well and good, but if not, there can be no criticism. The public service and federal exigency both demand that this territory be in telegraphic communications with the rest of the world, at whatever cost.
>
> There is nothing reasonable about this action of a government which has consistently tried to make Yukon pay for itself. [If the government] desires to place this important branch of the public service in the hands of cheap men it will only be a question of time when the bad effects of such a course will be manifest.[11]

To find a solution to the problem, J.B. Charleson was dispatched to the north to meet with the workers, many of whom he had hired. They agreed to abide by his advice, though it is hard to understand why, since in the past he had never shown much sympathy for their concerns.

Upon leaving Vancouver Charleson gave an interview in which he ridiculed the idea of there being any "serious trouble." He claimed, "The whole thing arose from the actions of a number of malcontents in the service who had become dissatisfied with the reduction of 17 1/2%." (The earlier imposed wage cut of 33 percent had apparently been reduced, but it was still a hard pill for the workers to swallow.) Charleson said the problem should be cleared up within a month.[12]

And he was right. In no time it seemed the strike was over, with the men agreeing to return to work at their previous pay rates. However, it soon became apparent that their wages had actually been reduced, to $82.50 for operators and $75.00 for linemen. There wasn't much the men could do; it was too easy for management to replace them.

Not long after the men went back to work, criticisms of M.W. Crean's "mismanagement" were heard in Ottawa. Once again J.B. Charleson was called upon to go west to adjudicate the problem. Accompanied by J.Y. Rochester (the "Government Auditor of the line") and Joseph Gobeil, who was still J.B.'s secretary, he made an inspection trip in the summer of 1903. Upon his return to Vancouver he gave an interview to the *Province*.[13] After expressing his reluctance to say anything about Crean until he had submitted his report to the DPW, he proceeded to make some unfavourable comments, not the least of which was that men in the stations south of Atlin had not been paid for months. The outcome of the brouhaha, about what we are not sure, was that Rochester was made acting superintendent of the Yukon Division and Crean was booted to Ottawa, where he was named a "technical assistant."

Gobeil Inspects the Line

In May 1905, Joseph Gobeil was given a new assignment. He became the Yukon Telegraph's first general inspector, a job that involved examining the line's operation and maintenance and making recommendations for improvements.[14]

Gobeil immediately began his inspection. Starting from the south end, for the next three years he travelled sections of the line each summer, recording the condition of the stations and the status of maintenance. He also described the physical features of the country, measured the distances between stations, and counted the number of live trees and poles used to support the wire.

Ashcroft to Hazelton, 1905

During the summer of 1905, Gobeil inspected the section between Ashcroft and Hazelton. He described the starting point, Ashcroft, as a busy town of 500 served by the Canadian Pacific Railway (CPR), the closest railway station to the Cariboo and Omineca gold fields. It was also the transfer point where the Yukon Telegraph connected to the CPR's line.

Table 3

Inspection Trip, 1905

	Miles Between Stations	Miles From Ashcroft
Ashcroft		
Clinton	33.50	33.50
Lake la Hache	68.50	102.00
150 Mile House	36.00	138.00
Alexandria	49.50	187.50
Quesnel	33.00	220.50
Blackwater	42.00	262.50
Bobtail Lake	37.00	299.50
Stoney Creek	32.00	331.50
Fraser Lake	21.00	352.50
Burns Lake	55.00	407.50
South Bulkley	27.00	434.50
Tyee Lake	52.00	486.50
Hazelton	50.00	536.50

The section between Ashcroft and Quesnel, originally built by the Collins Overland in 1865 and operated by the CPR until it became part of the Yukon Telegraph in 1899, followed the Cariboo Road. Shortly after it was taken over by the government, the poles and wire were replaced at a cost of $24,000. Interruptions along this section were infrequent.

Quesnel, situated at the confluence of the Fraser and Quesnel rivers, was "the point of departure for the unsettled northern interior of British Columbia." Two miles above the town the line crossed the Fraser, and at 11 miles it reached the first refuge cabin, "a log shanty 11x11 feet … now closed owing to Indians and others taking away the provisions." The office at Blackwater sat on the bank of the river, "a very turbulent stream running between high rocky walls and crossed over by a wooden bridge built by the provincial government."

The line continued to Bobtail Lake and Stoney Creek through gently rolling country, then crossed the Nechako River, "a noble stream, wide, deep and with a strong current." Gobeil recorded that the Fraser Lake office was located in the Hudson's Bay Company building and that the operator and lineman boarded with the HBC agent.

Beyond Burns Lake the line followed the Bulkley Valley to Hazelton. This section was not particularly difficult, except for the last portion, where there were two old trails, "one called the 'Hagglegate cut-off' and [the other] the telegraph trail. For some reason the old telegraph trail was chosen, although it is much rougher and some 10 to 12 miles longer." Gobeil concluded with his critical assessment of the living arrangement provided for the telegraph men: "The refuge houses and telegraph offices built along the line have all proven totally inadequate to meet the requirements. Most of them had no windows; some were at great distances from water, others were simply dug-outs, and the result was that the men had to help each other in erecting new buildings or extensions to the old ones. Most of the cabins originally put up are now used as storehouses or are altogether abandoned."

The main objective of the construction crews in 1900 and 1901 had been speed. They would move through an area, raise poles, string wire, and move on. Like a freight train passing in the night, they produced a tremendous explosion of energy, motion, and noise, which then faded away, leaving only silence. Providing decent facilities for those who came after was not a high priority. When the first operators and linemen arrived, they found only smallish log cabins with dirt floors and no interior furnishings. It was up to the men to make their new homes liveable. They were also left the task of building additional refuge cabins, which were referred to as ¼-, ½-, and ¾-way refuges.

The telegraph builders had not been sure how many cabins would be required, so they built the minimum. The result was that along some sections, the distance between cabins was excessive.

Gobeil's initial inspection trip was abruptly interrupted about 100 miles south of Hazelton when he was thrown from his horse, sustaining a broken leg. Natives packed him on a stretcher to the

The station at Bobtail Lake was built by the first linemen assigned to the area when they found that no adequate structure had been provided for them. The men in the photo are later occupants.

Men assigned to the 132-mile section between Quesnel and Fraser Lake found only one intermediate station, at Blackwater. When operator William Broderick and lineman Alex McDonald arrived at Bobtail Lake in the spring of 1902, there was only a small refuge cabin, an "impossible abode" totally unsuited to house two men. They quickly determined that in order to survive they would have to build a new station. Ottawa provided specifications for the building, but little substantive support. They were on their own. Fortunately, they were sufficient to the task.

Broderick and McDonald felled trees to fashion logs for the walls, and whipsawed boards for the door and window frames. They made the floor by smoothing off two sides of logs, laying them tightly together, then hewing them flat with adzes. The roof, the most important part of the building, was a more complex matter. They first set round poles tight together, then covered them with heavy clay. To provide a watertight top surface they laid on "scoops," similar to the tile system used in southern climes (California and Mexico), except longer and made of wood. They used straight clear poplar trees, split down the middle and hollowed out to make troughs. One layer was laid edge to edge with the open sides up. A top layer was then placed with the rounded sides up, covering the edges of the lower layer.[15]

The two men had been forced to build a suitable station, a warm and protected place in which to live and from which they could do their job of maintaining their section of line. Perhaps their superiors in Ottawa, when they neglected to provide adequate cabins, were counting on this sense of self-preservation.[16]

hospital in Hazelton, where he remained for three weeks.[17] He does not mention this incident in his report, but when sufficiently recovered he returned to the site of his accident and completed his trip to Hazelton. During this first trip Gobeil had inspected 536.5 miles of line and had counted precisely 8,975 poles. The following year he continued his inspection north.

Hazelton to Telegraph Creek, 1906

Gobeil reported that Hazelton, on the Skeena River near its juncture with the Bulkley River, contained a church, hospital, two hotels, several packer outfits, and a large Aboriginal settlement.

When he left Hazelton, he entered a much different country. The heavily wooded areas were susceptible to blowdowns and fires; the portions above treeline were vulnerable to heavy snows

Table 4

Inspection Trip 1906

	Miles Between Stations	Miles From Hazelton
Hazelton		
First Cabin	27.33	27.33
Second Cabin	21.70	49.03
Third Cabin	18.60	67.63
Fourth Cabin	14.86	82.49
Fifth Cabin	15.97	98.46
Sixth Cabin	16.69	115.15
Seventh Cabin	19.90	135.05
Eighth Cabin	18.83	153.88
Ninth Cabin	18.33	172.21
Echo Lake Cabin	34.50	206.71
25 Mile Cabin	22.36	229.07
Iskoot Cabin	16.71	245.70
Raspberry Creek Cabin	27.11	272.89
Telegraph Creek	30.84	303.73

and avalanches. Due to the difficulty of the terrain, 13 stations had been built between Hazelton and Telegraph Creek, with an average distance between them of 22 miles, the closest of any section of the line.

Gobeil found the trail after First Cabin rougher, more heavily timbered, and mountainous. Between Third and Fourth cabins the line made a very difficult ascent of Poison Mountain, named for foliage in the area that was poisonous to pack animals. North of Fourth Cabin the land flattened out and then ascended Babiche Hill, which was a source of trouble because of heavy snows and slides.

In an effort to overcome the frequent breaks in this section, there had been plans to replace the overhead line with an insulated ground cable. Unfortunately, the cable brought in was entirely unsuited for the purpose; it was the type of insulated wire commonly used indoors. A connection was never made, and, as Gobeil noted, there were now six coils of wire waiting to be removed.

The inspection job was a perfect fit for Gobeil, as it allowed him to exhibit his penchant for precise measurements, such as identifying the exact locations where the southern work crew stopped in 1900—1.3 miles north of Fifth Cabin—and where the line was completed in 1901—at a point "11 miles and 246 feet" north of Sixth Cabin.

Difficult as the route had been to this point, the worst was yet to come. The trail between Seventh and Ninth cabins was the:

> roughest so far ... simply a succession of deep canyons. The line is built up on the mountainside almost above timberline, and from appearances the valley of the south fork of the Nass River could have been followed to better advantage ... As the line raises toward the summit, there are more slides and falling timber. The nature of the country makes travelling very arduous.
>
> Between the Eighth and Ninth cabins the men have had to contend with snowslides in addition to the landslides and falling timber with which they have heretofore struggled

Young lineman Jack Wrathall with his dog in front of Fifth Cabin, between Hazelton and Telegraph Creek.

... Across the summit not a tree grows and poles have to be carried from five to six miles either way. When one considers that from a three to a four mile climb is required to reach this summit from either side, and that it is almost five miles across, one can form an idea of the task a repairer has to perform when he goes out in winter to find line trouble over this section of our system. I crossed this summit on July 10, and there were then from ten to 15 feet of snow on the level.

In the eight miles from Ninth Cabin to the crossing of the Bell-Irving River, a tributary of the Nass River, there had been a number of bad slides, leading Gobeil to recommend that the line be relocated. Beyond, after the area around Echo Lake, where the "country is simply a succession of swamps, beaver dams and beaver meadows," the trail improved. The remaining 100 miles to Telegraph Creek had a wider right-of-way and were in much better condition.

Over the 304 miles he inspected in 1906, Gobeil counted 7,944 poles, of which 1,100 were "planted" and 6,844 were listed as "trees," a clear indication that the telegraph builders preferred to use live trees that had been trimmed rather than cut poles.

In his summation, Gobeil again faulted the decision to build the line through the mountains, where it was vulnerable to heavy snows and slides. He noted that "about 55 miles west of the Sixth cabin the valley of the Kispiox river joins the valley of the south fork of the Nass River." He suggested that the line between First and Ninth cabins could be moved westward to good effect and that this new route would actually be 65 miles shorter. (It would have brought the line to the valleys chosen many years later for the Cassiar Highway.)

Although it is questionable whether Gobeil's suggested route would have been shorter, it undoubtedly would have avoided some of the problems encountered by passing through the Nass Mountains. In any event, there is no evidence that anyone seriously considered moving the line. It would have been difficult to gain backing for the cost of stringing 150 to 200 miles of new wire and building linemen's cabins, especially as the line was already receiving sizeable annual subsidies: $130,000 in 1905, $105,000 in 1906.

Telegraph Creek to Whitehorse, 1907

In 1907 Gobeil traversed the segment from Telegraph Creek to Whitehorse. After crossing to the west side of the Stikine River above Telegraph Creek, the line entered the village, which by 1907 consisted of a small trading post, two stores, a few dwellings, and the telegraph office.

From Telegraph Creek the wire followed the first 86 miles of the 150-mile Teslin Trail. Starting in gently rolling country, the trail rose to a summit, then parallelled several rivers and lakes through dead and burnt-out areas to the station on the Shesley River. From Shesley to the Nahlin River station the trail ascended a sparsely wooded summit, then dropped down to a marshy area where "sections of the corduroying have become so rotten that it is absolutely impossible to cross over them ... and long detours have to be made to get around the swamps and muskegs."

At Nahlin the telegraph line diverged from the Teslin Trail, heading northwest into lightly forested areas interspersed with

Table 5

Inspection Trip 1907

	Miles Between Stations	Miles From Telegraph Creek
Telegraph Creek		
Shesley Station	38.60	38.60
Nahlin Station	47.00	85.60
Nakina Station	46.50	132.10
Pike River Station	36.80	168.90
Atlin Station	18.40	187.30
Centre Cabin	35.50	222.80
Tagish	31.85	254.65
Whitehorse	55.50	310.15

swamps until it reached Nakina summit. The trail then descended steeply through a "wedge-shaped ravine of great depth" to the station at the Nakina River, followed by a three-mile hike up the other side.

After Nakina the trail was much easier to Pike River, a winter station, and then continued 20 miles along the rocky shore of Atlin Lake to the town, the terminus of the southern district. Atlin was a principal repeater and battery station, with 219 cells for transmissions and another 23 cells to operate the repeaters. It was a busy place. In addition to the daytime operator, a full-time night operator was employed.

From Atlin the line continued along the eastern shore of Atlin Lake, crossed the 60th parallel into the Yukon Territory, and then turned west to Tagish. Gobeil noted that there were few refuge cabins in this section, but that test poles, where the wire was brought down so linemen could attach their radio phones, were provided every seven or eight miles. From Tagish the line to Whitehorse followed Marsh Lake and the Yukon River, a section where there were few interruptions.

Gobeil included an inspection of the line from Tagish to Caribou Crossing (now known as Carcross), which was no longer part of the main line, but was maintained as an alternative connection to the White Pass and Yukon Route's telegraph. He also included some notes on a loop line to a mining area at Conrad City on Windy Arm that was operated from 1905 to 1907.

Comparing the several sections he had inspected, Gobeil concluded that, owing to the more favourable terrain, the Telegraph Creek to Whitehorse section was the easiest by far to operate and maintain. He summed up his reports with an assurance: Because his party had chain-measured the entire distance, he was certain that his distances were "absolutely accurate." However, some questions must have remained as to the reliability of his measurements, as the DPW did not automatically accept his numbers. For example, he calculated the mileage from Telegraph Creek to Atlin as 187 miles, about 30 miles less than previously estimated, but the department continued to list the distance in its annual reports as between 210 and 220 miles.

It took Gobeil three summers to inspect the entire southern district and the Atlin to Whitehorse portion of the northern district. It is not clear if the inspection continued to Dawson City, because in 1908 Gobeil was appointed assistant general superintendent of telegraphs in the DPW. Perhaps it was decided that further inspection was unnecessary, as most of the stations in this section were located along the Yukon River and the wire was easily accessible for repair and maintenance.

This is not to minimize the difficulties of keeping this section open; it had its share of problems, some unique to the river. In addition to interruptions due to blowdowns, fires, and floods, there were breaks when the smokestacks of river steamers hooked into the wire at river crossings and pulled out sections of line.

Gobeil's inspection trips had provided useful descriptions of the terrain through which the line passed and brief sketches of the living conditions of the telegraph men. These men deserve to be given further attention and recognition for their work and their lives in the bush.

CHAPTER 9

Life on the Telegraph Line

Some writers found romance in the Yukon Telegraph, that "great undertaking accomplished under difficulties hard to believe" and sustained by heroic men in isolated bush cabins struggling to preserve the link between Dawson City and civilization.[1] Actually, during its first years most of the operators were unsentimental old-timers. They took the job for any number of reasons. Some had been displaced by technological advances, others welcomed the solitude of the wilderness, and a few had drinking problems they wanted to overcome by drying out away from the temptations of John Barleycorn. The less-experienced younger men who took the job often looked upon it as temporary, an antidote to the depressed job market or a way to get a new stake. Few of them thought they would make it a career, and none of them saw any romance in the work.

Expert Morse-men were required only at the major battery stations. At the smaller, intermediate stations, designating one of the two men as the operator was misleading. In the remote areas over the course of a year, no more than a handful of messages might be generated, requiring the so-called operator to have little more than a rudimentary knowledge of Morse. The primary purpose of the bush cabins was to provide a base from which *both* of the men could inspect and repair the line.

These bush operators had few responsibilities beyond calling in every morning at 8:00 a.m. to assure the home office that they had survived the night and to report the condition of the weather. But even this minimal task could be a painful exercise for the unfortunate occupant of a frigid cabin where the fire had gone out during the night. One early winter morning, just as it was getting light, there came over the wire, in faltering dots and dashes, as if punched by stiff or untrained fingers, the message: "H o w — — c o l d i s i t f o r K r i s s t ' s s a k e ?"[2]

The men in the isolated stations engaged in a variety of activities to fill their hours. Some were avid readers, others tended vegetable gardens, did carpentry, or played a musical instrument. Listening to the phonograph was a popular way to recall that other, sweeter world. Early favourites included "Just a Baby's Prayer at Midnight" and "How I Miss You Dear Old Pal."[3] When battery-operated radios became available, a whole new world of entertainment and distraction opened up.

Almost every man, at one time or another, ran a trapline. Some earned more money selling furs than they received in salary. A few got rich. One trapper was reported to have made $5,000 in a season, but the usual take was about $300, which was worth a lot more in those days than it is today. A few men even managed to hold on to some of their money after they hit town.

A lineman-trapper displays his season's catch at Eighth Cabin.

Keeping occupied helped reduce the stress that resulted when two men were forced to live together in a small cabin. Those in the bush stations might not see another human being for months, especially during the dark winter when the weather kept them from venturing out. Under these conditions even the most compatible and forgiving among them might feel the strain of incessantly contending with the personality of another man, with his likes and dislikes, his annoying habits and idiosyncrasies. As one observer put it: "A man and a woman, living in isolation, can usually get along together indefinitely. They may quarrel at times but they will generally make up again. But instances are rare when men have lived together amicably in isolation for any length of time."[4]

One old-timer told the story of a sarcastic telegrapher who, toward the close of winter, became a little testy with his cabin partner. "'Listen,' he says, following a particularly long spell of bitter weather which kept both men indoors, 'I have listened to your curb[side] chatter for more than four long, weary months. It's getting so I'd welcome the tinkle of a drop of water falling from a leaky faucet in preference to your vapid vocalizing. If I had to choose a winter mate between you and a spavined cur, one of us now would be wagging a tail and yelping at the stars.'"[5]

Eventually, officials of the Department of Public Works realized that the reports they were receiving about the incompatibility of two men living together in a cabin were not isolated cases, but symptoms of the beast. DPW's answer was to send work crews out during the summer of 1905 to construct a second cabin at many of the stations. Thereafter, each man had more privacy, could eat what and when he wanted, and decide which phonograph record would be played, or when the radio would be turned on and off. And he no longer had to listen to the other fellow's snoring.

Living separately lessened the intensity of the relationship, decreased the friction, and allowed the men to choose when they wanted to socialize. They might enjoy an evening together, but at its conclusion the invited guest would retire to his own cabin. The improved amity could only benefit the quality of their work. They were more likely to cooperate when they had to repair a break in the line, a frequent occurrence during the first years.

Breaks at Nass Summit

The main line was no sooner completed in September 1901 than storms caused interruptions in the southern district. The most serious break, due to heavy snows and avalanches, occurred on November 8 in the high country of the Nass Mountains.[6] A repair crew of three men was sent from below Hazelton, a distance of more than 200 miles, which meant that the line would be down for weeks. The reason given was that the three, Jim Wiggins, John Dowd, and John McIntosh, were being reassigned to Seventh, Eighth, and Ninth cabins in the area of the break.

After reaching Hazelton, the three started north in a storm on November 24 and for four days took turns breaking trail through three feet of wet snow. Few refuge cabins had been built yet, so they were forced to find shelter as best they could, some nights camping in the open. To add to their troubles, Wiggins developed a nasty case of boils on his neck. Fortunately they were near Fourth Cabin, where the Native lineman, Charlie Martin, was known to be a wizard with herb poultices.

Assessing Wiggins's condition, Martin diagnosed that poultices would work, but they would take time. "Had there been no occasion for haste, no broken wire ahead, Wiggins unquestionably would have taken the slower treatment. But Dawson City was 'hollering' for communications with the outside world," and so he chose the quicker, if more painful, cure. Martin drew the boils out after applying hot water bottles. There were 11 in all.[7]

The party found the break during the first week of January 1902. It was located in the eight miles above treeline between Eighth and Ninth cabins, a country of "snowslides, perpetual glaciers, grizzlies and timber wolves." By the time they reached it, the poles and wire had been covered by 10 to 20 feet of snow. Luckily there was only one break, which they were able to expose and repair. The splice held up and the line worked fine under the snow until the following June, when a permanent repair was made.[8]

On this occasion the line was down for two months, an intolerably long interruption, which meant that messages to or from the area north of Ninth Cabin had to be channelled through the White Pass and Yukon Route's telegraph line between Carcross

The Telegraph Operator

Robert Service[9]

I will not wash my face;
I will not brush my hair;
I "pig" around the place—
There's nobody to care.
Nothing but rock and tree;
Nothing but wood and stone,
Oh, God, it's hell to be
Alone, alone, alone!

Snow-peaks and deep-gashed draws
Corral me in a ring.
I feel as if I was
The only living thing
On all this blighted earth;
And so I frowst and shrink,
And crouching by my hearth
I hear the thoughts I think.

I think of all I miss—
The boys I used to know;
The girls I used to kiss;
The coin I used to blow:
The bars I used to haunt;
The racket and the row;
The beers I didn't want
(I wish I had 'em now).

Day after day the same,
Only a little worse;
No one to grouch or blame—
Oh, for a loving curse!
Oh, in the night I fear,
Haunted by nameless things,
Just for a voice to cheer,
Just for a hand that clings!

Faintly as from a star
Voices come o'er the line:
Voices of ghosts afar,
Not in this world of mine;

Lives in whose loom I grope;
Words in whose weft I hear
Eager the thrill of hope,
Awful the chill of fear.

I'm thinking out aloud;
I reckon that is bad;
(The snow is like a shroud)—
Maybe I'm going mad.
Say! Wouldn't that be tough?
This awful hush that hugs
And chokes one is enough
To make a man go "bugs".

There's not a thing to do;
I cannot sleep at night;
No wonder I'm so blue;
Oh, for a friendly fight!
The din and rush of strife;
A music-hall aglow;
A crowd, a city, life—
Dear God, I miss it so!

Here, you have moped enough!
Brace up and play the game!
But say, it's awful tough—
Day after day the same
(I've said that twice, I bet).
Well, there's not much to say.
I wish I had a pet,
Or something I could play.

Cheer up! Don't get so glum
And sick of everything;
The worst is yet to come;
God help you till the Spring.
God shield you from the Fear;
Teach you to laugh, not moan.
Ha! ha! it sounds so queer—
Alone, alone, alone!

and Skagway—the system in use before the British Columbia line was built. During the new line's first winter it quickly became apparent that the section between Hazelton and Telegraph Creek would be the most difficult to keep open, particularly through the high country around Nass Summit.

These problems and others were documented in the DPW's annual reports. Especially illuminating are the reports of John T. Phelan (who became superintendent in 1906), which are chock full of information and statistics. They chronicle new construction and maintenance projects and list major interruptions, not only during the severe winters, but also during the summer months. One report, for example, notes that because the summer of 1906 was very dry, the line north of Nahlin Station suffered from extensive bush fires. One fire destroyed 130 poles, four miles of wire, and a refuge cabin. Although extreme heat held up the work crew, repairs were completed in three days.

During the winter of 1906–07, Phelan reported, sleet and extraordinary snowstorms between Hazelton and Echo Lake loaded up tree limbs, causing many trees to be uprooted and fall onto the wire. The men sent out to make repairs found the going difficult in the soft, heavy snow, but they were able to get the line back into service quickly. Farther north, the bank of the Yukon River had washed away at the Ogilvie wire crossing, requiring that the high poles be moved back 150 feet, increasing the span to 1,400 feet, said to be the longest in this part of Canada.[10]

To keep the telegraph in operation, the linemen regularly inspected their sections of wire to remove potential problems, and during the summer months, work crews were sent out to make major repairs. In 1907 a crew widened the right-of-way between Hazelton and Telegraph Creek and removed potential blowdowns. The following year the work continued beyond Telegraph Creek to Atlin, a section where many poles had already rotted away and needed to be "repoled." This process involved removing the pole from the ground, cutting off the rotted bottom part, then resetting the shortened pole back into the same hole. The advantage of this procedure was that the wire did not need to be removed from the pole to make the repair; the disadvantage, the wire was now lower and more vulnerable to damage. Of course, there was a limit to how many times a pole could be cut before it had to be replaced.

The rotting of cut poles was a continuing problem; live trees normally lasted a lot longer. Some trees, though, the ones that survived the axeman's trimming, in time might grow branches around the wire, which could cause other problems.

The widening of the right-of-way, and the repoling and replacing of poles, greatly improved the system's reliability. After 1907, Phelan's reports were usually models of confidence and optimism. Interruptions were infrequent and always speedily corrected within a few hours, so there was little or no delay to business.

Credit for the improved service must go in large part to the linemen, especially those assigned to the most isolated stations. They worked under difficult conditions that at times required them to put forth efforts that could tax a man's strength and endurance. Between these periods of exertion, and an occasional adventure, it was mostly mundane and boring work, performed in an often dreary and weather-beaten environment.

Death on the Line

Novice linemen quickly learned that living and working in the bush could be dangerous. Because many of their cabins were located far from settlements, and because they often worked alone, the telegraph men were acutely aware of their vulnerability to sickness and accident. They were prey to the vagaries of the weather and to the natural hazards of the land, most perilously the rivers and creeks they routinely had to cross. Spring was the worst time, when meltwater could turn a sweetly flowing creek into a frightening, turbulent deluge.

Jack Waller, the operator at Blackwater Station, tried to cross the Blackwater River at flood stage in a rowboat. "The boat capsized and Waller was dashed from rock to rock in the raging torrent." Only by grabbing an overhanging willow was he able to pull himself to safety.[11] Martha O'Neill at Port Simpson reported a drowning on the Skeena River in 1906. "Hank Boss, operator and his lineman, while covering their line section, capsized in the Kitselas Canyon. The river was at its most treacherous stage. Hank was carried by the current to a point of land and managed to drag himself to safety by some overhanging tree boughs; but the lineman, young Youngdall, was drowned and his body never recovered."[12] William Lanktree, the operator at Yukon Crossing, drowned at Rink Rapids when his canoe capsized on June 9, 1904. He is buried in Pioneer Cemetery in Whitehorse.[13]

In another burial ground, Gitanmaax Cemetery, which overlooks Hazelton, there is a granite shaft marking the graves of Gilbert McDonald and William Heinz, two operators who died within weeks of each other during the winter of 1907–08.

When McDonald was overdue returning from an inspection trip of the line and it began to get dark, Hunter Corner, his partner at Second Cabin, became increasingly concerned. Finally, around 7 p.m., Corner set out on the trail with a lantern, searching for his partner. Within three miles he came upon a huddled form in the snow. McDonald had been dead for hours, his body already frozen stiff. By backtracking on his partner's trail, Corner could see in the snow where McDonald had repeatedly fallen and struggled up, at the last crawling on his hands and knees in a desperate effort to get back to the cabin.

Because wolves were nearby, Corner dared not leave his partner. He devised a rope sling with which to hold the 175-pound body on his shoulders. Somehow he stood erect—a difficult feat on showshoes—and commenced the long, sad journey homeward. His progress was slow and painful as the rope cut into his shoulders and his snowshoes sank 18 inches into the snow. Over the last part Corner discarded his snowshoes and crawled, arriving at the cabin after 2:00 a.m. Two days later a dogsled arrived to take the body to Hazelton. There it was determined that McDonald had died from ptomaine poisoning.[14]

The other man buried in Gitanmaax Cemetery, William Heinz, was found dead in his cabin at Burns Lake. It seems there were two sides to Heinz's personality. R.G. McKay, a traveller who stopped at his station for a meal and an evening of good conversation, described him as having an inventive and resourceful mind and a keen sense of humour. To illustrate, McKay related Heinz's story of how he solved the problem of some troublesome wandering

146

cattle. In their eternal quest for scarce salt, cattle belonging to local Natives had been invading the station compound, eating everything within reach that contained even minute amounts of the essential compound. They had become pesky until Heinz decided:

> This thing has to stop, it has gone far enough. Consequently I placed a piece of metal at the corner of the shack, in plain view of the trail, and covered it with a generous sprinkling of salt, and connected it with a battery inside. By and by up came the cattle as if they owned the ranch. Presently a great big fellow, a self appointed leader, spied the salt, and rushed to lick it up to his hearts content. I watched until I was sure his wet tongue was touching the metal, and then I turned on the current good and strong. Well sir, that big ox, he just jumped right up in the air, and took to his heels with a muffled and terrified bawl. The rest were not slow to follow, but taking their cue from their leader, went tearing down the trail, till you couldn't see anything left of them for dust. After that, whenever those cattle had occasion to pass my place, they did so with due respect, treading softly, with their heads to one side, lest they should by any chance receive a sudden jolt again.[15]

The other side of Heinz's personality was darker, more melancholy and brooding. Only a month after McDonald's death, repeated calls to Heinz's station went unanswered. He had not called in his weather report for several days, a chore he had never been known to miss. Other linemen were concerned because they knew he was alone in his cabin in the middle of winter; his partner, William Clark, was on leave. Something wasn't right.

Jim Hodder, the operator at South Bulkley, 30 miles north, and Heinz's good friend, was instructed to find out what had happened. He walked all night and about 3 a.m. reached the cabin of a Native man who lived a mile or so from Heinz's station. The man said he had passed the cabin a day earlier. There was no smoke and the door was locked. "Me think him mamaloose [dead]." Hodder continued to the cabin, broke the door in, and entered the pitch-black interior, fumbling around until he found and lit the lantern. He then saw Bill Heinz dead in his bunk. On the table were three letters. The first was addressed to Hodder, the second to Heinz's brother, and the third to a girl in Vancouver.

Apparently, when Heinz was on leave the year before, he met a young girl in Vancouver's red-light district. They became great friends, although he was 50 and she only about 17 years old. He did not want to marry her, but rather to reform her, and he sent her money to help her find a new life. His efforts at rehabilitation did not seem to be working, and he began to fear for her future.

William Clark, who went on leave from Burns Lake in July, had intended to return much earlier, but he was delayed. This meant that Heinz was alone for more than six months, with too much time to brood about the fate of his young friend in Vancouver. Although

it was later determined that Heinz had been partially paralyzed before he died, some felt that he could have signalled for help. Years later Clark wrote, "You know Bill could easily have call[ed] up on the wire and told them he was sick. But I think poor old Bill was tired of this Old World and wanted to try another."[16] Those looking for the romantic angle said that Heinz had died of a broken heart.

The letter to Jim Hodder contained William Heinz's will, which left some money to his brother and some to the girl. Hodder carried out Heinz's instructions, sending her share of the money to the girl in Vancouver.

Lineman Jim Hodder at the monument in Gitanmaax Cemetery in Hazelton that marks the graves of linemen Gilbert McDonald and William Heinz, who both died on the line during the winter of 1907–08.

She wrote back a brief acknowledgement: "Received Bill's cheque OK." Nothing more. The men on the line subscribed handsomely to provide the monument in Gitanmaax Cemetery for the two operators.

Packers and Pack Trains

Also interred in Gitanmaax Cemetery is Cataline, the famous packer. Packing outfits like his had a long history of hauling goods and equipment into the remote areas of British Columbia. Soon after gold was discovered in the Cariboo and Omineca, packers were there to respond to the needs of the miners and businessmen. With horses and mules they would haul any item that could be broken down into 300-pound loads. Even after the roads came and the freight wagons took over, there were always more remote areas that needed to be supplied. The packers just moved their operations closer to the new wilderness.

Miners and settlers depended on the packers and often made arrangements months in advance for a load to be delivered to a certain place at a particular time. A packer was judged by his reliability, which was often affected by factors beyond his control. His schedule depended on the railroads and riverboats making shipments on time, and on the caprices of nature's seasons. Nothing moved until the snows melted and the forage for the animals began to grow along the trails.

The southern district of the Yukon Telegraph could not have been built without the packers, who hauled hundreds of tons of construction materials to the work sites. The coils of wire, boxes of insulators and side blocks, kegs of spikes, and provisions for the 100-man work crews had all been carried or skidded over the trails. Starting with short hauls, the distances increased as the work progressed farther from the depots at Atlin, Telegraph Creek, and Hazelton, until supplies were being hauled more than 100 miles.

Completion of the telegraph line did not end the need for the pack trains. Keeping the line in operation depended on supplying the men in the bush cabins with provisions. The government budgeted $30 per man per month, which comes to $720 a year for

The packers who guided the pack trains of horses and mules were essential to the progress of construction. Here, a heavily armed group poses in front of one of the newly built telegraph cabins.

each two-man station. Back in the early 1900s, this amount was enough to provide 3,000 to 4,000 pounds of provisions.

The operators and linemen relied on the packers to deliver their annual ration of supplies. After 12 months the previous year's larder might be running out—certainly the men's favourite foods were exhausted—and mould and rot would have taken their toll. There were also the special orders they looked forward to: books, games, tools, maybe a radio, and, for some, a case of rum, which would have to be tasted sparingly if it was to last for the next 12 months.

Word of the pack train's progress as it proceeded along the line from cabin to cabin was avidly reported over the telegraph wire. As it got nearer, the men's expectations kept rising, replaced by despondency if there was any delay. The supplies were welcome, but at times there were criticisms of the quality of some of the provisions. In 1904, lineman Guy Lawrence was waiting for the pack train at his cabin on the Nahlin River. When the train arrived,

Lawrence checked out the provisions and commented that although the government supplied them well, "the bacon and hams have arrived in a shocking state; covered with mildew and very shrunken. Evidently unsaleable in civilization."[17]

Tenders were let to haul the provisions from three distribution points: from Quesnel to the five cabins north as far as Burns Lake; from Hazelton to the two cabins south and First through Ninth cabins to the north; and from Telegraph Creek to the four cabins south as far as Echo Lake and the three north toward Atlin. The tenders were originally taken for a one-year period, later increased to three years.

Charlie Barrett held the first contracts to supply the cabins from Quesnel and Hazelton. Then Cataline took over until 1913, when he sold out to George Beirnes. For many years J. Frank Callbreath supplied the cabins out of Telegraph Creek.

The contracts called for the goods to be delivered by specific dates: the Quesnel section by May 15, the Hazelton section by July 1, and the Telegraph Creek section by July 10. These staggered dates recognized the different periods during the spring and summer when supplies could be shipped to the distribution points and when the trails were usually open. Quesnel could be supplied earlier by the wagon road, whereas Hazelton and Telegraph Creek were beyond reach of the riverboats until the ice on the Skeena and Stikine rivers broke up.

Pack-train deliveries from Hazelton and Telegraph Creek were limited to a three-month window (July, August, and September), the lifetime of the forage. Naturally, with these time constraints the packers wanted to start as soon as food for the animals was available, but they were wary of starting too early. It was safer to wait until the spring runoff had receded rather than risk trying to cross swollen and raging streams.

Since the pack trains could only cover 6 to 10 miles a day, the trip to the farthest cabins could take up to 30 days. If everything went as planned, they could supply all the cabins and return to their home base with time to spare, but if something went wrong, the packer might find himself in a race with the onset of winter. And things did go wrong, sometimes with tragic consequences.

Charlie Barrett lived an adventurous life. He operated his packing business year-round, in the winter running dogsled trains all the way to Dawson City. One year there was a mix-up on the telegraph-cabin run north of Hazelton. Barrett's outfit had returned without supplying Ninth Cabin, the farthest station on the route, 170 miles from Hazelton. Although it was late in the season, Barrett knew that he had to get provisions to the men at Ninth before winter set in. He figured there was still time to make a quick trip, so he started out again with his packhorses.

Halfway there he was stopped by heavy snows; the forage was covered, and the starving horses began to die. He had to turn around, but he was already devising an alternative plan, and on the way back he cached some of the horse carcasses high in the trees, out of reach of wolves and bears, to use later for dog food. Back in Hazelton he started out again, this time with 122 dogs pulling sleds loaded with the 4,000 pounds of provisions. In the depths of winter, and after "almost superhuman feats of endurance," he finally delivered the stores to the two lonely, and by now desperate, telegraph men at Ninth Cabin, "then crawled back to Hazelton with the remnants of his fine dog-teams."[18]

Barrett eventually sold his outfit to the man who was known throughout the area as Cataline. His given name was Jean Jacques Caux. He was born in 1829 in the Pyrenees area of France, near the border with Spain, and there are different stories about how he arrived in Canada, whether directly from Europe or via Mexico and the United States. Perhaps the confusion was caused by the variety of languages he used to communicate. He could speak French and Spanish and bits of English, Chinese, and some Native dialects. What is certain is that in 1858 he was in Yale on the Fraser River, hauling supplies into the Cariboo and Omineca areas, where he became well known for his honesty and reliability. No settlement or mining operation was too remote for his pack trains.

Cataline was described as being "defiant of eye" and "wiry of body," a man who never slept in a bed and took his baths in the winter by breaking the ice on the rivers. He could not read or write, but he had an amazing memory and could keep accounts in his head for months at a time, seldom being found wrong when settling up

Cataline, the famous packer, who carried provisions to the isolated telegraph cabins, with crew members, including chief wrangler Dave Wiggins on the left.

with his wranglers after two or three months on the trail. Cataline did not like to hire white men, preferring instead Chinese and Native packers. For many years his chief wrangler was Dave Wiggins, a Black man, and his manager was a Chinese man, Ah Gun.

No problem was too great for Cataline to overcome. Perhaps his most famous feat of packing "was when he loaded two mules with a piece of machinery weighing 670 pounds and packed it from Ashcroft to Manson Creek, nearly 400 miles." He accomplished this with a special stretcher carried between the two animals, which were reported to have survived the trial undamaged.[19]

Innumerable stories about Cataline present him as a colourful and independent character. One story will suffice to give a taste of the man. Perhaps because of a bad memory for names, Cataline called everybody "Boy." High station or low, to him everyone was "Boy." This idiosyncrasy was not universally understood or appreciated.

When the Yukon Field Force arrived in Glenora in 1898, Cataline was one of the packers hired to haul its tons of supplies to Teslin Lake. Colonel Evans, the officer in charge of the Force, "was a rather pompous individual who insisted upon everything being done according to military regulations." He and Cataline soon found mutual fault. The colonel did not appreciate being called "Boy," especially in front of the troops; Cataline complained about the army's incessant blowing of bugles, which upset his animals. "All tima blowa de buga, scara de mule, no gooda." He was most unhappy about the bugles in the morning when he was trying to gentle his mules into their workday and get them loaded.

> The trail was extremely rough and it was not unusual for a mule to fall, mire or meet with some other accident that would require immediate attention. One day a mule fell, rolled on top of its pack, and became helpless. Several of the soldiers attempted the rescue ... [without success. Colonel Evans] came up and took charge of the situation but only succeeded in making matters worse. When he had exhausted his few ideas he looked around and saw that Cataline had ridden up and had been quietly watching his efforts. He swallowed his pride and asked for help, "Oh Mr. Cataline, what will we do now?" Cataline, with a touch of triumph in his voice, replied, "Blowa da buga, Boy, blowa da buga!"[20]

Cataline was in his 70s when he took on the contract to supply the telegraph cabins. At the age of 83, when he was no longer able to accompany the pack trains, he sold out to George Beirnes.

During the early years, and until 1908, the contracts for hauling provisions included a payment of $1,000 for clearing the trails. Before the main pack train came through, an advance party would clear away fallen trees, repair bridges, and improve the footing of the trail. Even so, at some places where there were drop-offs, an animal was occasionally lost. Cataline's wrangler Dave Wiggins, for one, preferred mules to horses, as they were more sure-footed on dangerous mountain trails. There were other hazards: mudholes, slippery bridges, and fast-flowing streams. With good care, and barring accidents, animals might work for 15 years or longer, carrying packs that weighed 300 pounds, perhaps less as they got older. Hauling 3,000 to 4,000 pounds of provisions to each station required 10 to 15 animals, and trains of 100 animals were not unusual.

On the trail there was a routine that varied little from day to day. The crew rose at 2:00 a.m. and set about retrieving the animals, which had been allowed to browse through the night. Usually they did not stray far from the bell mare (the lead animal), which had been staked down. The previous night, when the animals were unloaded, the packs and saddles had been arranged in a semicircle in the order in which they travelled. After a few days on the trail, the animals became familiar with their positions and would line up in order, waiting to be loaded for the day's journey.

After breakfast and packing up the camp, the trail crew worked together loading the horses and mules. One man would put the packsaddles on, another the packs, and a third would cinch up the ropes and inspect the packing. Once they were all lined up, the bell mare would lead off, followed by the others, with a rider about every 10th animal. For a pack train of 70 animals, loading could take three hours or more.

Camping locations were determined by the availability of feeding grounds, and packers gave each place an appropriate name. North of Hazelton there was "Burning Camp," "Big Flat," "Old Kildo," "Wire Cache," and "Totem Pole Camp." Some of the older horses knew where the forage was located as well as the men did. It was usually nine o'clock before the men could turn in after making camp each evening, and then the next morning they were rousted out of their bedrolls well before sun-up so the whole process could start again.[21]

The pack trains hauled provisions for the Yukon Telegraph for more than three decades, although over the years the number of cabins gradually decreased. Around 1915, most of the cabins between Quesnel and Hazelton were dropped because they could now be supplied locally. In 1935 the section from Hazelton to Telegraph Creek was abandoned, in part because spring floods had washed out the bridges, making it nearly impossible for the pack trains to get through. The line north from Telegraph Creek to Atlin continued to be supplied for a few more years, although by that time there were only two stations operating.

CHAPTER 10

Superintendent Phelan and Operator Lawrence

The man in charge of the Yukon Telegraph during most of its existence was John T. Phelan, known along the line by his call letters, "PN." Born in 1859 to Irish parents in Quebec City, he started as an operator during construction of the line and was appointed superintendent of the southern district in 1902, and of the entire line in 1906, a position he held until his death in 1929. It was a demanding job. Working from his office in Vancouver, he had the formidable task of riding herd on more than 200 employees spaced out over 2,000 miles of telegraph line. They were not always easy to control, especially those in the isolated wilderness stations.

Phelan referred to the men along the line as his "boys," although as the years went by they were anything but that. He watched over them, "counselled them when in trouble, humoring and jollying them along when despondent."[1] He was proud of them, their work, and their sacrifices. A mutual loyalty developed between Phelan and his boys, although on one occasion his faith was sorely tested. That was when the international boundary between Alaska and the Yukon—the 141st longitude—was being surveyed using celestial positioning.

To determine the longitude's precise location, it was necessary to make certain measurements of stars at exact times. To ensure the accuracy of the time reading, the surveyors decided to use the chronometer at the U.S. Observatory in Washington, D.C. The time would be transmitted as a series of ticks over an open telegraph line all the way across the United States from Washington to Seattle, up to Ashcroft, and then over the Yukon Telegraph to Alaska. For the exercise to be successful, two conditions were required: a clear night sky and a completely open telegraph line.

After several attempts in 1904, all aborted because of unfavourable weather conditions, the organizers scheduled another try for what they hoped would be a successful measurement on New Year's Eve at midnight.[2] Phelan sent out instructions to every station on the line that no one was to go near a telegraph key at that hour. Then he confidently travelled to Seattle for the test, where he waited with other telegraph and government officials, both Canadian and American. At the appointed hour he listened as his manager at Ashcroft lined up the wire with Hazelton, Atlin, Whitehorse, then Dawson, which brought in Boundary and the connection to the U.S. military telegraph line in Alaska.

As midnight approached, the test began with the time-signal ticks from the banks of the Potomac to the wilds of the distant Yukon, 6,000 miles away. Phelan was proud of his boys for obeying instructions.

> But just as the American officials were warmly congratulating him there came a break in the regular beating of the chronometer pendulum. The American officials frowned. Surely, they intimated, this must be someone on the north line—the Canadian section. But "PN" smiled to himself. The interruption was not caused by any of his boys; of that he felt certain.
>
> They listened. Indistinctly at first, and then more clearly as the persistent one triumphed in the struggle with "time," came the call, "FN-FN-FN," and the sign "HN." Again and again the insistent signals rang out from the sounder. As yet the American officials did not know that "HN" was Hootalinqua, a lonely station on the Yukon River, and that the operator there was calling Five Fingers, a

The settlement at Hootalinqua, where the Teslin (Hootalinqua) River joins the Yukon River. It was here that a telegraph operator opened his line and ruined an attempt to survey the boundary between Alaska and Canada.

near-by station. But they soon did. For in a moment "FN" answered, and the astounded listeners heard the operator at Hootalinqua, quite unaware of the damage and indignation he was causing, calmly ask if a Siwash had been seen to pass up that way since dark.[3]

Phelan was incensed, but there wasn't much he could do. He could not fire the operator at Hootalinqua because he would not be able to get a replacement in to relieve him for several months. That was the end of the attempt to measure the boundary by using the telegraph.

Women on the Line

Phelan also had his "girls." He employed women operators in situations where a more timorous superintendent would have hesitated. He took a big chance in 1902 when he employed Martha O'Neill at Port Simpson. Another early female operator on the Port Simpson line was Lily Tomlinson at the Meanskinisht station, 35 miles downriver from Hazelton. She was later replaced by Martha

O'Neill's sister Katy, and it became a real family affair when brother Wiggs became an operator.[4]

The Department of Public Works included lists of operators in its annual reports, but only initials are provided for first names, so it is difficult, but not impossible, to spot the female operators. One sure way is to compare salaries. Male operators on the southern district were generally paid $75 a month, females $50. Even Martha's neophyte brother Wiggs started work at $75 a month while Martha, who by that time had several years' experience, was still working for $50. There is no indication in her memoir that she complained about this unfair arrangement.[5] Actually, she was better compensated than some other women who served the telegraph. They were called wives.

At locations in or close to a town, or along the Yukon River, it was not uncommon for the station to be staffed by an operator and his wife. As early as 1904, R.J. Barton and his wife ran the Pike River station south of Atlin.[6] Some years later Bill Hays and his wife were at Big Salmon, and Mr. and Mrs. Ed Morrison were at Lower Laberge.[7] Many of these women learned Morse code so that they could fill in when their husbands were away, and of course they did more than their share of station chores.

There were other females employed in paid positions, notably Mrs. LeBourdais, long-time operator at Clinton on the Ashcroft–Quesnel section, and Mrs. Bryson on the Lillooet line. These women were located at stations in towns, and their work was restricted to office duties.

It was very unusual for women, or girls, to be employed to make repairs to the line. One exception was the time Verna Vernon, a teenager, was called out in the dead of winter to repair a break. Because the regular lineman was not available, Louis LeBourdais, the operator at Quesnel, telephoned and asked her to find and repair an interruption somewhere near her home at Bouchie Lake.

> With heavy snow on the ground, she set out [on her horse] and found the break about half way. She tied the wire on to her saddle horn and tried to pull the ends together. They didn't reach so she had to splice another piece of line in.

Repairs completed, she then rode on to the stopping house [refuge cabin] at the lake, checking for breaks. The next day, she rode the twenty miles back home. It was a brave undertaking for one of such tender years.[8]

Guy Lawrence

John Phelan's career with the Yukon Telegraph spanned 30 years, surpassed by only one other man, Guy Lawrence. Through the years the two were to meet on several occasions, or as Lawrence would call them, "encounters with old 'PN.'"

Sydney Guy Lawrence was employed for a total of 41 years, from 1902, when he was hired as a temporary repairman at Atlin, to his retirement as an operator at Stewart in 1946. There were several time outs, including service in the First World War. Summing up his career, he wrote, "Like many another employee, I joined the Yukon Telegraph Service planning to spend just sufficient time with it to acquire a stake, but there was a fascination about it that bound me to it."[9]

Lawrence and his father left England in 1898 to seek riches in the Yukon gold fields. The younger Lawrence was a slight lad of 17, who barely looked his age, when the pair made their way to Wrangell and then up the Stikine River to Glenora, where they camped with the horde of other gold seekers lured by the promise of a fine wagon road to Teslin Lake. But unlike many of the others, who turned back when they learned of the difficult trail ahead, the Lawrences plodded on, eventually winding up in Atlin in the spring of 1899.

Guy and his father worked in mining for a couple of years until the senior Lawrence concluded that the family fortune was not likely to be made in Canada. He decided to return to England; his son opted to stay.

Guy was in Atlin in the fall of 1899 to witness the telegraph work crew stringing wire down the main street of town, and the following spring he watched as the long procession of horse-drawn sleighs made its way across Atlin Lake, hauling construction materials to complete the all-Canadian telegraph. Perhaps these experiences engaged his interest and influenced his decision when he was offered employment with the Yukon Telegraph.

His first job, in May 1902, was with the summer maintenance crew making repairs on the Yukon River section, at $75 a month. (He was not to earn much more than that during his next 40 years on the line!) The repairs lasted into the winter, which made the work much more difficult because after the river froze he could no longer use a canoe to move supplies. He had to pack everything on his back, not an easy task for a fellow who weighed no more than 140 pounds. In June 1903 he graduated to a permanent position as a lineman.

His initial posting was to the Pike River station, 20 miles south of Atlin. Here he experienced for the first time living in a cabin with someone other than his father. His new partner, Fred Gorrel, had been an operator with the line since it was built, was considered a good worker, and was well liked, but he had one flaw—as it turned out, a fatal one. He was not to be trusted with firearms; he was especially dangerous when he had been drinking.

On one occasion, when Gorrel, Guy, and a visitor had been imbibing freely, they decided to do some target shooting. As Lawrence recalled: "Fred stuck a ten cent piece on the trunk of a small tree and we all commenced to shoot at it [without success] …

Pike River Station on Atlin Lake, 20 miles south of the town, was a favourite picnic spot for locals. The man in the doorway wearing a Stetson hat is lineman Guy Lawrence, author of 40 Years on the Yukon Telegraph.

[Impatiently], Fred rushed into the cabin and seized his Winchester shotgun. I happened to be standing on the sill of the doorway and Fred came beside me, yelling out, 'I've got something that will make that ten cent piece jump.' Just at that moment the gun exploded and drilled a hole as large as a fifty cent piece right in the doorsill less than two inches from my foot."[10]

Notwithstanding the danger of living with Fred Gorrel, Lawrence felt that Pike River was one of the best locations for a lineman because it was close to a town with people. In the north, it was second only to the Yukon River stations, where boats went by all the time in summer and dogsleds passed on the ice in winter. The sociable young Guy often expressed his desire to be with people, a contradiction considering the kind of work he had chosen. Many years would pass before he was again assigned to a people-friendly station.

After only a few months at Pike, Lawrence was transferred to the isolated bush station at the Nakina River, 40 miles to the south. Knowing that he would need activities to occupy his time, he loaded his pack with a lot of things he thought he could use. In addition to winter clothing, a good supply of tobacco, and a rifle, he toted a camera, chessmen, and a banjo.

The trail to Nakina was overgrown and rough, with sections of soggy muskeg. The refuge cabins were inadequate; one located half a mile from the trail contained only a rusted-through iron stove and was occupied by millions of black flies. On the third day Lawrence reached the top of the bluff overlooking the river and hiked down the steep trail to his new station.

The cabin was a hovel. Set at the edge of the stream, it had "two small windows, a rough hewn door, and a pole floor which has ... large spaces ... between the poles, which must save a lot of sweeping."[11] On the bright side, Lawrence's new partner, Russell Pringle Hall, was the antithesis of Fred Gorrel. The son of a parson, he was the studious type, who spent much of his time with his typewriter, copying press material from the wire. And he was willing to help Guy learn the Morse code.

The construction crew had built a bridge across the river, but it had washed out and been replaced by a crude tramway consisting of two No. 8 wires, tightly wrapped together, from which a platform—a four-foot-long, 12-inch board—was suspended. The previous lineman had fallen 40 feet from this platform into the rushing water, fortunately not landing on any large rocks. To avert further mishaps, Lawrence decided to build a new bridge across the 90-foot span. He had completed one of the abutments by mid-November when a heavy, wet snowstorm turned his attention back to the telegraph. The line was down somewhere south, and both men started out to look for the break.

They had ascended the steep five-mile trail out of the ravine and were walking through Nakina Pass when they noticed a trickle of snow from the peaks to the east. Lawrence wrote: "Soon the trickle became an avalanche, and there was a terrific rumble of snow and large rocks descending ... soon poles were snapping off with the tremendous rush of air and simply disappeared under the rubble which must be from forty to sixty feet deep ... Where we had been walking only a few minutes before was [now] piled high with debris and unrecognizable."[12]

Lawrence and Hall both realized they were lucky not to be buried themselves. To reconnect the broken section, which was now covered by the avalanche, they strung spools of wire on top of the snow and raised the line up on small tripods, using tree poles. A maintenance crew would make more permanent repairs the following summer.

A few weeks later, news came over the wire that Fred Gorrel had had an accident at Pike. Not surprisingly, it involved a firearm. Gorrel was using his rifle to knock snow from low branches. He was holding the barrel when a branch caught in the trigger and the gun fired a bullet into his groin. A sleigh was sent to take him to Atlin for medical treatment, but he died before the doctor could remove the bullet. The men up and down the line mourned his death, remembering Gorrel as a cheerful man and a good operator who delighted in chatting on the line with the "boys."

The first year Lawrence spent at Nakina, winter mail service to Telegraph Creek by dogsled was begun over the trail from Atlin. Previously, the winter mail had come over the ice from Wrangell, but after too many accidents, some with loss of life, the river route

An early mail carrier at Atlin with his sled loaded and his dogs ready to hit the trail to Telegraph Creek.

was determined to be too dangerous and was replaced by the longer but safer trail to Atlin.

Norman Fisher was an early mail carrier, possibly the first. On his monthly trip he mostly followed the telegraph line, except for a section out of Atlin where he took a shortcut, away from the trail to Pike River Station, directly to the O'Donnell River, rejoining the telegraph line at Kuthai Lake. He normally hauled about 300 pounds of mail, plus a case of rum. The latter ensured that he would be cordially greeted by the linemen and invited in for a meal at the three telegraph cabins along the way, Nakina, Nahlin, and Shesley. The 220-mile trip took him six days, unless he was delayed by heavy snows. Fisher recalled, "It was the nicest job I ever had ... just you and the dogs and nobody to interfere with you." At night he would stop anywhere and just curl up with the dogs. "I had a bitch leader, nice and fat, she made a nice pillow and she didn't move much." He felt that he had learned more from the dogs then they ever learned from him: "how to be comfortable, where to be comfortable."[13] Later, two musher-mailmen carried the mail simultaneously, one starting from Atlin, the other from Telegraph Creek, passing at the midpoint. In 1933 the dogsleds were replaced by airplanes.

Guy Lawrence had a personal experience with the use of the mail service, or rather its misuse. At Nakina, after attending to his telegraph-line repair duties, he went back to working on the half-finished bridge. The result of his efforts was an impressive 90-foot-long structure set upon 15-foot-high abutments, the height the river rose during spring runoff. When he finished the job he figured he was due some recognition for his extra effort, so he wrote a letter to the DPW reporting on his achievement and hinting at reimbursement.

During the summer, when the Stikine was open, mail was delivered from Telegraph Creek up the line from cabin to cabin. Andy Johnson, the operator at Shesley Station, wired Lawrence, who by this time (May 1904) had been transferred from Nakina to the station at Nahlin, to tell him that there was an official-looking letter for him from the DPW. Johnson, instructed to open and read the letter, reported that it commended Lawrence for his public-spirited enterprise in building the bridge and included a cheque for $225. Lawrence was elated, if somewhat surprised at the generosity of the normally parsimonious department. His exuberance was short-lived. When the actual letter arrived, he found that although Johnson had truthfully reported the public-spirited part, the only other item it contained was an unbankable thank-you.[14]

The charade of Lawrence's cheque was but one example of Andy Johnson's practical jokes. The boredom of life on the line provided fertile grounds and a gullible audience for his creative imagination. Around the Christmas holidays, when he liked to extend the celebrating and was known to be in a cheerful mood, he was especially inclined to make up stories for the amusement of his fellow shut-in operators.

One winter he devised a story to explain why his line had been open and unattended for several hours. He claimed that while he was out on a repair job, a meteorite had fallen from the sky. "Suddenly there was a blinding crash, red glare, sulphurous fumes, a huge dark mass hurtling through the air which landed right in front of me." He was knocked unconscious. When he awoke he rushed back to his cabin to transmit a full report.

Most of the other operators were familiar with Johnson's penchant for trickery and got a chuckle or two from his carryings-on. One operator, however, wasn't in on the joke. Barney Taylor at

Atlin, who just happened to be a stringer for an Alaskan newspaper, sent in the story straight, and it appeared in the Alaskan and then the Vancouver papers. Pretty soon newspapers throughout the world picked up the meteorite story. There followed requests for interviews with Johnson and proposals to send reporters into the bush.[15] Despite denials, the story continued to gain attention, much to the amusement and distraction of the operators and linemen during their long, dark, and boring winter.[16]

Lawrence, who had learned Morse code and been elevated to the position of operator, welcomed his transfer to Nahlin.[17] Nakina was dark and claustrophobic, located in a deep canyon with mountains on both sides. Nahlin was more open, giving a greater sense of space, with a larger, brighter cabin. His new partner was also different. Rod McKay was a carpenter who had made the cabin more liveable by building much of the furniture.

The area abounded in game, and the men stationed at Nahlin had usually been able to make extra money trapping fur-bearing animals: lynx, marten, mink, and wolves. McKay loaned Lawrence six traps, which he set out on the telegraph right-of-way and tended until trapping stopped in April, when the animals' fur and skin began to turn black and could not be sold.

Boredom was a constant companion of many of the telegraph men in the bush stations, especially those like Guy Lawrence who enjoyed being around people. He stuck it out at Nahlin for three years, then went on leave during the summer of 1907. When he returned, it seemed that his experience "outside" had only heightened his determination to get out of the bush. He became increasingly restive in his lonely cabin.

On numerous occasions Lawrence had requested that Superintendent Phelan reassign him, to no avail. Exasperated, he finally left his cabin and headed out, first to Atlin and then to Vancouver to confront his boss. After a few days in Vancouver he "summoned up the courage" to call upon him, mainly because he wanted to collect his back pay.

Lawrence described Phelan as a jovial Irishman—until he got down to business, when he could be both a persuasive talker and a "verbal hard hitter."

As I entered his sanctum he arose with a genial smile and extended his hand. Gracious! I thought, this may not be so bad after all; but he was only getting me within range of his guns. Soon he began to fire them. In no uncertain terms he told me what he thought of my walking out of Nahlin Station as I had—walking out on one of the best jobs in northern British Columbia, a job for which there were literally hundreds of applicants ... He now told me the Department was through with me.

I got up from my seat and offered him my hand without a word, then walked toward the door. Just as I reached it, he said, "You better leave me your address. You men from the North are easy marks for city slickers."[18]

Two weeks later Lawrence received a call to report to Phelan, who, in a complete reversal of form, offered him the station at Blackwater, one of the most desirable locations on the line. Only 44 miles from Quesnel, it was on a wagon road with people passing every day. Lawrence was elated at his new assignment, where he would no longer be isolated and alone.

Phelan sent him off the next day with a letter to the present operator, who was much out of favour, informing him that Lawrence was taking over. He warned Lawrence not to tell anyone along the way of his destination, for fear that "this man might sell your entire annual provisions."[19] This was Lawrence's first face-to-face with Phelan. It would not be the last, as Lawrence was to take a vacation from the Yukon Telegraph on two more occasions, once to work for a private telephone company and the second time to serve in the Canadian army in the First World War.

CHAPTER 11

The Grand Trunk Pacific Railway

By the time the telegraph line was completed from Bennett City to Dawson City in September 1899, the stampede to the Klondike had reached its crest and was on the wane. Two years later, when the Yukon Telegraph's main line was in operation, only a fraction of the gold seekers who had made it to Dawson City remained. The others had abandoned their dreams of riches or moved on to other strikes, many to the one at Nome, Alaska. According to the 1901 census, of the 40,000 or so venturesome souls who had travelled to Dawson City, only 9,142 remained. During the following decades the population continued to go down, to 3,015 in 1911 and to 975 in 1921. The population of the entire Yukon, and the value of the gold produced, also showed significant declines.[1]

Fewer people meant fewer customers for the northern district of the telegraph. In 1905, the first year for which detailed statistics are available, the four major offices—Dawson, Boundary (where messages were relayed to the U.S.), Whitehorse, and Atlin—were the sources of 16,425 telegrams. Five years later the number was 9,537. More tellingly, in 1905 the north accounted for 61 percent of the business; five years later its share had declined to 22 percent. Notwithstanding this shift in volume, the north was still a significant source of revenue because of the higher tariffs for telegrams originating from these more distant stations. Conversely, the maintenance costs of this long line more than offset the higher rates.

By 1910 it was clear that a dramatic change had taken place. The statistics in Superintendent Phelan's reports illustrated this shift in business, as did Guy Lawrence's observation in 1907: "Down south the line is busier than ever, but up north the instruments are silent for hours at a time."[2] The tail was now wagging the dog. The original reason for building the Yukon Telegraph—to serve the Klondike—was no longer its only purpose, nor were the gold fields its primary source of income.

The south was where the action was, reflected in the increase in telegraph traffic and in the building of branch lines. Central British Columbia was growing, especially after the Grand Trunk Railway announced plans to extend its rails to the ocean, to become Canada's second transcontinental railway. The western section, named the Grand Trunk Pacific (GTP), would pass through Prince George and the Nechako and Bulkley valleys to Hazelton, then down the Skeena River to a new ice-free port called Prince Rupert. From Stoney Creek, 60 miles west of Prince George, the railway would parallel the right-of-way of the Yukon Telegraph.

As construction was to start from the Prince Rupert end and move eastward, it was important to establish communication with the new town, which was literally being hacked out of the wilderness. The government quickly responded by building a

The Grand Trunk Pacific Railway's new ice-free port at Prince Rupert, as it appeared in 1908.

branch line 40 miles from Aberdeen, opening an office on July 20, 1907.[3]

The promise of construction of the railway created a minor land boom in central B.C. The only drawback to settlement had been the lack of transportation to get products to market at an acceptable price. The railway would solve this problem, providing farmers and ranchers with an outlet for shipping their product both to the east and westward to the ocean.

F.A. Talbot Visits the New Garden of Canada

The anticipated effect of the railway was chronicled by the English travel writer F.A. Talbot, who in 1909 was exploring central British Columbia, collecting material for a book he would title *The New Garden of Canada*—which is exactly how he described the region. He wrote that its fertile valleys, with their thick, rich soils and ample forests, were excellent for growing crops, raising cattle, and harvesting lumber. The land was "ripe for development, silently calling the settler with its profusion of wild hay [and] tall grasses."[4]

Talbot and his party started by pack train from Prince George, following the planned route of the railway westward, which enabled him to observe the area before it was transformed by the GTP. Near Stoney Creek, Talbot first came upon the Yukon Telegraph. He was thrilled to see "trailed across the azure of the sky a thin dull-gray thread [of wire] stretching in an unbroken line from Vancouver to the far north."

Along the way he was able to talk with some of the telegraph men to learn how they were being affected. The first man he met was W.J. Milne, the operator at Stoney Creek, who was well aware of the prosperity the railway could bring. In anticipation he had purchased 800 acres of land, at an average price of one dollar an acre. Although he had started to clear the land, it was still impractical to raise a crop because of the high cost of cartage to market. He expected this would change when the railway was built.

Farther on, at the Nechako River crossing, Talbot was met by "a keen-eyed, taciturn, little fellow," Vital LeFort (or LeForce), who operated the ferry. His European name unknown, he had been called "Le Fort Vital," meaning "the strong life," by the Natives. Now in his 70s, LeFort had originally come to the area more than 40 years earlier to work on the Collins Overland Telegraph and had stayed on to prospect for gold. He made one of the first paying strikes at a place that became known as Vital Creek. Although he reportedly had a good claim, he did little to mine it and spent his years living in one or another small bush cabin, as "silent as a sphinx." He now survived on the fares he collected from travellers crossing the Nechako.

At Fraser Lake, Talbot came upon the local telegraph lineman, who complained about the frequency of interruptions caused by winds and fires that brought down pole after pole. He found it difficult to keep up with repairs:

Vital LeFort began his long working life in the north on the Collins Overland Telegraph, became a successful prospector, and for many years operated the ferry over the Nechako River at Fort Fraser.

> Last week I had been ten miles over my line towards Fraser Lake and had put a breakdown right. I got home late that night to find another interruption. I called up Fraser Lake. That was all right. It was on the fifteen mile stretch north that the break had happened. I was up in the early morning and off full pelt. A post had come down and there was a dead earth [this means the wire was grounded]. I put that right and returned home. As I rode up, dog-tired, my wife told me that there was another break. I called up Fraser Lake, and got through, then tried the other side, and found Burns Lake on the north did not answer. I was off again at

dawn, taking a blanket and a pocket full of provisions with me. I found a bush fire had been raging, and about a score of trees had dropped across the wire, bringing down two or three hundred feet of it, not far beyond where I was working the previous day.[5]

These back-and-forth repair trips, first north, then south, continued without let-up for two weeks. The lineman was kept hopping because of the importance of the line. A "tremendous" amount of traffic was being generated over the Prince Rupert branch, and any interruption resulted in a huge backlog of messages.

Although the frequency of interruptions was blamed on the weather and fires, it was as much a result of inadequate maintenance. Talbot observed many leaning and rotted poles. He asked one lineman if it was the poles that kept the line up or the line that held up the poles. "Hang me if I know," was the reply, "but I guess it's a bit of both." When one of the party's horses reared up and bumped into a pole, it proceeded to topple over, narrowly missing the rider.

Talbot asked how the local Indians had reacted to the telegraph, and one operator said that they accepted it and often rendered assistance by informing the linemen when they came across breaks. At times they might even prop up a pole that had fallen. However, on occasion this helpfulness had baffling results. One time when a lineman was out searching for the cause of an interruption, he was perplexed when he met his counterpart coming from the other direction. Doing some tests, they determined that the break was on the section he had just travelled. Carefully examining the wire on his way back, the lineman finally found the problem. A pole had partially toppled over, and a passing Indian, wanting to help, had looped a piece of wire around the top of the fallen pole and pulled it up to a nearby tree. Unfortunately, the wire he used was touching the line. As a result, the dots and dashes were simply running down the tree to the ground.

When Talbot reached the Bulkley Valley, he visited the McInnes Farm, run by two brothers from Scotland. They had come into the area on the telegraph construction crew and thereafter were employed as linemen. During this time they had acquired 160 acres of farmland, which they tended in their spare time. They became so enamoured of the potential of agriculture in the valley that they chucked their jobs with the telegraph to become full-time farmers.

As Talbot and his party got closer to Hazelton, they observed more people and activity, including felling gangs clearing the way for the railway. At Hagwilget they came to the wild canyon of the Bulkley River, with near-vertical rocky sides plunging 80 feet to the rushing waters below. A few years earlier it would have been impossible to cross the canyon at this point without using the amazing cantilever bridge the Natives had built. It was an ingenious construction for people lacking formal training in the structural principles of this type of bridge.

From each side of the gorge they had extended two huge tree trunks and anchored them down with tons of boulders, earth, and debris. Each trunk was supported by a diagonal brace, also anchored into the cliffs. The gaps between the large trunks were spanned with two more logs, and here is the ingenious part. These

The last in a series of unique cantilever bridges built by the Natives that spanned the Bulkley River at Hagwilget near Hazelton.

logs were supported from above by a truss-like construction in which diagonal braces supported a horizontal member that in turn held up the logs bridging the gap. The entire structure was originally lashed together with willow thongs, later replaced by wire. "It is a crazy-looking affair, and when you venture on, it creaks, groans, and swings as if threatening to collapse at every footstep." Yet it had fulfilled its purpose, "though white men prefer to look at, and not to walk upon it."

This frail-looking structure had been the sole means of crossing the river at this point until a few years earlier, when the province erected a suspension bridge a short distance downriver. Examining the new bridge, the Natives were intrigued by its cables and wires. They did not understand their significance and concluded that they must be ornamental. Since they liked the effect, they decided to embellish their own bridge in the same way. They strung and attached wire, some of it dating to the Collins Overland Telegraph, in a haphazard fashion, creating the erroneous impression that the structure was their attempt to build a suspension bridge. The wire may have supplied some support, but it could not change the fact that they had built their own style of cantilever bridge and merely used the white man's wire for decoration.

Talbot's journey on the telegraph line ended at Hazelton, where he boarded a river steamer to travel down the Skeena to Prince Rupert, observing along the way the work being done on that section of the new railway.

Problems for the Telegraph

From Stoney Creek to Hazelton the railway parallelled the telegraph line, passing through valleys that were wide enough for both lines. The new construction threatened only minimal inconvenience to the operation of the government's telegraph.

This compatibility changed radically on the 200-mile Port Simpson branch (now called the Prince Rupert branch), which ran on the north side of the Skeena River, the same side the railway would occupy. The rocky, steep terrain had made it impossible for the telegraph men to build a trail along the line. They had used boats to gain access to the cliffs in order to erect their poles and wire, continuing the practice by using launches to maintain the line. Difficult as stringing a single strand of wire through this area had been, it was nothing compared to what the railway builders had to overcome. The cliffs overhanging the river restricted the location and the width of the railbed. In some places the tracks had to be built on the right-of-way of the telegraph, causing considerable disruption. Thousands of tons of rock had to be removed. Work crews used dynamite to blast the rock away from the cliffs, and then as many as 3,000 "navvies," or unskilled labourers as they would be called today, descended upon the debris to clear the railbed of rubble.

Railway work began to cause problems for the telegraph line during the latter part of 1908, when survey parties occasionally cut down trees that fell across the wire. The real difficulties started the following spring, as described by Superintendent Phelan:

Railway construction on the Grand Trunk Pacific from Prince Rupert, eastward for one hundred miles, began in May, and, as the railway parallels the telegraph line, and, in some places, usurps our right of way, innumerable interruptions were of daily occurrence during the months of June, July and August, mainly due to the clearing of timber for the one hundred foot wide railway right of way. As the telegraph line and railway follow the base of heavy timbered bluffs for great distances, and, as the fisheries regulations prohibited the contractors from falling the timber into the river, the line was in places completely destroyed. Although extra linemen were placed in railway camps, in some cases only two miles apart, they could not keep pace with the interruptions, and every expedient was resorted to keep the business moving. Four new telegraph offices were also installed at intermediate points to facilitate the location of breaks, confining the movement of the linemen to the sections affected. In some places, where bald mountains rise sheer from the water, iron rods were used [to attach the wire to the cliff], and the line placed as far as possible out of the line of danger, but blasting operations later caused further damage, and this is still of daily occurrence at one point or another, along that portion of the line. As it was anticipated that railway construction would cause us trouble, a general repair gang was started from Hazelton on the opening of navigation in May, and the line reconstructed its entire length, and, where possible, the line was diverted to escape damage from railway construction work. After the line had been reconstructed, and the greater part of the timber clearing completed, interruptions were reduced to a minimum. Traffic on this branch has increased at a rapid rate, and, a much greater and continued increase is looked for, especially at Prince Rupert, when the townsite at that point is placed on the market.[6]

By the summer of 1911, after two years of work, the most difficult section of the new railway had been completed. The remaining terrain along the river to Hazelton was less constricted, and the work proceeded with fewer interruptions of the telegraph. At the same time that telegraph crews were working along the Skeena to accommodate the construction of the GTP, another crew was employed 100 miles to the north, completing a new branch line.

The Grand Trunk Pacific Railway, here under construction east of Hazelton, was built parallel to the Yukon Telegraph.

Branch Line to Stewart

When significant mining activity developed at the head of the Portland Canal around Stewart, the DPW decided to build a line to the Skeena branch, connecting at Kitsumkalum, near present-day Terrace. It would provide service to mining properties at places like Goose Bay, Alice Arm, and Aiyansh, and later to the Anyox copper smelter. Starting from Stewart, the work crew followed the Portland Canal for 37 miles, then struggled over two very rugged heights of land, too steep for packhorses. Through these sections, "every pound of materials and supplies had to be packed on men's backs, making the work slow and expensive." Construction began in September 1910 and was completed a year later on August 31, 1911. During its first winter the new branch performed well, except for a few snow slides along the Portland Canal.[7]

With the construction of the Stewart branch, the Yukon Telegraph system was almost complete. The last major addition was the Bella Coola branch, built off the main line from 150 Mile House and completed on November 30, 1912. Because of the lack of settlements along its 329 miles, it was operated as a composite system, a combination of telegraph and telephone. There were three telegraph offices: one at each end and one midway at Kluna. At points in between, 11 telephone offices were established, operated by commission agents who received a percentage of the telephone charges.[8]

After 1912 a few short extensions were added, and some sections were rerouted, such as the line between Port Simpson and Prince Rupert. It had always been difficult and dangerous for linemen to get to the poles along Work Channel, the fjord-like inlet running south from Port Simpson, when they needed to make repairs. After the Prince Rupert branch was up and working, a new line was built around the coast, and the Work Channel section was abandoned.

The Composite System

After 1912 the heady era of rapid expansion of the southern district was over, and the Yukon Telegraph entered a period of programmed maintenance and conversion. More sections were converted to the Railway Composite Telegraph-Telephone System, known as the composite system for short. Although previously it had been possible, with proper equipment, to use telegraph wires to transmit voice messages, the new composite system was a great improvement. The newer lines had been provided with this equipment, and some old lines were converted.

An advantage of telephones was that they could be set up at almost any location—roadhouses, farms, ranches, mining camps, and canneries—and they allowed people to talk to others along the line. For long-distance transmissions, a customer no longer had to travel to the distant telegraph office, but could simply call in the message from his local telephone office to the closest telegraph office, where it was transcribed into Morse and sent down the line. And the telephone did not require an operator with knowledge of the Morse code. It was a portent of the advancing technology that would soon make the telegraph obsolete.

From the beginning, maintenance of the telegraph had been a concern, but as the system grew and matured it became a never-ending struggle to keep more than 3,000 miles of line in working order. Poles rotted at an alarming rate; only a few years after construction, a section would need to be repoled or replaced. Their short life was due to a combination of factors, principally the species of softwood used and the swampy condition of the ground into which many of the poles were sunk. In an effort to keep ahead of the rot and to reduce the number of times linemen were called out to make emergency repairs, a schedule of regular pole replacement was adopted for the entire line. The cost of maintenance became an even larger part of the telegraph's budget, but it was an essential expense if the line was to operate effectively. Work crews were in the field each summer replacing thousands of poles. The breaks caused by fire and storms continued, but overall there were fewer reports of lengthy interruptions.

Guy Lawrence at Blackwater

The coming of the railway created a land boom in central British Columbia that not only attracted speculators and settlers, but also provided opportunities for the telegraph men to share in the bounty of prosperity. One of the operators upon whom fortune smiled—who was in the right place at the right time—was Guy Lawrence, who had been surprised and delighted when Superintendent Phelan assigned him to the Blackwater station, the first office north of Quesnel, which was in the centre of the action.

In the summer of 1908, Lawrence boarded a train for Ashcroft, where the horse was king: "The men wore chaps and high heeled boots with large rowel spurs; a silk bandana tied loosely around his neck, and a black Stetson wide-brimmed hat on his head. Every adult man favored a long, drooping mustache."[9] At Ashcroft he booked passage to Quesnel on a Cariboo Road stagecoach. During the 225-mile ride, Lawrence passed many of the telegraph stations whose operators he had conversed with over the wire. He went past Clinton, 115 Mile House, 150 Mile House, Soda Creek, and Alexandria, but there was no time to visit as the stage rumbled along over the bumpy roadway, pausing only to change teams of horses every 20 miles. They did stop for meals, usually at farmhouses, many dating to the Cariboo gold-rush days of 50 years earlier. The charge for each meal was 50 cents, and the table "absolutely groaned under the weight of delicious home cooking, each family seeming to vie with the other to provide the best meal." After three days Lawrence arrived at Quesnel, the end of the road and the stage line.

Quesnel in 1908 was a bustling town, filled with people heading north, including Lawrence, who still had 42 miles to go to his station at Blackwater. After crossing the Fraser River on a ferry attached to a cable, with the current of the river supplying the motive power, he hitched a wagon ride with an old farmer. The trail/road was in the process of being improved, but there were still tree stumps to be navigated. He and the farmer pried and pushed the wagon through these obstacles, and in the early afternoon of the fourth day they reached the crest of a hill overlooking the Blackwater River. Just beyond the bridge that crossed the river, Lawrence could see a very small, flat-roofed cabin, his new home for the next five years.

Waiting for him was J. Ward, the operator he was replacing. Ward had a good business going, providing travellers with lodgings and wretched meals. At first Lawrence suspected he was skimming government provisions, but later cleared him of the charge. He was just making money any way he could, and he was very successful at his sideline. In the evening Ward suggested a game of stud poker, one of Lawrence's joys and weaknesses. His earlier gaming experiences had not often been successful, but on this occasion luck was with him. By midnight Lawrence found himself the owner of a poke of dollars, a horse and saddle, a six-horse barn, and 160 acres of land. The next morning Ward had to ask to borrow his old horse to get himself and his gear to town. It seemed a hard thing for a man to have to do.

Two days later the lineman, George Duclos, returned after an unauthorized leave to spend time with his wife and four daughters. When Lawrence told him about skunking Ward at poker, Duclos burst his bubble: "Well, the cash will be useful for a bottle or two of rum, but the horse is a bad stumbler and as for the land, he does not actually own it as he hasn't yet proved up on it [and] the barn is ready to fall to pieces."

Lawrence soon settled in at Blackwater, continuing the business of providing services to travellers. He also began to look for some land he might acquire. The maxim "The early bird gets the worm" applies not only to ornithology, but also to land speculation, and Lawrence was up early enough, and in the right place, to take advantage of what was happening around his station.

A steady stream of land seekers was moving into the area, the vanguard of those hoping to ride the rails of economic opportunity and prosperity provided by the railway. Within weeks of his arrival, Lawrence and his lineman-business partner Duclos had expanded their hostelry by erecting a bunkhouse and a 20-horse stable. They provided meals and lodging for the travellers and feed and shelter for their animals, all at reasonable prices. And when the stage line was extended beyond Quesnel, they were ready to accommodate the passengers and the eight-horse teams.

Although Lawrence mentions in passing that telegraph traffic was very heavy, his work did not seem to distract him from his business interests. Even the 160 acres he had won at poker turned out to be a decent piece of land, suitable for growing feed for horses. He discovered that it also contained remnants of the original

Collins Overland Telegraph built in 1866. There were strands of wire and some old insulators, which he later learned were prized by collectors.

Duclos frequently spent nights with his family in town. On one occasion he did not return; he had quit the telegraph. His replacement, Monty Montgomery, was an equally enterprising fellow, who immediately proceeded to build a large cabin for himself and his wife, with an attached private room for female travellers. The flurry of enterprise continued unabated when Lawrence built a larger house, into which he moved the telegraph office. While all this was happening the telegraph business was flourishing "enormously."

Prince George, 50 miles away, was attracting scores of settlers. Since the telegraph did not go through the town, a private telephone company was established to serve the community's needs. For long-distance service, the DPW permitted the company to run a telephone line to the Blackwater station, which increased volume so much that a second operator was hired to handle the telephone business. Lawrence, speaking as a true telegrapher, was skeptical, observing that "phone messages were proving to be full of errors and causing much grief."

However, his cynicism did not deter him from accepting a job with the new company soon after. He resigned his position with the government to run the private company's telegraph/telephone system in Prince George. Lawrence was convinced that "it was a golden opportunity to get in on the ground floor of a new booming community." He sold his land, house, and horse, gave his share of the bunkhouse and stable to his partner, and moved to Prince George.

To his disappointment and disillusion, Lawrence found the work demanding and the new environment confining, and soon wished he was back at Blackwater. Burned out after two years, he petitioned Phelan to take him back, which Phelan did, assigning him to the station at Fort Fraser. His stay was short, however, only 15 months. The War to End All Wars was raging, and in January 1916 Lawrence enlisted, "since the army by then was taking older men." He was 36 years old.

Thus ended Lawrence's first stint with the government telegraph. From his employment in 1902 as lineman at Pike River to his enlistment in the army, with the exception of the hiatus at Prince George, he had been part of the growth of the Yukon Telegraph. He still had a long way to go to complete the 40 years in the title of his book. But even at this early date, few others had been with the line as long.

CHAPTER 12

Gunanoot, Airplanes, and Floods

So far, this study of the Yukon Telegraph has made only passing mention of the Aboriginal peoples who inhabited the land before the invasion of gold seekers, settlers, and telegraph builders. Ignoring the fact that the Natives had their own culture, accounts at the time validated their lives only as they related to the objectives of white men.

The Native people served the newcomers by guiding them over ancient trails, hauling their outfits, and at times saving their lives. For example, when Peter J. Leech, one of the Collins Overland explorers, was wandering around the Nass Valley in 1867, looking for a route for the telegraph, a Native man showed him the way back to "civilization." On the Ashcroft Trail, Natives were at the river crossings to ferry the gold seekers, their outfits, and pack animals across. And as the Hudson's Bay Company factor at Fraser Lake told Hamlin Garland: "An Indian won't let even a white man starve to death."[1] Some Natives worked for the Yukon Telegraph, such as Charlie Martin, the lineman at Fourth Cabin, and Simon Gunanoot.

Simon Peter Gunanoot

Simon Peter Gunanoot,[2] a member of the Gitksan people, was involved with the Yukon Telegraph from its beginning. The line was built through the traditional lands of his band in the Hazelton–

Simon Peter Gunanoot in the Gitanmaax Cemetery in Hazelton among the elaborate Aboriginal spirit (or burial) houses.

Kispiox area, where his family held rights to extensive hunting and fishing grounds. An expert hunter and trapper, a shopkeeper and fur trader, Gunanoot was a prosperous family man with a wife and two children. This all changed on June 18, 1906, when his world was turned upside down.

The fateful events started at the Two-Mile Hotel outside Hazelton, where Gunanoot was drinking with some friends. As the night progressed, the drinking turned to drunkenness for Gunanoot's party and also for some other men in the tavern who were not his friends. According to one version,[3] slurs were cast upon Gunanoot's wife by one Alex MacIntosh, described as the product of a Native woman and a Hudson's Bay Company Scotsman, and by Max Leclair, a French sailor. A fight ensued between Gunanoot and MacIntosh that resulted in no serious physical damage to either party. But Gunanoot's remarks after the fight were to have a profound effect on later events. Witnesses testified that they hazily recalled Gunanoot mumbling "[he] was going for a gun and would come back and fix him."[4] It was the last time anyone saw MacIntosh or Leclair alive.

About seven the next morning, MacIntosh's body was found. He had been shot in the back as he rode his horse. Leclair was found soon after, shot in exactly the same way. When the police learned of the fight and Gunanoot's threats, he became their prime suspect, and when he and his brother-in-law, Peter Himadam, fled the area, it seemed an admission of guilt. The police set out to arrest both men.

For the next 13 years the B.C. Provincial Police and the Royal North West Mounted Police scoured the British Columbia wilderness, but Gunanoot was always a step ahead, although not a very big step. He did not flee to some far-off land, but stayed in the country he knew so well, the 100 miles of wilderness between what is now called Mount Gunanoot and the Groundhog Mountain–Bear Lake area. After the intensity of the initial search had died down, Gunanoot was joined by his family, and although frequently forced to move his camp, he was able to work a trapline and occasionally venture into town to sell his furs. Gunanoot felt so secure that he was reputed to have come into town one time to view an early motion picture.

A $1,000 reward was offered for information leading to his arrest, but there were no takers. Regardless of how many search parties were sent out, Gunanoot's mastery of the bush enabled him to avoid detection.

The Yukon Telegraph passed through the southwest corner of Gunanoot's sanctuary, and he travelled the linemen's trail with impunity. He was very familiar with the telegraph, having been employed in its construction and later with the pack trains that hauled provisions to the wilderness cabins. Often the linemen knew where he was, but either out of sympathy or fear they never reported him to the police. In fact, the existence of the telegraph line was useful to him. As one observer concluded: "If there had not been cabins with friendly linemen and emergency food supplies available, it is doubtful that he and his companions could have eluded capture as long as they did."[5]

Although the telegraph line was usually an advantage to Gunanoot, it could also be used against him. When search parties received information about his whereabouts, they were able to wire ahead to other police units. The union-busting Pinkerton Detective Agency, which had been hired to join the search, used the telegraph during the winter of 1909–10 to relay instructions; agents also filched supplies from the refuge cabins. The charge to the government for Pinkerton's short-lived services was $11,000.

After years of failure, frustration, and expense, the government's enthusiasm for the chase waned. Nothing had been accomplished, and the police continued to be embarrassed by their inability to find a small group of wandering Natives. When it become apparent that without the cooperation of local people, both Native and white, Gunanoot was not likely to be found, active pursuit was replaced by a waiting game.

The years had also taken a toll on Gunanoot and his family, who were tiring of the need to remain constantly alert, to move their camps, and to suffer the hard winters in the bush. Both sides were eventually ready to find a solution to the standoff, opening the way for a telegraph man to play a pivotal role as an intermediary.

Tommy Hankin was born in Hazelton and probably knew Gunanoot. He started with the telegraph during construction as a water boy and worked his way up to lineman and then operator, a career that was to last off and on until the Hazelton–Telegraph Creek section was shut down in 1935. From 1906 to 1909 he was the operator at Seventh Cabin, followed by a gap in his employment when he ran a trapline and guided big-game hunters.

In 1913, while camping with two hunters in the Skeena–Stikine high country, Hankin was approached by Gunanoot and Himadam. Hankin offered the two a meal, and thus began a relationship that was to grow in trust and eventually enabled Hankin to assist Gunanoot when he decided to turn himself in.

> [On one occasion] Hankin was camped about 12 miles from his cabin near what is now Hankin Mountain, 50 miles north of Bowser Lake, when Gun-Ah-Noot reappeared from the dark woods. He was alone and they traded some caribou meat that Gun-Ah-Noot had for some of Hankin's bacon and beans. Then they sat throughout most of the night and talked.

Gun-Ah-Noot spoke with emotion of his exile. Death had taken his father and one child and he was tired of running. He asked if the government would treat him fairly if he surrendered. Hankin said he didn't know but promised to help.[6]

Hankin spoke to his friend George Beirnes, the packer, who contacted a prominent criminal lawyer, Stuart Henderson. Henderson agreed to handle the case, and after several aborted attempts he got together with Gunanoot in Hazelton in March 1919. After hearing his story, Henderson assured him that he would have no difficulty winning an acquittal.

The lawyer persuaded Gunanoot to turn himself in, and in June the former fugitive was taken into custody for trial in Victoria. After 15 minutes of deliberation the jury acquitted him. It had always been a weak and circumstantial case, but the passage of time, and possibly the laxity of the prosecution, contributed greatly to the speedy conclusion.

Gunanoot was free to resume his life of hunting and trapping, now no longer fearing apprehension. In 1933 he succumbed to pneumonia and was buried near his father at Bowser Lake, in the wilderness he loved so much. *Finis* the story, except for the unanswered question: Who killed MacIntosh and Leclair? Information uncovered by Pierre Berton and other writers suggests that Gunanoot was indeed the murderer.[7]

Unique Personalities

While the Gunanoot story was unfolding, there had been other, more mundane, developments along the Yukon Telegraph.[8]

There had been a change in packing contractors. George Beirnes had taken over Cataline's packing business, which included the contract to deliver provisions from Hazelton to the telegraph cabins. Beirnes, who came from Ontario as a young man to make his fortune in the Klondike, had worked on the construction of both the White Pass and Yukon Route's railway and the Yukon Telegraph. He arrived in Hazelton about 1906 and became involved in the packing business, acquiring a large ranch in the Kispiox Valley where he kept as many as 80 pack animals. When he got the contract to supply the telegraph stations, he changed his stationery letterhead to mimic a royal appointment. He was now "Packing contractor to the Canadian Government."[9]

George Beirnes' first experience hauling for the telegraph in spring 1913 was auspicious. When he was ready to start on the trail, the wide Skeena River, which had to be crossed, remained at high-flood stage much longer than usual. Beirnes waited as long as he could for the water level to go down. Finally he could delay no longer. The whole countryside turned out to witness what promised to be the riskiest crossing of the Skeena ever seen. Everyone watched as Beirnes took to the water astride the bell mare, followed by the other 75 horses that plunged in after their leader. As they got further out, fighting the pull of the water, their heads began to look like black specks in the distance. "And [then] they saw Beirnes land, dripping wet and laughing, on the opposite bank and wave his hand at them. For he lost never a horse that time!"[10]

The linemen and operators waiting for Beirnes to deliver their provisions were a mixed bunch, each a distinct personality. As a group they probably weren't much different from the general type of man who ventured into the north, but individually they certainly were different one from the other. In a letter to Louis LeBourdais, the Quesnel operator who collected interviews with veteran telegraphers, C.W. Mitchell recalled the antics of some of the men he got to know as an operator on the section between Hazelton and Telegraph Creek.[11]

One of these was George Smith, the operator at Ninth Cabin and a very successful trapper. Each time he went out on his triennial leave he took a sizeable amount of money—as much as $7,500. One time his poke lasted three weeks in Vancouver. The next time he was more frugal and made it all the way to his hometown, Buckingham, Quebec. As he neared his destination, he missed a train or a boat. Undaunted, and apparently still retaining much of his poke, he chartered a tugboat to take him the rest of the way. To show that he had not completely reformed, he also hired an orchestra to accompany him.

On Smith's return to the line, since some of his money remained unspent, he was able to afford five gallons of overproof rum. He hired a horse to carry the load and started out from Hazelton. According to Mitchell, "He got as far as First [Cabin] where old Garrity was the operator. They both got drunk. Next day Geo Byrne's [George Beirnes'] pack train came along with the year's grub for the line. The whole bunch got drunk. Byrnes himself came along three days later and found pack horses along the trail for miles with their packs still on. They fixed it up and I don't believe [Superintendent] Phelan ever knew about it."

There are innumerable stories about the drinking habits of some of the men, who took every opportunity to imbibe their favourite overproof rum. Guy Lawrence writes about ordering bottles of rum to be brought to his isolated cabin by the annual pack trains. The mail carriers were also known to deliver booze with the letters from home.

One critical observer of the character of the telegraph men was Harper Reed, a surveyor and long-time Indian agent at Telegraph Creek. Reed was not an easy man with whom to find favour. Lawrence's dedication in his *40 Years on the Yukon Telegraph* reads: "This book is dedicated in tribute to the employees of the old Yukon Telegraph Line, many of whom gave their lives to maintain the Service."[12] In the margin of his copy, the irascible Reed, commenting on this inspirational message, wrote: "Excepting Joe Hicks [at] Nahlin, old Moose McKay & one or two others, the gang were a squaw-chasing ... bunch of so-called white trappers, bootleggers & no-good trouble makers. H.R."[13]

In his letter to LeBourdais, Mitchell included a story about a very different personality, W.T. Weeks, the miser at Seventh Cabin. When he went out on leave, rather than spend any of the money he had accumulated from three years work in the bush, Weeks hired out to drive a team of horses. During his two months away, in Vancouver or wherever he went, he spent as little as possible. Any "new" clothing he purchased came from used-clothing shops.

He was as frugal with money as he was foolish with firearms, a failing he shared with a few other linemen, such as the late Fred Gorrel. Their fondness for holding a rifle by its muzzle seems to have been a common, and deadly, practice. One time while out working alone on the line, Weeks grasped the muzzle and managed to trip the hammer, discharging a bullet into his chest. Although badly injured, he was able to cut into the wire and send a message about his condition, adding that he would try to get to the cabin of an Indian two miles away.

A doctor was sent out from Hazelton to treat Weeks at the Indian's cabin. "There was no doubt that [Weeks] was badly wounded. When the doctor commenced to cut off his undershirt [though] he raised a howl—he would about as soon die as ruin a shirt."[14]

C.W. Mitchell himself did not fit into any neatly defined category. He seems to have been a sober, sensitive, and sensible man, although a bit of a hermit. He genuinely enjoyed the solitude of his work on the telegraph and appreciated the beauty of the country. He closed his letter to LeBourdais with a bit of poetry and an apology to Lord Byron:

> There is pleasure in the pathless woods;
> There is rapture in the lonely shore;
> There is society where none intrudes,
> Where horned owls hoot and night hawks soar;
> Not that I love man the less but nature more.[15]

This idyllic setting was brutally shattered by the First World War. The army needed telegraph operators, and some of the men volunteered for service, including Guy Lawrence, who couldn't wait to sign up. In service he was given extensive training in "Army Signals," adding the Continental code to his knowledge of the Morse code. He served with the 67th Battalion of the Canadian Expeditionary Force, spending some of his time in the front lines. He did not dwell on horrendous wartime experiences, preferring to recount less painful, and perhaps amusing, stories, such as the one about his lucky foot. While he was in a foxhole, a mortar burst dangerously close to his left foot, the same foot that Fred Gorrel at Pike River had missed blowing off by inches. In each instance the "lucky foot" had escaped without injury.

Immediately after he was discharged, Lawrence once again headed for Superintendent Phelan's office, confident that he would be quickly rehired because of his patriotic service to his country and his long experience with the Yukon Telegraph. But Phelan hadn't changed. He could not resist giving Lawrence a hard time and told him that since he had resigned to join the army, he could not expect to receive preference in being hired back. Then he brought out his ledger, which contained the work records of every employee who had ever served on the telegraph. He noted the black marks against Lawrence's name for leaving his post. They argued, and then suddenly Phelan offered Lawrence a job at Stewart, the small mining town at the head of the Portland Canal.

Once a flourishing mining camp, the area was now depressed, the population down to 17 souls. The local postmaster, who didn't have much mail to deliver, was serving as the telegraph agent. To accommodate Lawrence, the government rented part of an ancient building for an office, with a sleeping room in the rear. A butcher shop occupied the other part. "Every time that butcher hit his meat block my office relay would jump, with the result that many strange symbols found their way into code."[16]

The line from Stewart to the Skeena followed the Portland Canal, then went overland to the company town of Anyox, with its nasty copper smelter. Over the years the acrid chemical fumes from the smelter corroded miles of telegraph wire. Not only was the wire disintegrating, but the fumes had also killed all the vegetation for miles around. Dead trees regularly fell onto the wire, engaging the linemen in a constant battle to keep the line open.

The government did not want to give up on the branch line because some of the mines were planning to restart, which would increase the telegraph business in Stewart. It was Lawrence's assignment to get the telegraph back into shape. He was told to press the linemen to keep working at what must have seemed to them a never-ending and thankless task.

Northern Flights and Floods

At about the same time Lawrence was confronting the corrosion problem of the Anyox wire, the operator at Telegraph Creek, 200

The copper smelter town at Anyox was served by the Yukon Telegraph branch from Stewart. The line was difficult to maintain because the fumes of the smelter corroded the wire.

miles to the north, had a different kind of dilemma. As part of a test to show that airplanes could fly great distances, the U.S. Army Air Service sent four two-seater deHavilland bombers on a flight from New York City to Nome, Alaska. In the Yukon they were to stop at Whitehorse and Dawson City so the pilots could rest and refuel. As there was no suitable airfield at Whitehorse at the time, all available hands were called out to clear the area above the town. The work was accomplished in time and the planes landed, refuelled, and flew on to Dawson City and from there to Nome, arriving on August 23, 1920. It is claimed that these were the first airplanes to fly in the Yukon and Alaska.

On their return trip south, after refuelling at Whitehorse, the pilots ran into foul weather and three of the four planes were forced to return. The fourth, apparently with greater incentive, went on to Wrangell, "as the pilot was in love with a nurse there."[17] When the weather cleared, the three planes started south again and headed for Telegraph Creek, where they landed in a big hayfield on the Diamond C Ranch. The ranch was owned by Frank Callbreath, the packer who for many years held the contract to haul provisions to the telegraph cabins.

Because the undercarriage of one of the planes had been damaged in landing, all three crews stayed in the area to wait for parts to be sent upriver from Wrangell. When the parts arrived and the repairs had been completed, all the pilots needed to take off and continue their flight was a favourable weather forecast. This was easier said than done. The telegraph office at Telegraph Creek could receive the reports from Hazelton, but because the ranch was 30 miles from town, the operator had to figure out a way to get the information to the pilots in a timely way. According to one published report, this is how it was done: "Men were stationed at set times each day on heights of ground, one some distance from the telegraph office, the other several miles from the ranch. If a good weather report came in over the wire from Hazelton, the man at the Telegraph Creek end was to set off a charge of Dynamite. When the second man heard the blast go off, he in turn was to set off another charge to be heard at the ranch."[18]

The three pilots and their engineers had been at the ranch for 20 days, and everyone in the area had been invited to see the planes, the first to fly in the Cassiar region. When an acceptable weather forecast was received, the operator alerted the relay dynamiters to signal Callbreath's. The whole town turned out to watch the planes. To honour their new friends, the pilots dipped their wings

Four U.S. Army airplanes at Dawson City on a test flight from New York City to Nome, Alaska, in 1920.

before heading south. One local woman, Emma Brown, who had been having labour pains while waiting for the planes to fly over, was then able to go home to give birth to her daughter.[19]

Compared to all the activity in the south, the northern district was dormant most of the time. Maintenance requirements were minimal, and when breaks did occur they were relatively easy to locate and repair. The calm ended in May 1925 when the Yukon River flooded, causing extensive damage to the telegraph line.

It was not unusual during break-up for slabs of ice to be pushed into a jam, or blockage, that acted like a dam, building up water behind it. Eventually these jams would break, loosing a torrent that would quickly raise the level of the river. In years past any resulting flooding at Dawson City had been limited to the city's lower streets, causing inconvenience but little damage. In 1925, however, the ice buildup above the city, as far upriver as Selkirk, went on for days until the blockage was enormous. When the dam burst it unleashed the worst flood in the river's known history, a massive surge of

An ice jam on the Yukon River above Dawson City, similar to the one that sent flood waters down the river when it broke in 1925, causing extensive destruction of the Yukon Telegraph.

water and ice that inundated Dawson, causing great damage and cutting off communications with the outside world.

Fifty miles upriver, the telegraph station on Ogilvie Island, where the wire crossed the river, was completely swamped. Water was shoulder-high in the office, and outside, the ice stood in 10-foot mounds. To survive, operator Guy Swineheart climbed to the roof, where he built a fire to keep warm and subsisted for three days on soda crackers and tea. The *Dawson News* reported that the eternal optimist was seen "clicking away as usual" with his key, although the wire was down in both directions.[20]

Cabins along the river were swept away, and the tons of moving ice scoured the riverbank. Those sections of the telegraph line that had been the easiest to build, because they were closest to the river, were the most affected by the flooding. Miles of poles along the shore were undermined and collapsed. Telegraph service was not re-established until June 1, nearly three weeks after the ice broke.

The problems the flood caused the Yukon Telegraph produced mixed signals. On one hand they indicated how vulnerable the land line was to the powerful river. But on the other, as the *Dawson News* pointed out, the extended interruption showed how important the telegraph was to the Yukon, especially to the steamboats during the season of navigation.[21]

Keeping track of the boats that travelled the Yukon River between Whitehorse and Dawson City had become an important function of the telegraph stations along the river. They reported on the progress of the boats, called for help when they had problems, and provided telegraph service for the passengers. In fact, the final justification for retaining this section of the land line long after other sections had been replaced by wireless was the service it provided the river steamers. When they stopped running in 1952, the telegraph line was abandoned.

Chapter 13

The Wireless Experiment, 1925

In 1899 the general superintendent of the Dominion Telegraph Service suggested that $10,000 be included in his budget to experiment with wireless telegraphy.[1] The government's interest in the potential of the new technology intensified when, two years later, Guglielmo Marconi successfully transmitted a radio signal from Lizard, England, to St. John's, Newfoundland. Soon after, Marconi met with W.S. Fielding, Canada's minister of finance, and J. Israel Tarte, the minister of public works, to discuss the government's use of his wireless system. Everywhere, Marconi reported, he found a "disposition to facilitate his operations."[2]

Initially, interest focussed on employing wireless to bridge waterways; one of its first applications was across the Strait of Belle Isle between Newfoundland and the mainland. On the west coast, it was used to communicate with shipping. A station was set up north of Vancouver, and on the treacherous ocean side of Vancouver Island, the telegraph stations along the Lifesaving Trail (later the West Coast Trail) were augmented by wireless.

The vast distances over which messages had to be transmitted in parts of Canada made the use of wireless (soon to be called radio) an attractive alternative to the telegraph, especially in areas where land lines were difficult and costly to maintain, such as the wilderness sections of the Yukon Telegraph. In July 1906 both the Marconi Company and the DeForrest Company submitted bids to

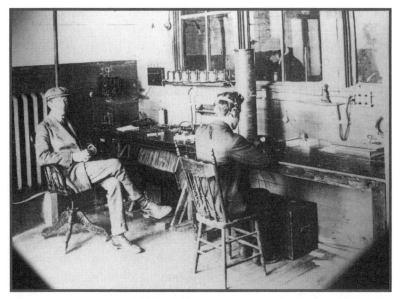

The inventor of wireless, Guglielmo Marconi, in the Glace Bay, Nova Scotia, office of his Wireless Telegraph Company in the early 1900s.

install a wireless system over the 1,200 miles between Quesnel and Whitehorse.[3] Nothing came of these proposals from private industry, but there were people in government who began to question the high cost of maintaining the land line to the Yukon.

The original rationale for the all-Canadian route was no longer valid. The fear of American annexation had passed and the location of the Alaska boundary had been negotiated. Communication with the north was now possible through two U.S. routes: the Army Signal Corps line from Boundary to Eagle, and the White Pass and Yukon Route's telegraph to Skagway. Both of these land lines were connected to the underwater cable to Seattle.

In the reporting year 1909–10, the 16 stations between Atlin and Hazelton, with the exception of Telegraph Creek, generated a total of 109 messages; Telegraph Creek was the source of 163 messages, mostly from outfitters and traders.[4] There was little justification for continuing to operate this portion of the land line. Only nationalism, pride, and vested interest stood in the way of change.

In 1911 the commissioner of the Yukon, in a letter to the Governor General, inquired about the possibility of replacing sections of the land line. He was concerned about the frequent interruptions of service, arguing that wireless would perform more effectively. His request was rebuffed on the grounds that, overall, the present service was satisfactory and that when there was a break, messages could be sent over the American line through Alaska.[5] In other words, wireless was not needed as it was now okay to use the American system to transmit messages from the Yukon (ignoring the corollary that this made the Atlin to Hazelton section unnecessary, with the exception of a connection to Telegraph Creek).

In fact, it was not uncommon for government offices, including the Department of Public Works, to route messages over the American cable-land system via Seattle, Valdez, and Eagle–Boundary. G.D. MacKenzie, the Yukon gold commissioner, complained that a recent telegram from the deputy minister of public works, J.B. Hunter, had arrived from Eagle rather than over the government's line. "Your telegram is not an isolated case, as quite a large percentage of the telegrams that originate in the various departments at Ottawa are forwarded in this way."[6]

Using this sort of evidence, the advocates of wireless argued that if the government itself was not using the land line, then the land line should be replaced. The continued expense of operating the line, which they claimed was significantly greater than the operating cost of a wireless system, could not be justified. DPW officials with an interest in the telegraph line disputed these figures and questioned the reliability of wireless, especially in the north, where weather abnormalities could affect transmissions. This exchange was a harbinger of the debate to come, one that would include a sometimes rancorous turf war between two departments of government.

First Wireless Attempt

One of the first, and as it turned out, benign, attempts to introduce wireless in the north was a scheme to set up a wireless station at Whitehorse. In 1919 the town was given the honour of erecting the first wireless tower in the Yukon Territory. The task was assigned to the local Royal North West Mounted Police detachment, Inspector W.J. Moorhead commanding. The inspector put Constable John Banks in charge of the detail, assisted by the local school's headmaster, Mr. Gilpin, presumably because he knew something about telegraph codes.

The plan was to erect two 100-foot wooden towers on the bluffs overlooking the town, where the airport is now located. Copper wires would run from the poles to a building below the bluff, which contained sending equipment. Because 100-foot trees were not available, several Jack-pine poles were spliced together with bolts and wire.

When the poles were ready to be erected, Inspector Moorhead assembled a suitable delegation of local dignitaries, politicians, and business principals. After all, this might be a hallmark day in the history of communications in the north.

Using a team of horses to pull, and thrusting levers under the poles to push, Banks and his police detail successfully raised the poles into their six-foot holes and secured them with guy cables. All seemed to work perfectly, and congratulations were in order. "It was a stately sight," Constable Banks reported. "Tall and slim they stood with the … copper wires gleaming in the sun … I felt proud. [The commanding officer] came over to shake my hand publicly and I was almost in tears. He told me that he had chosen me for the job because I was tenacious. I wasn't too sure what he meant as he had never been too friendly to me before, but as we were both Irishmen, I took it kindly."[7]

Shortly though, with a quickening of the wind, the spars began to sway, causing a whiplash effect on the dovetailed joints that had been used to connect the several sections of trees together. Although secured by iron bolts, they were clearly under strain. It was an embarrassing moment, "one of those moments which plant lines on the face and turn hair a distinguished grey," according to Banks. "I looked at the C.O. and he looked at me … Someone yelled 'Timber' and before our astonished eyes the whole ensemble crashed [to the ground]." It took a while for the shock to wear off and for Constable Banks to realize that he was the only one remaining on the field.

When he returned to barracks and entered the mess hall, Banks expected to be the subject of his mates' jibes. Instead he was met with cheers, and his meal was served by the cook himself, who, in a fine Belfast accent, said, "Don't worry, Jack. You can't win them all."[8]

Although this effort failed, the agitation to bring wireless to the north continued. The promoters of wireless did not want to shut down the Yukon Telegraph completely. They only wanted to operate the long-distance system, to set up stations at population centres in the northern district at Atlin, Whitehorse, and Dawson City. From these main stations, messages would be sent over the airwaves to the rest of the country and to the world. A feeder system of intermediate stations would still be needed, and this function would be left for the land line, be it a telegraph or telephone system. Employing wireless, advocates argued, would overcome the land line's vulnerability to fires, storms, and all the other intractable earthbound problems that caused interruptions. It would be more reliable and cost less.

The land-line people did not at first respond forcefully to counter these claims because there were no specific proposals, but they knew it was only a matter of time. They did suggest that there was evidence that radio waves were erratic and could be adversely affected by atmospheric conditions, such as the aurora borealis. Nor did they accept the cost-savings claim. But the discussion was academic, since no government agency was as yet prepared to sponsor a wireless system. The Department of Public Works, which was the logical candidate and was using wireless in other parts of its system, was not ready to give up on its investment in the Yukon Telegraph's land line.

For years the agitation to replace the land line continued in the halls of Parliament and in the press. Some newspaper reports, allegedly planted by wireless advocates, contained questionable facts, the most debatable that the annual cost of maintaining the land line was $250,000. The discussion might have remained within these two august bodies indefinitely, except for the intrusion of the Department of the Interior.

In 1923 that department, proffering the explanation that it needed to improve communications with its officials in the north, contracted with the Royal Canadian Corps of Signals (RCCS or

Signal Corps) to set up a wireless system. To accomplish its mission, the Signal Corps, under the direction of the Department of Defence, created the Northwest Territories and Yukon Radio System (NWT&Y). The new organization's first assignment was to establish a link between Dawson City and Mayo, a silver-lead mining area 100 miles to the east.

Teams of signalmen were sent to Dawson and Mayo, where they erected towers, set up radio equipment, and began transmitting by telegraph key, i.e. not yet by voice. After some initial radio wave surfing, contact was made, and the system opened for business on October 23, 1923. The cost of a telegram from Mayo was set at $1.50 for a 10-word day message or a 50-word night message.[9] Because the messages sent to Dawson had to be retransmitted over the land line, the Mayo line could be rationalized as just another branch of the Yukon Telegraph.

The next year, however, a fundamental change was made. The NWT&Y Radio System was extended to include a station at Fort Simpson and a transfer station at Edmonton, which was connected to the Canadian National Railway telegraph. The Yukon now was served by a second Canadian connection to the south, making the land line through British Columbia even more redundant. "The radio connection with Edmonton rapidly replaced the Yukon Telegraph as Dawson City's main link with the outside world."[10]

Turf War

The next step in the demise of the Yukon Telegraph was the Signal Corps' move to replace sections of the land line. The army's first objective was to have all messages originating from Atlin and stations to the north channelled through Dawson City. The line between Atlin and Telegraph Creek, which still generated over 100 messages a year, would need to be retained for the present, but there was little justification for continued operation of the line south of Telegraph Creek to Hazelton. Clearly, this section, the one most vulnerable to interruptions, most difficult to maintain, and most costly to operate, could now be abandoned, along with the 11 maintenance stations that produced few telegrams and practically no revenue. Thus began a turf war between the Department of

Public Works and the Department of National Defence, acting for the Department of the Interior.

What factors would determine the outcome? The actual performance of the wireless system? Its ability to operate under all atmospheric conditions? The number and duration of interruptions? Perhaps, but outweighing all other considerations was the war of words, the perceptions more than the facts. And in this battle the army made some tactical blunders, most notably its penchant for making exaggerated claims for its service, and roused the sleeping lion by denigrating the telegraph service.

The Signal Corps presented its wireless system as a panacea for the isolation and dangers of life in the north. It was, for example, prepared to equip government survey parties, which each summer went into the bush, with portable sending and receiving sets to keep them in touch with the outside world. And there were commercial and humanitarian applications. According to Colonel Elroy Ford, head of the Signal Corps, mining companies operating in areas beyond telegraph lines could profitably use the system in their work, and they would be able to summon help should illnesses or accidents occur. Lonely trappers and miners "in the land of six months winter, who make a study of the dot and dash method of communications, will also be able to bring themselves in touch with the doings of civilization." Ford was able to conjure, in his own mind at least, the picture of a crusty old prospector, snug in his warm cabin, intently listening to his little wireless instrument as it tapped out in Morse code the latest happenings in Vancouver and the price of gold on the London exchange. A wonderful vision it was, but one more suited to advertising copy than to reality and the needs of miners.

These inflated assertions were harmless, and perhaps they even provided a chuckle or two, but when the colonel went on to criticize the government telegraph as "operating at a considerable loss" and likely to be "done away with ... and replaced by wireless communications," he was making claims that were guaranteed to be resented.[11]

Statements like these only served to raise the hackles of DPW officials who were responsible for, and who took great pride in, their Yukon Telegraph. Some of these men had been associated with the line from its beginning, most notably Joseph E. Gobeil, who began his career with the department as J.B. Charleson's secretary during construction. After a stint as the first general inspector of the line, he rose through the ranks to become general superintendent of the entire Dominion Telegraph Service. His evaluation of the factors involved in the proposed changeover to wireless were well informed, if a bit skewed toward preserving the land line he had helped to build and operate for so many years.

Gobeil and other department officials were particularly sensitive to the criticisms that their line was inefficient and inordinately costly to maintain. According to them, the claim that the line cost the Canadian taxpayer $200,000 to $300,000 annually was a downright falsehood, based on figures provided by the Signal Corps, and its allies, that were circulated repeatedly by irresponsible newspapers.

These newspaper reports and interviews gave the impression that the entire land line could be replaced by wireless with significant savings. Typical was an article that appeared in the *Toronto Daily Star*, stating: "The maintenance of the [land] line alone cost Canada in the neighbourhood of a quarter of a million dollars a year. [Therefore], it is the intention of the government to scrap the old government telegraph line from Hazelton, B.C. to Whitehorse" and to replace communications in the far north with wireless.[12] At the time this article appeared, in March 1924, there was no plan to "scrap" the land line, but as no source for this information was provided, it was difficult to refute. However, as the rest of the article dealt with the Signal Corps' plans to establish additional radio stations in the north, the implication is that it was the source.

Gobeil was incensed by these planted newspaper stories that were "without foundation and not based on facts." In memos to Deputy Minister of Public Works J.B. Hunter he pointed out "that wireless with all its wonderful ability of leaping vast distances and establishing communications between far distant points, does not give local service, except at such places where the stations are installed, and can only reach the hundreds of intervening

points through the very landlines they are supposed to replace."
He provided figures showing that shutting down the Hazelton–
Telegraph Creek section would save about $47,000, less the cost
of building and operating the replacement wireless stations. He also
analyzed the cost of setting up the wireless stations at Dawson and
Mayo compared to building a land-line branch. Although he had
not been able to secure the exact costs, he drew upon knowledge
of other radio towers to estimate the price for the two at $77,636,
with annual upkeep of $37,960. He figured that a land line could
have been built for $27,500, with annual upkeep of $6,000.[13]

In a separate memo, Gobeil undertook to set the conditions
for a wireless takeover and to anticipate problems that might
arise. He suggested that if the wireless people stated they were
prepared to handle the Yukon traffic, DPW should shut down the
Hazelton–Telegraph Creek section, but not abandon it entirely.
The section should be maintained on the chance that it would
need to be reactivated should the wireless performance be
judged unsatisfactory. The shutdown should start in February or
March, the period when wireless was least likely to be affected
by atmospheric interference, and extend into the more difficult
summer months. If problems arose during the summer, the land
line would be re-established.

Gobeil also advised that the wireless rates must be competitive
with those of the alternative U.S. lines through Eagle and Skagway.
He was concerned that the new rates via Edmonton might be higher
than the U.S. rates and perhaps even higher than the land line's
rates via Ashcroft.[14]

Within days of Gobeil's memo, Hunter wrote to the Department
of the Interior, inquiring if they were ready to take over the Yukon
traffic.[15] In response, O.S. Finnie of Interior replied:

The Department of National Defence is operating this
system for us and on enquiry at that Department, I am
informed that the wireless system is now in a position to
handle, expeditiously, any traffic which may be turned
over at the above points [Edmonton, Fort Simpson, Mayo
and Dawson]. It is assumed, however, that in abandoning

the landline, you will leave intact that portion between Atlin and Dawson. This part of the line is required for the convenience of those residents in the Southern end of the territory and for the steamboats plying on the Yukon River and in the Atlin country.[16]

Given this assurance, on March 23, 1925, the Department of Public Works severed the land line of the Yukon Telegraph by shutting down the section between Hazelton and Telegraph Creek. Thereafter, messages from Telegraph Creek northward were sent to Dawson City, for transmission by wireless to Edmonton.

The department, not convinced that the Signal Corps could do the job, made contingency arrangements, as Gobeil had advised, to ensure that it could reactivate the section on short notice by retaining some linemen to maintain the wire. Of the 11 stations, 6 were permanently closed and 5 remained staffed: Second, Fourth, Sixth, Eighth, and Echo Lake cabins. The average distance between stations was now 40 miles, which doubled the responsibilities of the linemen.

The Experiment Ends

The years of noisy agitation and disparagement of the land line's performance gave the impression that there was widespread support for the takeover. An antiquated 70-year-old system of communications was being replaced by a new, less costly, more

Charlie Janze and John Jensen, veteran linemen at Eighth Cabin, whose jobs were threatened by the replacement of the telegraph land line with wireless.

efficient technology. Who could object? But amazingly, almost as soon as the wireless system was put into operation, the complainers began.

One of the earliest and most insistent was the editor of the *Dawson Daily News*, who within a week informed the government that he was no longer able to secure dispatches of the Canadian Press Service because they were prohibited from being sent over wireless. These dispatches, he claimed, were essential to the operation and the very existence of his newspaper.[17] The people who handled the weather reports from the Yukon were also not happy. Previously their reports had been sent free to the meteorological service in Toronto; now they were being charged the full rate. There were grievances about the inconvenience caused by the wireless's circuitous routing of messages to Edmonton, but by far the most numerous complaints were about the higher rates.

The Signal Corps had blundered by initially establishing a tariff schedule sure to infuriate its regular customers. Rates were higher than those of the land line and much higher than the rates charged for messages sent through the American system. As the Yukon Telegraph continued to forward the messages generated by its stations over the cheapest route, for a time many messages were sent via Skagway or Eagle.

J.F. Callbreath, the packer-businessman in Telegraph Creek, was raising hell in newspapers and letters, one to the British Columbia Chamber of Mines. He said that previously a telegram sent from Telegraph Creek directly to Vancouver had cost $2.05. Now, sent via Edmonton, it cost $5.25. He claimed that these charges would seriously impede the economic development of the Cassiar region, which was just beginning to witness a revitalization of mining. The minister of mines passed the complaint on to J.H. King, the minister of public works, who responded that as of April 20, new rates had reduced the cost of a message to Vancouver to a more reasonable $2.50. He then added a few comments for the record:

This result [shutting down the Hazelton–Telegraph Creek section] was achieved by Members of Parliament having since 1918 advised the closing of that Section of our Yukon Main Line ... and operating same by wireless, ably seconded by British Columbia newspapers who repeatedly advertised that such a course would enable the Government to affect an annual savings of $250,000. Now that this action has been taken as strong, if not stronger, criticism of this Department's action is forthcoming because they have been given what they have been clamouring for.[18]

He concluded by pointing out that the actual saving from the shutdown was about $20,000.

As spring turned to summer another problem loomed on the horizon. The DPW had to decide if the change to wireless would be permanent and if the remaining stations between Hazelton and Telegraph Creek should be shut down or resupplied. Regardless of the mounting criticism, the department was reluctant to end the experiment, wary of being charged with not giving wireless a fair chance. On the other hand, if the land line was going to be reactivated, the linemen's cabins had to be provisioned for the next year, and soon. Normally the pack trains were on the trail by July 1. Any later and they might run into foul weather and the loss of feeding grounds for the animals.

George Beirnes, whose pack trains had supplied the cabins north of Hazelton for years, was pressing for a decision. If the horses he was reserving for the government were not going to be needed, he wanted to employ them elsewhere. On June 4 Gobeil urged the department to make a decision, fearing that it would be put in a "very awkward position" should it want to provision the cabins a month or six weeks later and the pack train was not available.[19] Within two weeks, Deputy Minister Hunter agreed to resupply the cabins,[20] but he was not yet ready to announce the termination of the wireless experiment.

It was well into July before the decision was made: The land line would be reactivated on September 1. Apparently this information was not widely circulated. It remained a secret outside the department, with the result that the complaints about wireless, and demands that it be replaced, continued right up to September 1.

The *Dawson Daily News*, as late as August 20, again complained that it had received no press-service news since June. A wireless officer, apparently unaware that the land line was to be reactivated on September 1, advised the editor that he could not guarantee press service until sometime in September, claiming that daylight static made proper functioning of the radio impossible. The editor warned that if the land line, which had given very satisfactory service, was not opened soon, the *News* would have to give up publication.[21] On the same day, an impressive group of Dawson and Yukon leaders, including the head of the White Pass and Yukon Route, sent a telegram calling for the immediate reopening of the land line.[22]

The long agitation in Parliament over the use of wireless was summed up in an exchange between George Black, the Yukon's Conservative MP, and Minister King. Black started (July 17) with a complaint: The wireless telegraph rates in the Yukon are discriminatory. King, who had been waiting for someone to find the wireless wanting, eagerly responded (August 1) with an "I told you so" letter. He delighted in informing the MP that he tried to warn people like Black, who so strongly urged wireless in the Parliament, that there would be problems. Black, admitting no fault, returned (August 26) a "sarcastic" (according to King) note implying that any idiot could solve the rate problem. On September 17 King responded with equal vitriol, suggesting that Black have someone explain to him how telegraph rates were structured. He concluded the fun with an effort to placate the member: "Now that the land line is in operation, old rates in force, and your grounds for complaint are removed, it is hoped that the tranquil and effective course of business over the Yukon System as existed previous to March of this year will again prevail."[23]

Although the army had lost the land-air battle, it continued the war of words, a recounting of which is informative only in that it sheds light on the limitations of the military mind when placed in a situation where civilian values dominate.

After the wireless experiment was scuttled, newspaper articles appeared in which Superintendent Phelan was quoted as stating, quite accurately, that wireless was being replaced because of dissatisfaction with its service. In a flurry of letters to the DPW, G.J. Desbarats, the deputy minister of national defence, called attention to Phelan's "public criticism of the Department of National Defence" and demanded that his utterances be investigated. Deputy Minister Hunter replied that, according to complaints in the DPW files, the newspaper articles were correct and no further action was necessary. Desbarats answered with a wonderful example of feigned ignorance and chutzpah:

I may say that not only have no legitimate complaints reached this Department but, on the contrary, we have received many reports expressing satisfaction with the prompt service which has been all the more appreciated in contrast to the interruptions, sometimes of many days duration, to which the old telegraph line was inherently subject.

[On the subjects of public service and lines of command]: I would remind you that the Department of National Defence is responsible for the operation of this system and in consequence any complaints which may have been or may be received by any officer of the Public Service of Canada should be referred to me, so that prompt steps may be taken to investigate and where necessary correct.[24]

Hunter's reply summed it all up:

From 1911 when the installation of wireless to supplant the land line service was first mooted, numberless reports were made by this Department pointing out the difficulties in the way, yet pressure was constantly brought to bear until this Department was practically forced to abandon, under protest, its land line, and now that wireless has failed to live up to representations made by your Department, this Department is practically taken to task on account of various articles appearing in the press due to the muddle caused by your wireless installations. Why this question of re-opening the land line to traffic, due to unsatisfactory wireless service, has been almost a daily topic of interest from Vancouver to Dawson from March to September, and you state that you have not had a legitimate complaint. Strange this Department received them all, the general public may have been under the impression that this Department was responsible for conditions which arose from the insistence that our line be closed and the business handed over to your Department.[25]

The land line was back in business as before, except for those six cabins that had been abandoned and the 12 telegraph men who had been laid off. However, the battle of words and accusations would go on well into the next year and beyond[26]—to no effect. The Yukon Telegraph land line would survive for another decade, until it came under threat from more powerful forces, those of nature, and the Department of Public Works itself decided to replace it with a radio system.

CHAPTER 14

Transition: From Telegraph Line to Telegraph Trail

The wireless experiment had been judged a failure. Nevertheless, even the most loyal telegrapher realized that it was only a matter of time before the land line would be replaced by a combination of telephone and radio.

Each year more telegraph keys were replaced by telephone receivers, and economies dictated by Ottawa continued to reduce the number of stations and employees. Nowhere were these cutbacks more apparent than on the wilderness section between Hazelton and Telegraph Creek, where the original 11 stations had been reduced to five. Stations on other sections of the main and branch lines were also being closed or replaced by the telegraph-telephone composite system.

Although less severely affected by reductions, the northern district between Atlin and Dawson City was also undergoing change. The successful erection of a radio tower at Whitehorse in the early 1920s, enabling wireless transmissions to Dawson, meant that the intermediate stations, which had never generated many telegrams, were no longer needed to keep the line open for through messages. The primary function of the stations along the Yukon River was now to serve the needs of the steamships that plied the river during the summer months. They had in large measure become adjuncts to the growing tourist trade.

The earlier promising tourist industry, which had been short-circuited by the First World War, began to recover and flourish after the war. The White Pass and Yukon Route, taking advantage of its unique position as operator of both a railway and a fleet of steamships, offered expeditions combining rail and river travel. Tourists could board a train at Skagway for Whitehorse, where they commenced a voyage by riverboat to Dawson City. Or passengers could detrain at Carcross to board excursion boats for Atlin, where the company had built a large hotel. By 1925 these trips were attracting more than 5,000 visitors annually. White Pass's plan was to develop a string of vacation hotels along its route, as other railways had done. This goal was never fully realized, in part because of the depressed economy of the 1930s.

Even crusty old "every-man-for-himself" Dawson City began to mellow and acknowledge the need for a modicum of civic control if the economic potential of tourism was to be realized. The Yukon Order of Pioneers, wanting to "create community spirit," discussed ways to make the town more inviting to visitors. They suggested that tourists be provided with information about some of the area's attractions: the Dome that overlooked the town, Robert Service's cabin, and the scenic Moosehide Trail. But before the tourists could

The Atlin Inn was built by the White Pass and Yukon Route to accommodate tourists who were ferried across Atlin Lake on the MV Tarahne, *which is seen docked nearby.*

be let loose, it was imperative to clean up the "ghastly atmosphere" of some of the town's vacant lots.

Most visitors to the primitive north were prosperous members of the middle and upper classes. They were willing to "live rough," but only up to a point—they expected a degree of gentility during their sojourn. There were exceptions, the few who were attracted because they wanted a more intense exposure to wilderness and had a greater appreciation of its wonders and beauty. Like Hamlin Garland before them, they wanted to experience the untouched wilderness before it was gone. They may also have been harbingers of the notion that though the primitive world must be conquered, it need not be mutilated in the process.

Expeditions to Dawson City and to Atlin could satisfy most travellers. However, these places were relatively civilized, with settlements, RCMP posts, and telegraph offices. The adventurous explorers had to look elsewhere. One area that was off the beaten track was northern British Columbia, a region that was still largely untouched save for the intrusion of the Yukon Telegraph.

The trail that followed the wire was originally intended only for the use of the linemen making repairs and for the once-a-year pack trains that delivered provisions to the telegraph cabins. Local Natives, trappers, and a few big-game outfitters also travelled on sections. Occasionally it was used for longer trips, such as the one made in 1924 by John Noland, an Atlin guide who drove a herd of horses all the way from Hazelton to Atlin.

Although none of the early users of the trail had much interest in bringing it to the attention of a wider audience, word began to spread. After the Grand Trunk Pacific Railway was completed in 1914, travel to Hazelton became much easier, and by the 1920s the "Telegraph Trail" began to attract more independent travellers, some for the wilderness experience, others with more practical ends in mind.

For those looking for an oasis free from the stimuli of modern living, relatively unpopulated and undisturbed, where wild animals flourished, the area between Hazelton and Atlin was ideal. The Telegraph Trail provided a convenient entrée, and the linemen in their cabins promised a modicum of safety and support.

Diamond Jenness on the Trail

Although information about the Yukon Telegraph had been available in newspaper and magazine articles for years, the distinction of bringing the trail to the attention of a larger audience goes to Diamond Jenness, who published an account of his 1924 hike several years later in the *Canadian Geographical Journal*.[1]

Jenness was not a typical adventure hiker. Rather, he was a well-known and respected anthropologist, a student of Aboriginal culture, who had accompanied Vilhjalmur Stefansson on his landmark Canadian Arctic Expedition (1913–18).[2] The primary purpose of Jenness's 1924 trip was to report on Aboriginal artifacts along a section of trail north of Hazelton. He started in February with a guide, Angus Beaton, who knew most of the telegraph men along their route with whom they had arranged to stay.

The party travelled on the wagon road into the valley of the Kispiox River, which Jenness described as one of the "beauty spots of British Columbia." They soon came to a ruined church and an abandoned farm known as the Cock and Bull Ranch. Jenness related the story of a missionary who came to the area to establish a Native mission:

> His outfit comprised, among other things, a bull and a cow, a cock and a hen, and a cooking stove. To cross the river he made a raft, and placed his stove in the middle, with the cock and hen on top inside a wooden crate. He then attached the cow to the stove by a stout rope, leaving the bull to swim across unaided.
>
> All went well until he reached midstream, when the raft struck a submerged snag and up-ended. The stove sank to the bottom drowning the cow and the hen. The cock, escaping from its crate, drifted ashore unharmed, and the bull crossed without misadventure. Supported by cock and bull the missionary established a ranch and built a church; but soon he converted the church into a barn. A year or two later his bishop arrived to inspect the new mission and opened the church door. Only one worshipper met his gaze—an angry bull.[3]

Twenty-three miles from Hazelton, Jenness and Beaton passed the ranch of George Beirnes, the outfitter and packer. Shortly thereafter they began to see blazes that identified places where there was good camping and browsing for the pack animals. They also came upon the characteristic sign for a Native camp: a face formed by cutting two notches for the eyes and one lower down for the mouth.

The wagon road ended at First Cabin, where the trail began its ascent over the snowy divide between the Kispiox and Skeena watersheds, which required the use of snowshoes. The men camped at the halfway refuge between First and Second cabins, not far from the beaver meadow known as "Boneyard Camp," where in the fall of 1901 the construction party on its way out to Hazelton was forced to shoot its starving pack animals. In 1924 the bleached bones remained to tell the tale.

After Second Cabin, Jenness and Beaton went on to Old Kuldo, a deserted Native village. It had been an intermediate station on an old trading route, one of several "grease trails" in the area, between the mouth of the Nass River and Kisgegas, a village on the Babine River. The Natives from the Nass carried boxes of the oily oolichan, or candlefish, to trade with the interior people for furs. The fish oil, or grease, that dripped from the boxes being transported gave the trails their nickname. This flammable oil was used in candles or as a condiment with meats. When the people at Kuldo tried to exact a fee from the traders to pass through their area, it caused ill will. The Nass Indians attacked the village, and the few people who survived the massacre moved away.

Jenness ended his 60-mile trip at Kuldo, extolling the land he had passed through as one of the richest hunting and trapping grounds in British Columbia. There were fox, marten, wolverine, black and grizzly bear, goat, mountain sheep, increasing numbers of moose, and enough caribou to "content the most insatiate hunter."[4] Evaluating the location and condition of the trail, he was less complimentary. As others before him had done, he concluded that the telegraph builders would have been wiser to select a route that followed the Skeena River valley rather than going over the height of land with its heavy snows.

Jenness experienced only a short section of the trail. Other travellers were intent on trekking the entire distance between Hazelton and Telegraph Creek, and perhaps beyond. They began to show up in increasing numbers at the line cabins, more often than not seeking the assistance of the telegraph men. The distance was so great, 330 miles, it was unlikely that a hiker could have carried sufficient provisions for the entire trip. Only those with pack animals, or those skilled at living off the land, could expect to get all the way through without being resupplied. For a while longer, though, even the most woefully uninformed or ill-equipped could hope to succeed—with the help of the linemen.

Roughing it in the Bush

In addition to explorers like Jenness, the trail attracted travellers who ventured into the wilderness for more desperate reasons. They were fleeing from the pressures and problems of the outside world: the Great Depression and the growing threat of war.

The telegraph men in the bush were able to keep up with world affairs from the news reports that came in over the wire and by listening to their radios, which by the 1920s were standard equipment in the line cabins. They were well aware of the misery being caused by the Depression and of the millions of men in the south looking for work, where every job opening drew 500 applicants. They were thankful they had jobs with regular paycheques and "three squares a day."

Some hikers who came along the trail had given up on the cities and were hoping to find work in the small northern towns. The various motives of these travellers are revealed in the stories of Armel Philippon, the "two Fritzes," and a man known only as the "Russian Communist."

One of the distressed men who headed north looking for work was 23-year-old Armel Philippon.[5] He and a partner started from Vancouver driving an old Model-T Ford. Their assets consisted of little more than the automobile, which they sold to the Hudson's Bay Company manager at Hazelton for $35 worth of supplies. Poorly equipped, scantily provisioned, and inexperienced in bush lore, they set out to walk north 330 miles to Telegraph Creek. When their food supply ran out, they planned to survive on the small game they would shoot with a .22 rifle. But as their journey progressed, they came to rely more than they had intended on the succour of the telegraph linemen as they went from station to station, literally begging for food.

The linemen were generous, but by midsummer their own supplies were beginning to run short as they awaited the arrival of the pack train with their annual delivery of provisions. The allotment of 3,000 pounds was more than adequate for two men for a year, but if too frequently shared with hikers it could be seriously depleted before the next year's delivery. Therefore they tried to feed their guests from nature's larder, with the animals they killed, the fish they caught, and the berries and edible plants that grew around them.

It was difficult going for Philippon and his partner. The distance between stations, after half were closed in 1925, was now 40 miles or more. There were other hardships: millions of ravenous mosquitoes, streams swollen by runoff, and the Nass Valley—"a tangled swamp ... overlaid with wind-falls and braided with streams and bogs, the trail an illegible mush." The two trekkers would not likely have survived this section, much less attempted it, if the telegraph cabins and linemen had not been available.

Eventually the two men reached Telegraph Creek, where they rested for a few days and feasted on salmon from the Stikine River, provided by local fishers. They then pushed on to Dease Lake, looking for work. Eventually Philippon settled in the area, where he prospected for gold along the streams and was forever known as the man who hiked from Hazelton.

The linemen, regardless of their distance from the events of the outside world, were well aware of the growing menace of war in Europe. Acutely sensitive to the legacy of war were those telegraph men who had served in the Great War, which had cost the lives of so many of their generation. With fascism on the rise in Italy and Germany, they feared that another conflagration was threatening.

In June 1933 these portents of tragedy, seemingly so distant from the wilds of British Columbia and the Yukon, were brought home to lineman John Sutherland at Echo Lake when two young

Germans appeared at his cabin door. He called them "the two Fritzes" because he could not pronounce their names. When the Fritzes were children, both their fathers had been killed in the Kaiser's war. They told Sutherland that they did not want to be cannon fodder in the war they felt was sure to come under Hitler. They had jumped ship to get away from what was happening in Germany and were now men without a country. The north was where they hoped to make a new life. After a few days at Echo Lake, where they were well supplied with food, they continued on their way. No more was ever heard of them.[6]

Sutherland had another visitor during that fateful summer: a man he called the "Russian Communist," who was hiking from San Francisco to Moscow. His story was that he had been mixed up in the San Francisco longshoremen's strike, protesting the loading of scrap iron for Japan. In the ensuing violence a policeman

had bopped him on the noggin. It was then that he decided to walk to Moscow because, as he explained, "any more head hits might make him lose his mind or go insane."[7]

Apparently the man had already lost much of his good sense. As soon as the linemen spotted him on the trail, they followed his progress from station to station, as they did with all travellers. When he did not arrive as expected at Echo Lake, Sutherland set out in search of him. He found the poor fellow at a refuge cabin, in bad shape and sick, the result of a toxic brew. He had found a one-pound can of coffee, dumped the entire amount into a coffee pot, and boiled up

John Sutherland, lineman at Echo Lake, called this fellow the "Russian Communist" because he was hiking the Telegraph Trail to return to his native land.

a "knock em out knock em down brew of black coffee so strong it had knocked him out for 24 hours."[8]

The Russian told Sutherland that he intended to float down the Yukon River to the ocean, where he would flag down a Russian whaling ship to carry him across to Siberia. The telegraph men were able to keep track of his progress until Whitehorse, where he left the land for the river. After that he became just another traveller who had passed along their trail.

The linemen were pleased to have guests, happy to have someone different to talk to. They fed them and allowed them to rest for a few days, and when the travellers moved on, the linemen gave them enough food to keep them going for at least the next 100 miles. But it was a short travelling season, four months at the most, and after the weather turned colder in September, there were no more trekkers, only the occasional musher with his dogsled.

Mushing in the Bush

One musher on the Telegraph Trail in 1933 was a traveller of a whole different stripe. Clyde Williams was a raw 18-year-old in 1900 when he was dumped on the mud flats at Valdez along with the horde of gold seekers headed over the glacier for new strikes around Fairbanks. He was a tall skinny kid, whose appearance almost immediately gained him the lifelong nickname of "Slim." Unlike most of the others, he was not there primarily to find the valuable yellow metal. He was out for adventure. He wanted to see Alaska, to find out what was over the next mountain.[9]

And adventures he had. He made many long trips by dogsled, did his share of prospecting, mostly unsuccessfully, and ran traplines. But his main interest was breeding sled-dog teams—or, rather, dog-wolf teams. For 25 years he bred and trained mixed teams, seeking to combine the tireless running power of the wolf with the more malleable traits of the dog to produce an animal with strength, toughness, and a kind of human understanding. Slim claimed that he had bred the best teams in Alaska. It was this confidence, this braggadocio, that got him involved in the long trip south.

Slim was living in Copper Center, Alaska, 100 miles northeast of Valdez, when he learned that another musher was planning to drive a sled-dog team all the way to the Chicago World's Fair. When Slim bragged that his team was the only one capable of making such an arduous trip, his "friends" publicized his claim in the local newspaper. The word spread from there, and after one thing led to another, he found that his original goal of visiting the Chicago World's Fair had been expanded to include blazing and publicizing the route for an international highway. The road to connect Alaska to the lower 48 states would include sections of the Telegraph Trail.

In November 1932 Slim set out from Copper Center in minus 40° weather. He was travelling light, planning to live off the land. In order to conform to the anticipated route of the highway, he went the long way around via Chicken, Forty Mile, and Dawson City, then headed south to Whitehorse and eventually reached Atlin. Slim then entered a wilderness that would not be relieved for 550 miles. His exact route is not known, but he almost certainly followed the Telegraph Trail from Atlin to Telegraph Creek and went part of the way on it from there to Hazelton.

He got lost more than once, suffered snow blindness, broke through lake ice, and, near the end, ran out of snow, reaching

Clyde "Slim" Williams with his dogsled on his 1933 trip from Alaska to the Chicago World's Fair. Note that wheels were added to the sled for travel on roads.

Hazelton on May 15, 1933. The planned three-month trip had taken twice as long. At Hazelton the road began, first to the Cariboo Highway and then east to Chicago.

After adding bicycle wheels to his sled, he continued with his dog team down the road, a strange sight for motorists, although he travelled mostly at night to spare the exhausted dogs from the warm weather. Newspapers reported his progress and he was greeted and feted in many of the towns along the way. In September, after 2,000 miles of highway mushing, he finally reached the Alaska Exposition at the Chicago World's Fair. After a brief rest he headed for Washington, D.C., where he hoped to continue to promote the highway.

Reports of his amazing adventure made Slim a celebrity and brought a great deal of attention to Alaska and to the Telegraph Trail. However, his trip was of minor interest to the bachelor linemen in the bush cabins compared to the visits of adventurous women hikers, of which there seems to have been a disproportionate number.

Chapter 15

Women Hikers
in the 1920s and 1930s

A surprising number of Telegraph Trail hikers were females. Perhaps it only seems that way because their experiences and stories were more intriguing to male journalists. There was one woman, however, whose only interest in travelling the trail was to get back to her native land.

Lillian Alling

Lillian Alling arrived in the United States in 1925 from Russia, or maybe from Poland.[1] She worked for a while in New York City, where she found neither happiness nor contentment and longed to return to her family. Lacking funds for steamer passage across the Atlantic, she turned west, vowing to walk across the continent all the way to the coast of Alaska. From there she would find passage across the Bering Strait to Siberia and then continue her trek to her home.

On a spring day in 1927, Alling set off on her 6,000-mile journey across the United States and Canada to the Bering Sea. She was 25 years old and small, almost petite, weighing no more than 100 pounds. But she was one strong walker, capable of covering 30 miles in a day. She carried only a small backpack containing blankets, clothing, and a few camping supplies; shelter and food would be where she found them.

From reading books in the public library (she is reputed to have had a rudimentary knowledge of English) she learned about the Telegraph Trail, which she chose as her route through northern British Columbia. By late summer Alling had reached Prince George, then clocked another 270 miles on roads to the village of Hazelton, where she planned to start north on the trail.

At the first line cabin she was met by telegrapher Bill Blackstock, to whom she appeared "gaunt and ragged." He felt that she was in no condition to travel farther, especially with winter coming on. To deter her from continuing, he alerted the provincial police, who escorted her back to Hazelton. Although "she pleaded for permission to continue her journey, her shabby clothing and shoes, meagre supplies and deteriorating physical condition" argued against her ability to survive the approaching winter.

Lillian Alling in 1927 during her ambitious and arduous trek across North America to return to Russia, travelling partway on the Telegraph Trail.

To keep her from going on, the police detained Alling, even though they had no legal reason to hold her. For her own good she was taken to court. When the police found she had an iron pipe in her pants, they charged her with carrying a concealed weapon. She was found guilty and, unable to pay the $25 fine (she had only $20), sentenced to two months in the Vancouver jail. It seemed a harsh punishment, but was the best solution to stopping her suicidal hike.

Alling grew stronger in prison, and when she was released she got a job working in the kitchen of a Vancouver restaurant, where she waited out the winter until she could resume her odyssey. When spring arrived she was off once again, hiking north toward Alaska. But this time the authorities were waiting for her. When she reached Smithers, 700 miles from Vancouver, police told her that a condition of her being allowed to continue was that she report to every telegraph cabin between Hazelton and Telegraph Creek so they could keep track of her progress.

With the help of the telegraph men, she made rapid progress. Her safe passage was reported from station to station and she soon reached Eighth Cabin, but once again she appeared to be weakening. Jim Christie and Charlie Janze, the linemen at Eighth, were appalled by her pitiful appearance: "Her clothes were in shreds, [her] exposed skin sunburned and swollen from insect bites." They convinced her to rest for a few days, fed her some hearty food, and supplied her with used clothing.

Christie accompanied her over treacherous Nass Summit, intending to turn her over to Scottie Ogilvie, the lineman from Echo Lake who was coming south to meet her. Ogilvie never showed up. Apparently, when attempting to cross a swollen and raging Ningunsaw River, he slipped and went under. When the water receded to its normal level, his body was found tangled in driftwood. Upon hearing of the tragedy, Alling is reported to have commented, rather unfeelingly, as she observed the low water: "How could a man be so dumb as to drown in a dry creek?"[2] Some of his fellow linemen buried Ogilvie's body near the riverbank, where they held a short service that was transmitted over the telegraph wire to the men at the other cabins.

Alling's travels provided a novel diversion for the linemen as news of her progress was reported up the line. They were generous in their offers of shelter, food, and supplies, and curious about her reasons for attempting such an arduous journey. When asked, she replied simply that she was going to Russia. What more did they need to know?

After a brief rest at Telegraph Creek, she continued on, passing several telegraph cabins on the way to Atlin. Before entering the

Scottie Ogilvie, the lineman at Echo Lake, started south from his station to meet and help Lillian Alling, but drowned attempting to cross a stream.

town she stopped at the Murphy homestead on the O'Donnel River. It was there that Marie Murphy snapped one of two known photos of Lillian Alling. It shows a face that "reflects fatigue but ... creates a compelling portrait of resolve."

From Atlin she walked to Carcross, then to Whitehorse, where the ever-glib press labelled her "The Mystery Woman." She reportedly reached Carmacks, then Stewart, and was later seen in a small boat drifting down the Yukon River. Thirty-nine days after leaving Whitehorse she arrived in Dawson City, where she spent her second winter.

Alling worked in Dawson to make some travelling money, but with spring break-up she was off again, last seen floating down the river in a somewhat larger boat on her way to Alaska. Thereafter, reliable information about her progress is murky. There were a few unconfirmed reports: that she was seen at the river's mouth, that she was seen trekking toward the village of Wales, where the Bering Sea narrows. No one saw her cross.

The Lillian Alling story apparently ended at the edge of the windswept Bering Strait. She is remembered as a very brave and determined women, albeit a foolish one, who might have found a safer and more sensible way to get back to her home. Many years later, a story out of Siberia told of a woman on the waterfront about 1930 who said she had walked across America.

Anna Mae Ullman

Another Yukon Telegraph Trail hiker, a few years after Alling, was Anna Mae Ullman, a 19-year-old American who was born in Manitoba, but had most recently lived in California.[3] Little more is known about her background, but her motivation for hiking the Telegraph Trail seems to have been purely for adventure and to see the country. Starting from Vancouver in April 1932, she hitchhiked to Hazelton, where she was keen to visit the Gitanmaax Indian Cemetery before starting for Telegraph Creek.

Carrying a 40-pound pack, the first day she covered 20 miles before darkness overtook her. She set up her camp, unconcerned about spending the night alone in the wilderness. "I chopped some lower branches off a spruce tree, started a fire, unpacked my camp outfit, and put some water on to boil for tea." After her meal she spread out her blankets and tarpaulin, took off her boots to dry by the fire, and slept under a tree.

She arrived at First Cabin the next day, but before she could continue on, she too was met by a provincial police officer. He warned her against travelling any farther at that time of year because the melting snow of early spring made the trail too dangerous. With the help of the police, Ullman was able to get a job as a cook at the nearby ranch of George Beirnes, where she spent the next three months flipping sourdough hotcakes for his wranglers.

In July she started off again, only to find the trail was still wet and the going rough. There were mudholes to be waded, crude wobbly bridges to be crossed, and the relentless rain to be endured. There was water everywhere, and her pack got heavier and heavier. Some creeks she walked through rather than chance the slippery footing on the low bridges. The fourth day out she met a party of Natives, whose leader, Simon Gunanoot, insisted she have breakfast with them. This was after he had been acquitted on murder charges (see Chapter 12). Ullman knew his story, and she "plied this almost legendary man with questions."

Day after day she plodded on, often staying the night in the telegraph refuge cabins. At one refuge she came upon a lineman and one of George Beirnes' packers, who were building a new cabin. After she washed her filthy clothes in the nearby lake, Al, the lineman, provided a wonderful treat, a supper of fried ham, potatoes, tea biscuits, and chocolate pudding. She was allowed to stay in the old cabin while the two men camped in a tent. When she retired she listened in the dark to the cries of loons on the lake and the patter of the tiny feet of mice running through the cabin. She figured it was time to get up the next morning when one ran across her face.

When the two cabin builders headed out, she hitched a ride for her backpack on one of their horses and travelled with them to Sixth Cabin, where they met the pack train, which had been hauling provisions to the telegraph cabins, on its return trip to Hazelton. Ullman was now again on her own, facing more days of tramping through mud and sodden forests. Finally the country opened up as the trail rose above treeline toward the pass through the Nass Mountains. She was able to stride through fields of beautiful wildflowers, where the only guide to the trail was the never-ending telegraph wire. Near the summit she stopped briefly at a refuge cabin to have lunch and to carve her name, the date, and the words "Going north on the hoof."

But her exhilaration was short-lived when the trail once again descended into the trees and the wet. She soon came to a cable-car crossing over Goat Creek.

A single five or six-strand cable stretched across the creek. The "carriage" is made of a few boards held together by a crosspiece at each end. Telegraph wire is looped under each end of the carriage and attached to two pulleys which run on the main cable. A small box is nailed to one end of the carriage. I put my pack into this box, climbed onto the carriage and unfastened the wire hook which kept the carriage from sliding across toward the other end of the cable. The carriage went across easily.

This crossing was accomplished without incident; not so a crossing farther on. At the Bell-Irving River, in an effort to escape the maddening multitude of mosquitoes, she camped out on a gravel bar at the edge of the river. Unexpectedly, during the night the river rose 1.5 feet. When she awoke she found the gravel bar completely surrounded by rushing water. Fortunately, Charlie Janze, the lineman at Eighth Cabin, was travelling behind her and helped her get to the other side and on her way again. She crossed the Ningunsaw River on cables, then hiked past beautiful Echo Lake.

Anna Mae spent her last night on the trail in a refuge tent. It was probably the most miserable night of her trip. The rain came down in torrents, the tent leaked, and her food cache had shrunk to one lonely biscuit. But in the morning the sky cleared, and in the distance she could see "a silver thread in the bright sunlight," the Stikine River, and beyond it was Telegraph Creek.

Throughout her trip she had been offered every assistance by the telegraph linemen, frequently accepting their hospitality and staying in their cabins. She could not have survived without them.

Anna Mae ended her hike at Telegraph Creek, where she got a job in the kitchen at Ira Day's ranch near the mouth of the Tahltan River. In her spare time she hiked, and later snowshoed, throughout the area. In town she got to know Jack Wrathall, the lineman at Shesley Station, and his wife Lucy, who invited her to spend some time with them during the Christmas season.

Ullman started out for their place a few days before Christmas, snowshoeing up the trail along the Tahltan River and looking for the crossing of the Telegraph Trail, which she intended to follow to the station. The weather was not bad, about minus 10° Celsius, but when she did not show up at Shesley, word went over the wire to look out for her. The linemen south of Telegraph Creek, who had met her earlier, were asked how experienced a hiker she was. Charlie Janze remembered her "as a little slip of a girl with a lot of personality and determination." She was good about following trail directions and had never been lost as far as he knew.

But now she was lost. Somewhere along the river trail she decided to take a shortcut, became disoriented, and lost her way. Several days passed before she finally stumbled upon the

Telegraph Trail. Exhausted by her effort and weakened by the cold, she lay down to rest and to sleep, the "sleep from which there is no awakening."

Few people were travelling at the time; most had already gone into town for the holidays. Fortunately, Tahltan chief Joe Coburn came along with his dogsled. He found her, semi-conscious, sitting on the side of the trail about 20 miles from Telegraph Creek. She was in bad condition; her hands and legs were frozen. He loaded her on his sled and got her to a refuge cabin, where he started a fire and began to rub her hands with snow, for an hour, for two hours. He knew that circulation was beginning to return when, even though she was still only semi-conscious, she began to scream and moan with pain. He had saved her hands.

The 70-year-old chief then wrapped her in his fur robe, tied her to his sled, and made a dash to town, arriving dead tired himself after midnight on Christmas day. During the early-morning hours, people worked feverishly to save her feet and legs, then telegraphed for the mercy plane from Atlin, where there was a hospital. She was flown out that day, but it was too late. The gangrene was well advanced, and both of her legs had to be amputated below the knees. She was flown to Vancouver for more treatment and therapy. The last anyone on the telegraph line heard about Anna Mae Ullman was that she had been fitted with artificial limbs and was working in Vancouver.

Chief Joe Coburn saved Anna Mae Ullman's life when he found her unconscious in a snowbank along the Telegraph Trail and got her to medical attention in Telegraph Creek.

Thea of the Yukon

That same summer of 1932, when Anna Mae Ullman was hiking the trail, another woman, calling herself "Thea of the Yukon," was also attempting to walk from Hazelton to Telegraph Creek. At Eighth Cabin, Thea wrote a letter to Louis LeBourdais, a friend and long-time telegraph operator at Quesnel (see letter on following pages). In it she writes vividly about her experiences on the trail and describes how essential was the help of the telegraph men. They not only provided bed-and-breakfast service, but also acted as clothiers, entertainers, and trail guides.[4]

"Thea of the Yukon" Frances in 1942, ten years after her trek on the Telegraph Trail.

Thea writes about the helpfulness of the telegraph men and the good times she had at their cabins, but during her journey these were the pleasant exceptions. By the time of her trip, the number of occupied telegraph stations had been severely reduced. The distance between them was now 50 to 80 miles, which meant that during most of her hike she carried all her food and supplies and spent her nights alone in refuge cabins or camping out. Only occasionally was she able to listen to a radio, do a jig, and sleep in a cozy bed.[5]

Mary Joyce

Another traveller during the 1930s—a very unusual one—was Mary Joyce, a private nurse who had moved to Alaska to tend Hackley Smith, an injured First World War veteran addicted to drugs.[6] As a cure, he had been advised to get involved in outdoor activity, so he purchased a lodge on the Taku River, not far from Juneau, where he

8th Cabin - Home Station
August 9, [1932]
Yukon Telegraph Trail, B.C.

Dear Louis,

Well here I am on top of the world. This is not a trail but a mud hole. Yesterday I only did a little over four miles, and it took me from 8:30 until 2 o'clock. I spent the night at the last 3/4 cabin and then got to Mooney Creek. The only way I could see to get across was on the emergency cable that has two hand locks. In time I got up enough courage to go across that way and managed to take off, only to have the locks open and dump me. Luckily I landed at the edge of the creek and not in the middle. I tried again but gave it up, sat down and cried and called myself a coward. After an hour I started back for the cabin and saw a sign that led me to a narrow bridge. I was so shaky by that time that I just crept on it.

I made the four miles to 8th [Cabin] in almost tears as the flies and mosquitoes fairly devoured me. I got into mud over my knees. The worst thing was that I lost my balance altogether and went backwards right in the worst mud hole. After fighting weeds and willows, I finally arrived at 8th, where I was received royally. Mr. Jansen turned his cabin over to me; he went and bunked with Mr. Janze. Both my hosts are treating me fine.

I had to take a day off in order to wash out the mud. We're all having a grand time, three dogs and a cat with frozen ears comprise the rest of the family. Mr. Janze got a new radio and so tonight I was cutting up generally, such as dancing a ballet and a jig.

But seriously, this is a terrible trail. It takes all day to do about 10 or 15 miles, and one is exhausted from wading glacial creeks or else crossing them on slippery logs, and from here to ninth cabin there are cables. The mud, especially after the pack train has been over the trail, is unbelievable. I have to put my stick down and if it holds a few inches I put my foot there. The weeds are taller than a tall man and often hide the trail so that you must feel your way.

From 4th Cabin to 8th I wore Mr. Smith's shoes (rubber) and now my hosts here have given me a taller pair, which I shall wear with two pairs of linemen's socks.

My own breaches are patched with the legs of a pair Mr. Ironsides gave me at 6th. I also have a pair of corduroys which Mr. Ironsides brought along with him on the line and I wore from 7th to 8th. The men are all peaches and try to do everything to make one comfortable at the home stations.

Mr. Smith, when I got in at 4th, even pulled my shoes and socks off, bathed my feet and put a brand new pair of socks and moccasins on them. He escorted me over his line, that is he went ahead and cut brush, even insisting upon packing me on his back over a few places where I could not find a foothold because of the mud, both feet having been hurt two days before. (A mosquito is doing a jig on this paper to the music.)

It rained here for more than two weeks straight and I have gotten accustomed to being a dripping being.

Traveled for nearly a week with Arthur Hanlien [sic], a former Indian outlaw called Simon Peter Gunenot [Gunanoot] (who had formerly helped to build this line and trail), and a little man who is trailing along with them. I had an interesting time, tho the traveling through mud was most difficult. They were very good to me.

Bread is baking. It is going on to eleven o'clock P.M. It seems as if I have never known any other kind of life, just living in log cabins, fetching water and bathing out of two pails, washing mud out of my clothes, oil lamps and candles. As for food I am doing very well. But the going is terrible. There is no other trail like this in the world.

This is a messy letter, and I hope you will get it sometime as Mr. Beirnes is coming back with the pack train and will take it back. I am going to turn in soon as I must do a little more mileage tomorrow.

The radio is playing a lovely melody. My remembrance to everyone.

Thea of the Yukon

and Mary began to raise and train dogs for mushing. When Smith died a few years later, he willed the lodge to Mary, who continued to work with the dogs.

When the attractive Mary was named Miss Juneau in a beauty contest, she was invited to compete in the Miss Alaska Pageant in Fairbanks. She could have flown, but decided instead to give herself and the dogs a workout by mushing their way to the contest. Over the trails and rough roads of the time, it was about 800 miles from Taku Lodge to Fairbanks. She started a few days before Christmas 1935, travelled up the Taku River, and then went west to Atlin, no doubt along a portion of the still-active telegraph line. From Atlin she continued to Tagish, Carcross, and Whitehorse, then toward Fairbanks along the route that would later become part of the Alaska Highway, averaging about 20 miles a day. She tried to plan her progress so that she could stay in a settlement each night, but when she couldn't she camped out and dined on her own moose mulligan stew.

Mary Joyce did not complete the trip by dogsled. After three months on the trail, time ran out and she was forced to fly the

Mary Joyce set out to mush her dogsled from Juneau to Fairbanks in 1935 to participate in a beauty pageant.

last several hundred miles to Fairbanks. Although she did not win the Miss Alaska contest, in recognition of her remarkable journey through the bush she was made an honorary member of the Order of Pioneers of Alaska. Why did she do it? "I wanted to see the country and experience some of the things the old-timers did when they climbed over the Chilkoot Pass or walked from Valdez to Fairbanks ... And I just wanted to see if I could do it."

It is not likely that many travellers would have risked the wilderness of British Columbia if it had not been for the existence of the Telegraph Trail. It provided a route through the bush, tramways at stream crossings, and stations and refuge cabins for shelter. Most essential were the telegraph men, who assisted the hikers and could always be depended on for a handout when supplies ran low.

After the section between Hazelton and Telegraph Creek was abandoned in 1935, there were few independent travellers who ventured onto the wilderness trail—only Natives, trappers, big-game outfitters, and perhaps the occasional adventure seeker who was prepared to live off the land.

CHAPTER 16

Literate Linemen

During the final years of the wilderness section, two linemen assigned to stations in the area recorded their experiences. Richard Landry and John Sutherland wrote magazine articles about their lives at remote telegraph stations, and Sutherland compiled a lengthy memoir.[1] As a bonus, both were amateur photographers. Along with Guy Lawrence's reminiscence, *40 Years on the Yukon Telegraph*, and Louis LeBourdais' interviews and articles, the accounts of Landry and Sutherland are the only recollections of life and work on the telegraph line that I have uncovered.

Richard Landry

Richard Landry titled one of his articles "I'm A Wilderness Hermit,"[2] referring to his years as an operator/lineman at Echo Lake and later at Nahlin. He did not regret his solitary life; rather, he relished being surrounded by the creatures of the wilds in an "unspoiled paradise." He hunted for meat and trapped for fur, but mostly he just liked to watch and photograph the animals he came across, especially the moose.

Landry observed the big animals in the bush and from his front window, recording their characteristics and habits in their struggle to survive in a world of dangers and predators. After he had lived at Echo Lake for several months, the moose learned that wolves would not go near his cabin, and they began to regard the area

235

around his station as a safe haven. It became a sanctuary where cows came to calve.

On more than one occasion, motherless calves wandered into his yard, and he would bottle-raise them, often to his regret. The "mischievous little devils" repaid him by breaking into his garden and pulling up the vegetables. Sometimes they even clambered through a cabin window and soon made the inside look like a "cyclone had visited." When that happened, he swore that he would never befriend one of these "brats" again, but they were difficult to resist. "My heart softens [when they] stick their little heads under my arm and beg for tidbits," he wrote. "Once you pet a baby moose, it becomes almost impossible to get away from it. I tried to take a picture of a calf one day, but found I couldn't get him far enough away from the camera. Finally I put down my camera. I carried him several yards, then ran back. When I turned around, ready to snap his picture, the calf's nose was right up against the lens."

During his frequent hikes to inspect his section of line, Landry had many opportunities to observe moose behaviour. Once, while resting beside a campfire, he looked up to see a large cow and calf ambling down the trail, the calf in the lead. When the calf saw him it stopped. The cow raised her head to test the wind, but was unable to smell Landry, for what little wind there was, was in his favour. Then she walked past the calf, stopped, and tested the wind again.

> Slowly, the calf edged nearer. Finally, he was in front of the cow. He braced himself against her chest, as if trying to keep her from coming any closer to me. The cow came forward, however, pushing the calf ahead of her for several yards, then stopping to test the wind again before advancing further. The calf finally took fright and ran back down the trail a short distance. He stood there waiting for the cow.
>
> I couldn't quite understand it. She had her big ears straight up, sniffing the wind as if she could neither see me nor hear the snapping and crackling of the fire. I sat perfectly still and looked her over carefully. Her shoulders, mane, ears and huge nose were all grey. Then I noticed

that her eyes were all of one color—creamy white. Now I realized why her five-month-old calf had tried to turn her back! The mother was stone blind—probably from old age. I whistled softly several times. She turned, then, and trotted back down the trail, her calf leading.

Encounters between moose and man did not always turn out as benignly as this one. There were times when Landry was forced to scoot up a tree to avoid a protective cow or an aggressive bull. He also came across examples of the dangers the telegraph wire could pose for moose, and the damage the animals could wreak on the line. On one occasion, when scouting out a break, he found it had been caused by a bull moose. The wire had become tangled in the animal's antlers, and the bull had pulled out several poles and ploughed up a couple of acres of ground before breaking loose and departing with a hundred feet of telegraph wire wrapped around his head. Other moose were not so lucky. Landry came upon the carcasses of bulls, their antlers tangled in the wire, that had become immobilized and starved to death.

He also witnessed the results of human encounters with the more dangerous residents of the wild. In an article in *Alaska* magazine, Landry recounted the tragic story of Louis Dumas, the lineman at Eighth Cabin, the next station south of Echo Lake.[3]

Linemen patrolling their sections were expected to keep in contact with the adjacent stations, reporting their location at the end of each day. Dumas notified Landry that he was setting out to inspect his section, which extended halfway between Eighth Cabin and Echo Lake. Early one evening, when he had not heard from Dumas, Landry began to worry. With James MacDonald, an old trapper who had a cabin 10 miles away, Landry set out on the trail to look for Dumas. In two days they hiked to the end of Dumas's section and began their search. The two men expected the worst, but certainly not what they found.

Dumas had shot a mountain goat and was in the process of dressing it out when a grizzly came from behind and grabbed him. Unable to get to his gun, which was leaning against a tree, he had tried to fight the bear off with his knife, without success. There was blood all around—blood from the goat, from the grizzly, and from Dumas, whose body was terribly mauled. His blood-drenched hunting knife was still tenaciously clutched in his hand, so tightly held that it could not be pried from his fingers. MacDonald and Landry buried him on the site with the knife still grasped in his hand.

Landry was sure he had confronted this animal before. He believed he had met it one time when he was patrolling without his rifle, and the monster had scared 10 years off his life. It was the biggest grizzly he had ever seen, and when it reared up and advanced toward him he was sure he was a goner. Only by persistently banging on a pot did he finally get the bear to back off. As a result of this encounter, Landry swore he would never again venture into the bush without his rifle. When he completed his patrol and returned to Echo Lake, there was more bad news. The grizzly had paid a visit. It had busted in the door and "thrown everything outside, even the kitchen stove."

Months passed after the death of Dumas, and both Landry and MacDonald forgot about the bear. Then one night the old trapper appeared at Landry's door in an agitated state. As Landry told his story:

On his way home he had visited some of his traps. Arriving at his cabin at dusk, as usual he lit the fire, put on a pot of beans, got some water boiling for his coffee, and started to remove his heavy clothes. While waiting for the coffee water to boil, he sat down to read. At his elbow was a one-pane window, about 12 x 14. Suddenly, with a bang the window shattered, and a huge grizzly bear poked his head through. It so surprised the old man that he grabbed the first thing handy, the pot of boiling water, and heaved it in the bear's face. With a loud WHOOF the head vanished. The brute plowed a furrow in the snow with his scalded nose for about 50 feet. In the meantime, the old trapper had put the bar across the door and reached for his rifle. He was just in time, too. His cabin door had only small hinges. The grizzly gave it one bang with his paw and the hinge at the top busted. The door teetered on the crosspiece, then with another bang everything broke. The old trapper emptied his .303 rifle in the bear's head and the bear fell half in and half out of the cabin door. When he was dead, the trapper took his dog and walked the 10 miles to my station.

The two men went back to the trapper's cabin and examined the bear. It was very old, its teeth worn down and broken. And when they rolled him over they saw six festering knife wounds. He was the rogue that had killed Dumas and scared Landry.

The section of line assigned to the linemen at Echo Lake was a nightmare to maintain, especially during the winter months. The area's heavy snowfalls and slides caused frequent interruptions and made travelling to repair breaks extremely difficult. After struggling with these demanding conditions for several years, Landry applied for a transfer. It was granted, and in late 1932 he was moved north to Nahlin Station to take over for old Joe Hicks, who was retiring. His replacement at Echo Lake was John Sutherland.

John Sutherland

Sutherland was a step ahead of many of the men employed by the telegraph.[4] He was no cheechako, coming to the job with considerable experience living and working in the bush. The son of a railway man, he was only 16 when his father died, leaving a wife and six children. As the eldest son, John no doubt felt responsibilities beyond his years. After high school he took a position as a junior clerk in a Vancouver branch of the Royal Bank of Canada, but soon realized that he preferred to work outdoors. After two years he quit the bank for work in logging camps on Vancouver Island.

At the age of 20 he decided to see what was up north in British Columbia's vast wilderness. In March 1926 he set out, first by train to Hazelton, then by snowshoe 330 miles on the Telegraph Trail to Telegraph Creek, then a further 70 miles to Dease Lake, where he found work in a placer mine. Spring was probably the worst time of year to travel through the area, as the trails were turning to mush, then mud, and many of the creeks were raging over their banks with runoff. This was his introduction to the Yukon Telegraph and to the rigours of life in the north, and the beginning of his learning the skills he would need to survive in the bush. Returning south at the end of the mining season, he spent the winter with his family in Vancouver.

The following year Sutherland headed north again, this time by boat to Stewart, where he worked on a railroad construction project. In this small town he likely became acquainted with the local telegraph operator, Guy Lawrence. By this time Lawrence was a 25-year veteran of the Yukon Telegraph, a man well into his 40s, while Sutherland was just starting to find a life in the north. But not quite yet, for once again he returned to his family to wait out the harsh winter weather. It was to be his last trip south for many years.

In 1928 Sutherland again hiked the Telegraph Trail, this time during the summer months. And this time he stayed through the winter to work a trapline he had purchased on the Whiting River, 50 miles north of Telegraph Creek. He remained in the Cassiar–Atlin area for the next 12 years. For the first five, when not tending his trapline, he lived in a cabin he had built three miles north of Telegraph Creek in an area known as the woodyard.

The winters in Telegraph Creek were dreadfully dreary. For six months after the Stikine River froze up, the only way in or out of the settlement was by dogsled. During the winter of 1931–32 Sutherland found himself at loose ends, as he did not need to return to his trapline until April or May. He had developed a splendid sled-dog team that loved to work and pull a sled, so he decided to try his hand at the lucrative business of hauling freight from Atlin. The going rate that year was one dollar a pound. A good team of six dogs, like Sutherland's, could haul 400 pounds, worth $400—good pay for a month's work.

If the money didn't convince him to make the trip, the dogs did. Each morning they would jump up, looking at him eagerly, hoping to be harnessed to the sled, only to slump back down when nothing happened. It was clear what they wanted to do. They were almost human in their excitement and joy when he started to bring boxes back to the cabin to load onto the sled. There was much wagging of tails and little whines where before there had been just dull, motionless silence.

Sutherland was ready to start from Telegraph Creek on Christmas morning, carrying mostly dog food. It was a good year to travel, as several other freighters were using the trail, which helped to keep it packed down. Even so, after a fresh snow the trail could become "heavy," and there often appeared a "shadow," a driver who waited for someone else to go first and break trail. With the light load and good weather, it took Sutherland only seven days to mush the 220 miles to Atlin.

In Atlin Sutherland immediately started to assemble the cargo for the return trip. Since there was no liquor store in Telegraph Creek, booze in one form or another comprised most of his load. On the list were four cases of Lemon-Hart rum and a case of mixed spirits: two bottles each of gin, curaçao, bourbon, and wine, and four bottles of whiskey. "Blackie" Irwin, the town brewer, wanted a 50-pound can of malt. The rest of the load included two quarts of wine for the Anglican missionary, and several roasts of fresh pork for people who had tired of a steady diet of moose. Including the 200 pounds of food for the dogs, the total weight to be pulled was at least 600 pounds.

Sutherland and his dogs left Atlin on January 8, following the more direct route blazed by the mailmen, which joined the Telegraph Trail partway along. The load was heavy and the trail rough, and over the first section the team was able to make only 15 miles a day.

When he reached the Dixie Lakes, 30 miles from Atlin, he hoped to make better time over the flat ice. But he found that there was overflow on the first lake and feared that the heavy load might plough into a foot or more of freezing water. To decrease the pressure on the ice he brought out a second sled, which he had been carrying for just such a contingency, and split the load, thus lessening the chance of breaking through. One dog was separated from the team to pull the smaller sled.

Crossing the second of the Dixie Lakes, Chips, the lone dog who was pulling the second sled, made it clear that he did not like this arrangement at all. His whole "hangdog look" indicated that he felt he was being discriminated against. Dogs trained to work together as a team can become depressed if they are separated and made to work alone. Chips acted so downhearted and hurt that, after Paddy Lake, Sutherland put him back pulling with the other dogs. Paddy Lake, Sutherland reported, was where the mailmen's trail joined the Telegraph Trail; from there to Telegraph Creek, the telegraph stations and refuges were available.[5]

Through Nakina Gorge and over Nakina Summit, Sutherland was forced to break the load down and haul it in relays. While the team was moving up to the summit with the last load, a violent blizzard blew up, and only after four hours of floundering through the swirling snow and biting cold was Sutherland able to find the refuge tent, the only shelter available. More accurately, the lead dog found the shelter, as for hours it had been too dark for Sutherland to see anything.

After a miserable cold night the storm subsided and the skies cleared, but as many northerners will tell you, this is often a sign that it will get colder, much colder. Starting at about minus 40° Fahrenheit, the temperature kept going down during the day. Whenever Sutherland stopped, the dogs were restive and had their tails between their legs. They kept fidgeting from foot to foot, as if to say "Get going; it's too cold to stand around."

John Sutherland's sled-dog team hauling supplies (mostly booze) from Atlin to winter-locked Telegraph Creek in 1932. The second sled is pulled by Chips, who did not appreciate being separated from his teammates.

When he reached the refuge cabin 30 miles before Nahlin Station, Sutherland got a roaring fire going, unhitched and fed the dogs, and moved his cargo inside. He did this every night to guard against freezing. Upon opening the case that contained the wine bottles, he found that the extreme cold had frozen the wine, pushing out the corks until an inch of icy wine stuck up from the necks of the bottles. The hard liquors had fared better. They were only partially frozen into slush.

When the temperature dropped to minus 55° Fahrenheit, Sutherland decided to hole up at the refuge until the cold snap ended before proceeding to Nahlin. While he was there, the two mailmen passed through, one headed toward Atlin, the other to Telegraph Creek. They were behind schedule, so despite the cold they hardly stopped in the cabin. Each grabbed a quick meal, passed out on the bunk for a few hours, and then was off on his appointed round. Sutherland, in no hurry, stayed a week, waiting for the bitter cold to abate. When the temperature got up to minus 40° he resumed his journey, heading for the two remaining telegraph stations at the Nahlin and Shesley rivers. Nahlin was about halfway from Atlin; Shesley was 60 miles beyond and only 45 miles from Telegraph Creek. Sutherland stayed for a day with Joe Hicks at Nahlin, then with Jack Wrathall and his wife at Shesley.

On the last leg of his journey he passed through the Salmon Lake Indian Reserve, where he came upon an old woman living in an open tent. He took a photograph of her in front of the tent, tending her fire with her little Tahltan bear dog.

Later, Harper Reed, the Indian agent, told him that the woman he had seen was Mother Chrisanne, who was around 110 years old. Reed said she had borne many sons and, even in her later years, continued to travel widely: to town for Christmas, to fish camp for the salmon run. What impressed Sutherland so strongly was "that she had just weathered a cold snap of 10 days, during which the thermometer held at 70° below zero [minus 55° Celsius], in a draughty tent when the same cold snap held me in a snug refuge cabin."[6] Sutherland concluded his trip at Telegraph Creek on February 11, a month and three days after leaving Atlin.

During John Sutherland's winter trip from Atlin to Telegraph Creek, he came across Chrisanne, an Aboriginal woman reputed to be 110 years old.

The following winter, in November 1932, Sutherland began his career with the Yukon Telegraph, the result of an unusual interview process. It started when he was hired to transport Richard Landry's replacement, Fred Appleyard, and his gear to Echo Lake. On showshoes and with backpacks and six fully loaded dogs, the two men made good time, reaching their destination in six days without incident.

Sutherland deposited Appleyard at Echo Lake with some trepidation. By 1932 the number of stations had been severely reduced. Although Echo Lake was normally staffed by two linemen, at the time a second man was not available. Consequently, there was no one at the station to teach the inexperienced Appleyard how to survive a northern winter. He was immediately thrust into a situation in which he alone was responsible for maintaining 30 miles of line both north and south of his cabin.

Sutherland headed back toward Telegraph Creek to tend to his trapline. On his way a big storm hit, what locals called a "big flop," and it was soon snowing an inch an hour. At Iskut Station, 45 miles from Echo Lake, he learned that the wire had gone down somewhere to the south, in the direction of the new lineman's section.

Appleyard had hardly had time to get organized in his new home when he was called out to locate and repair a break. At first light—what there was of it in the blowing snow—he started south from Echo Lake to look for the cause of the interruption. He was equipped with a clip-on phone so that he could stay in touch with the other stations. At Iskut, the linemen and Sutherland waited anxiously for his reports, concerned because he was so new to the job. And sure enough, about 8:00 p.m., when Appleyard clipped his phone to the wire, they learned that he was having problems.

He had lost sight of the wire several times during the day in the blinding, swirling snow. He made camp with his two dogs and was soaking wet, cold and hungry. He told about finding a dry spot under a big spruce tree and putting his outfit next to the trunk and sitting with his back to the trunk and starting a big fire. In a short time the heat of the fire had melted the snow laden branches of the tree and before he knew what was happening he was drenched to the skin as well as what grub he had and also a couple of blankets. Now he was cold and hungry and lost too as [in] his circling around looking for the wire in the dark he had lost all sense of direction.

The other linemen had an idea of where he was. They told him to keep his head and at first light to find a creek and follow it; it should take him to one of the refuge cabins. Sutherland knew that Appleyard's life depended on his getting out of the weather. He decided to head back toward Echo Lake to see if he could help, hoping that he would be in time. Eventually he found Appleyard, who had luckily stumbled across a refuge cabin where he managed to dry out and get warm. The new man seemed to be physically okay, but Sutherland related that "he looked terrible, with strained face and staring eyes as if he had just been shaking hands with the grim reaper … His cheeks were shrunk and hollow from the mental ordeal he had suffered."

When Superintendent J.J. Dore in Vancouver learned of Sutherland's volunteer effort to help, he immediately hired him as a lineman at $110 per month and "found" (lodging and food), and assigned him to Echo Lake with Fred Appleyard. The two men were stationed there for several years, and unlike some other pairs of linemen forced to live together, they developed a close friendship.

Ten years older than Sutherland, Appleyard had served as an officer in the Great War, and although it was nearly two decades later, he still retained some troubling memories of his experiences. He had survived the war without injury to his body, but carried a wound of the mind that could not be quickly cured. There were two cabins at Echo Lake. Normally, at nightfall Sutherland went to his cabin to sleep, but at times Appleyard hinted that he wanted him to stay, saying that he would enjoy his company overnight.

One night when Sutherland stayed he was awakened by an "anguished cry." Upon lighting a lantern he found Appleyard standing in the middle of the cabin with a look on his face that, Sutherland said, "I had become familiar with in other … men returned from the battlefields of Europe." As Appleyard slowly awakened from his nightmare, he began to talk in a low voice about one of the terrible moments in the war that came back to him in his dreams.

> It was one early morning just after he was given the rank of captain on the Somme … He had taken a group of five men out on a reconnaissance patrol … They had come to a pillbox near a farmhouse. Fred told his men to wait in the pillbox while he alone would reconnoitre the farmhouse and come back for them … It was a cold frosty morning and he told the men not to light a fire, as any sign of smoke

would advertise their presence and draw fire from the Germans. The men were chilly and evidently one of them set fire to some paper. This was all the German artillery needed and they dropped a shrapnel shell into the air vent in the top of the pillbox ... When Fred returned a few minutes later he found the remains of his five man squad plastered around the inside of the pillbox.

This was only one of Appleyard's nightmares from the past, one of several. But they recurred less frequently as time passed and he felt freer to talk about them with Sutherland, who had a kind and sympathetic ear.

When Appleyard and Sutherland took over at Echo Lake, the number of stations with linemen between Atlin and Hazelton had been reduced to seven: Fourth Cabin, Eighth Cabin, Echo Lake, Iskut, Telegraph Creek, Shesley, and Nahlin. The distances between occupied cabins had doubled and even tripled, now requiring linemen to patrol 30 to 40 miles in each direction.

Fred Appleyard, John Sutherland's partner at Echo Lake Station in the 1930s, was a veteran of the First World War. His haunting memories and nightmares of the war receded the longer he lived in the bush.

At Echo Lake, Appleyard worked the north section and Sutherland the south, which was known as one of the "heaviest" on the entire line. It was not a popular assignment, as the prodigious amounts of snow that blanketed the area each year could produce 10-foot snowpacks and frequent slides.

Sutherland documented the difficulty of keeping the line open in a portion of his work report for January 1934.

Work Report January 24–31, 1934

January 24—Remained at refuge. Raining and snowing, (time to stay put when a weather change occurs, [usually] indicating line trouble. It has changed from steady snow to rain.)

January 25—South on open wire to 12 mile refuge.

January 26—South to 19 mile refuge, repairing one break at 15 miles.

January 27—Spliced thirty breaks in wire on 9 slides between 19 and 23 mile refuges. (there was 4 miles between for this reason: it is a snowslide area. The rain on snow had caused numerous slides all along this section, as well as south to 8th cabin and Charlie Janze.)

January 28—Sunday. South to 29 mile refuge cabin no trouble, wire still open south, [Meaning that the break was not in his section.]

January 30—South to 41 mile refuge. Repaired one break at 39 miles. (This refuge is on the west bank of the Bell-Irving River, there is a cable crossing here for summer high water, but can snowshoe across in winter.) After repairing break at 3 P.M. wire was still open south of me so continued on to 9th cabin [abandoned]. Wire south still open.

January 31—South to slide 2 miles from 9th cabin. About a mile of wire had disappeared under the slide. Crossed the slide and found no spare wire to run another span to connect line together again, found none handy so decided to sit down on slide for a while and wait for Charlie Janze to arrive from the south as I knew we were due to meet momentarily, although there had been no contact between us since the snow had turned to rain on January 24.

Sutherland eventually found the cause of the open wire, but it had taken him more than a week, plus the time it would take to return 50 miles to his home station. He had spent his nights in the refuge cabins, which he described as "Circles of Warmth," the lineman's only defence against the weather. They were equipped with a pole bunk, blankets, cooking utensils, a "B.C. camp stove," and a crosscut saw. A relay and a telegraph key connected to the telegraph wire enabled the lineman to keep in touch with the other stations. A regular chore was to clear the cabins' roofs of snow so that they would not collapse under the heavy load.

With the exception of the heavy snows, Echo Lake was an ideal assignment. The trapping was good, hunting for moose was excellent, the lake contained trout, and the ground around the cabin was suitable for growing vegetables. Moose and potatoes were tasty supplements to the canned meats and dried vegetables supplied by the government.

As part of his early telegraph education, Sutherland learned to stay away from "pegboards" during electrical storms. Every station and refuge cabin had one of these boards nailed to an inside wall. They were used to connect the heavy-gauge wire from outside to the smaller wires connected to the telegraph equipment. The outside wire was attached to a metal strip on the board. The metal carried the current to holes in the board where the lighter wire could be held in contact by pegs, hence the name pegboard.

One time when Sutherland was with Charlie Janze at Eighth Cabin, where thunderstorms were a daily occurrence during the summer, he received a vivid lesson in the power of lightning. The two men were sitting and talking, waiting out a storm, when a bolt of lightning hit the line. Instantly the electricity travelled down the wire into the cabin to the pegboard, from which a five-foot bolt zapped into the room. Sutherland got the scare of his life, but old-timer Janze told him there was nothing to worry about. All he had to do during an electrical storm was remember to stay six feet away from the pegboard.

At each cabin there was also a simple device called a "jumper," a two-foot piece of ordinary telegraph wire. When wrapped around the two wires going into the cabin, it cut the cabin out of the system.

This would prevent the equipment inside from causing an opening in the line, which could occur when a wire inside was separated or shorted out because of condensation. When a lineman arrived at a cabin, the first thing he did was remove one end of the jumper, thus getting power to the pegboard. The last thing he did when leaving was to reattach the jumper.

During his years at Echo Lake in the 1930s, Sutherland observed a trickle of men, singly and in pairs, starting to pass along the Telegraph Trail. "They were the forerunners of the displaced [and] dispossessed, the refugees from the new darkening war clouds of all the ism's that were to erupt in World War Two." There were also those fleeing the hopeless conditions of the Great Depression.

The bush could be a perilous place for the inexperienced and ill-equipped, although the linemen were always willing to assist these travellers as they passed through. They felt a responsibility for them and took pride in ensuring their safety, but there were times when they were not able to avoid disaster.

One day while patrolling near the Bell-Irving River, Sutherland came upon a distraught Englishman, "wild-eyed and incoherent." After Sutherland calmed him down, the man related that he had just lost his travelling companion and their outfit in the river, which was high and running fast. Escapees from the Depression, the two had started north hoping to find work in one of the small towns. They had travelled on the Telegraph Trail without incident until reaching the Bell-Irving, where they built a small raft. The river was flowing rapidly, but with poles they slowly made their way across. On contact with the far bank, in a split second the raft was spun and bounced into a deadly sweeper (a fallen tree that hung over the river), which upended the raft and dumped his partner and their outfit into the water. The Englishman had been on the side of the raft nearest the bank and was thrown onto the sweeper, where he was able to cling to branches and scramble up the trunk to shore. As he grabbed the limbs he caught a glimpse of the raft and his partner as they disappeared forever in the black current of the swiftly flowing stream.

Chances were a million to one that the man had survived in the icy water that can shock and chill within minutes. Sutherland regretted that he had not been able to escort the two men safely through his section, but there was nothing more to be done. He considered a search for the body so that it could be properly buried, but dismissed the idea as likely to be a futile undertaking, and certainly a risky one. The conventions of civilization could not always be observed in the bush. The Englishman, now travelling alone, continued his trek north, Sutherland, his patrol south.

The incident was a reminder of the dangers regularly faced by the linemen, who in the course of their patrols were required to cross many of these streams. Sutherland had learned to "treat the rivers of the north with prudence, that discretion was always the better choice than valour."

As the seasons began to change and travel on the trail ended for 1934, Sutherland and Appleyard prepared for another long winter at Echo Lake. It would be their last, and they probably knew it. The Department of Public Works Wireless Service was already erecting radio towers at Hazelton and Telegraph Creek. It claimed that they would be used only as emergency replacements for the land line when it went down. None of the linemen believed the government's explanation.

Thus, when unusually high floods in the spring of 1935 tore out bridges and damaged sections of line, the department's decision to shut down the Hazelton–Telegraph Creek section was not unexpected. What may have been a surprise to Sutherland and Appleyard was the way in which the announcement was made. On August 1, 1935, they received a blunt, impersonal message over the wire: "Abandon station, no supplies ordered." They were later told to pack up their personal gear, leave everything else in the cabin, lock the door, and head out to Telegraph Creek. This was the first section of line that Sutherland was forced to walk away from. It would not be the last.

What the departments of Interior and Defence had been unable to achieve in 1925, the Department of Public Works itself accomplished 10 years later. The earlier effort had been a hostile takeover of one department's turf by another. This was an intradepartmental transfer to the Wireless Service, one that was probably long overdue.

Regardless of the cause of the change, it was the end of a job for most of the linemen. A few were transferred to other stations, others retired; short-timers like Sutherland were simply let go.

The closing of the wilderness section signalled something more. It was the end of an era, if the Klondike gold rush can be called an era. Long after the country's attention had shifted to other, more sombre matters, the land line had continued to provide a link with the Klondike and those mad days of exuberant optimism. It was, after all, the Yukon Telegraph, as much a visceral as a physical reminder of that time, of the liberating adventurous spirit of the north.

For a while longer, sections of the telegraph would continue to operate, but it was not the same. The chain of the all-Canadian Yukon Telegraph line had been broken. However, the wire in the wilderness still had one last hurrah, one final role to play.

CHAPTER 17

The Second World War and the Alaska Highway

A few years after John Sutherland was told to walk away from Echo Lake, the Department of Public Works decided that all the line cabins between Hazelton and Telegraph Creek would never be needed again. They were declared surplus property and offered for sale, with all their contents, to the highest bidders. Ottawa calculated that the cost of salvaging the stoves, blankets, tools, and other furnishings would be greater than their value. What today would seem a very good deal for a fully equipped cabin did not at the time attract much interest; the highest bid for Second Cabin, for example, was $40 from John Crosby of Kispiox.

Consequently, when the B.C. Indian Commissioner requested that the cabins be made available for use by Natives, the department readily agreed and voided the earlier sales.[1] The disposal of the cabins was the final step in the abandonment of this section of the telegraph line. Within a few more years the remaining wilderness portion between Telegraph Creek and Atlin, already reduced to the two stations at Shesley and Nahlin, would also be closed.

At the same time that the land line through British Columbia was being shut down, American interests were promoting an alternative use for the abandoned Telegraph Trail. Boosters for opening up Alaska argued that the only thing standing in the way of developing the territory's abundant natural resources (its forests, minerals, and fisheries) was the lack of a highway connecting it to the lower states. Canadians who wanted greater access to northern British Columbia and the Yukon put forward similar arguments.

Three routes were proposed, labelled A, B, and C. There was agreement as to where the road should end—in Fairbanks—but each route began at a different town. Route A, the Telegraph Trail Route, started from Hazelton and more or less followed the Telegraph Trail to Telegraph Creek, Atlin, and Whitehorse, then headed northwest to Fairbanks. Route B was similar to Route A, but ran to the east of the Telegraph Trail. Called the Inland Route, it commenced at Prince George and went north to Watson Lake, then Dawson City, before turning west to Fairbanks. Route C was entirely different. It started from Edmonton, used existing roads to Dawson Creek, then went northwest through British Columbia and the Yukon to Whitehorse before heading to Fairbanks.[2]

The most vociferous backers of each route were the politicians and entrepreneurs who saw a road bringing economic benefits to their regions, much as, 40 years earlier, southern officials and business interests had sought to entice Klondike stampeders to travel through their cities. There also were "civilians" who joined the campaign. The best known was Clyde "Slim" Williams, a long-time advocate of the Telegraph Trail Route, who had mushed his dogsled from Alaska to the lower states during the winter of 1932–33 (see Chapter 14).

Slim Williams Hits the Road Again

The reporting of his earlier adventure had made Slim a celebrity of sorts and had pointed his life in a new direction. He got married and gave up his trapline for the lecture circuit. Possessed of a wealth of practical knowledge of the north, he was an appealing speaker with a great reservoir of stories he used to charm and stimulate his audiences. And if his enthusiasm sometimes ran ahead to embellish a story, or even to add an adventure, where was the harm? It might have happened that way. In his appearances, he also continued to

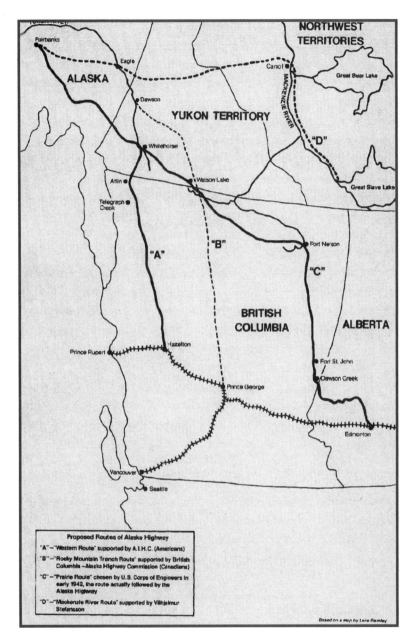

Map of proposed routes A, B, and C for the road to connect the
Lower 48 to Alaska. Route A included portions of the Telegraph
Trail, but Route C was chosen to be the future Alaska Highway.

beat the drum for an Alaska highway and became known as Alaska's most vocal unofficial spokesman for the international highway.

After a few years of city life and lecturing, Slim grew restive and bored. He began to look for a new challenge. After his first trip he had kept in touch with highway engineer Donald McDonald, the prime advocate for the Telegraph Trail Route. McDonald encouraged Slim to venture on another journey through the wilderness—to make some "noise for the highway." All Slim needed to make up his mind was a know-it-all government official saying that a road could never be built. When Louis Johnson, the U.S. assistant secretary of war, declared that a road to Alaska through British Columbia was not feasible, Slim decided on the spot that he was the man to show it could be done. He would prove to the world that the route was suitable for motor travel by riding a motorcycle over the trail the following summer.[3] One might question if riding—actually, an equal amount of pushing, towing, and ferrying—a motorcycle through the bush was sufficient evidence to show that a road was practicable. But in Slim's mind it was, and anyhow, such an audacious journey was sure to generate a lot of publicity.

The cynic might say that it was a hare-brained stunt by a man in his 50s who may have been looking to prove something other than the trail's viability. But it was an idea that also appealed to other men, and to one man in particular. At a meeting of the Adventurer's Club of Chicago, Slim was approached by John Logan, who was familiar with his earlier exploits. Williams invited the 25-year-old to come along. Logan recognized the potential significance of the journey should the highway be built, but his primary reason for enlisting in the cause was his youthful spirit of adventure.

Since neither man had any previous experience with a motorcycle, their first order of business was to learn how to ride one. Then they began to make plans for the ambitious 2,250-mile journey, more than half of which was through a roadless wilderness criss-crossed by streams and muskeg. They judged that it would take them three months.

On May 14, 1939, the two trailblazers, after some surreptitious practice on their 250 BSA motorcycles, were ready to start on their adventure, accompanied by a last-minute addition, a young husky presented to them by supporters. Blizzard would prove to be a good companion, but a handful to control.

From Fairbanks they intended to follow about the same route Slim had taken with his dogsled seven years earlier. First they headed southeast toward Dawson City, through an area that in 1939 offered only a few short sections of roadway but many miles of trails, most unsuitable for motorcycles. The trip started slowly. The trails were so rough that it took them two months to traverse the 225 miles to Chicken, Alaska. The motorcycles, although essential to justify the feasibility of the route for motorized travel, were being pushed more than they were being ridden. On July 25 Slim and John entered Dawson City, where they were given an enthusiastic welcome. By mid-August they were in Atlin, ready to start upon the most difficult part of their journey, the 550 miles of wilderness to Hazelton.

The *Atlin News-Miner*, naturally a big booster of the telegraph route, wished them success. "Some people may think they are crazy, but we take our hats off to them and shall be happy to hear they have reached Hazelton safely, which should speak loud words for the Atlin–Hazelton route for the future Hi-Way."[4]

The Telegraph Trail was the real test. Although the linemen had kept the section from Atlin to Telegraph Creek open, there were numerous streams and creeks to cross and bogs and swamps to get through. Blowdowns were especially troublesome. While a man could step over a fallen tree, manoeuvring a 220-pound cycle over or around it was a much more difficult and time-consuming task.

Their work was reduced by half because they had temporarily abandoned one of the cycles, sending it ahead to Hazelton. Even so, to get through the wet and boggy sections they had to lay down a pathway of small trees to support the machine, repeating the process again and again. The incessant rains kept the streams high, which posed additional problems. At some crossings they were able to use the linemen's tramlines to carry the cycle across; at others the platforms were too small. When they could not ford a stream, they built a raft to ferry the cycle.

When Slim and John reached Nahlin Station, the halfway point between Atlin and Telegraph Creek, they were down to their last cup of gasoline. They had arranged to have a supply of fuel sent to Nahlin with the annual pack train, but relying on the pack train was always a gamble. They were elated when the operator at Nahlin, Richard Landry, informed them that their resupply had arrived safely. Filling up the cycle's gas tank, they motored on to Shesley Station. From there the trail was greatly improved, and they (or rather one of them) rode on the old Teslin Trail into Telegraph Creek, which they reached on September 14.

Time was beginning to be the enemy. The days were getting shorter and fall was well advanced when they crossed the Stikine River and set out for Hazelton. There were no longer any telegraph cabins with helpful linemen to speed them on their way and to send messages ahead reporting on their progress. Fortunately, at Telegraph Creek they had purchased a horse, which they put to good use carrying their outfit and, when the gasoline supply was exhausted, towing the motorcycle.

The two adventurers followed the telegraph line much of the way, diverting to other trails to avoid the higher terrain, where snow was already falling. As they were completely out of touch, when their estimated date of arrival at Hazelton came and passed there was apprehension for their safety. But on November 9 they finally reached the town, Slim Williams leading and John Logan astride the motorcycle being ignominiously towed by the horse. They were bearded and filthy, and each had lost 20 pounds. Slim was suffering from pneumonia and was immediately hospitalized.

Hazelton was the transition point from the drudgery of hauling the motorcycle over bush trails to actually riding it—and the second cycle, which had arrived at Hazelton—on roadways, with gas stations and places to eat and rest. To accommodate Blizzard, they employed a local mechanic, Ernie Clifford, to convert the two bikes to a four-wheeler with a platform welded between to hold the dog and their outfit. The arrangement worked fine except for turning corners, which could be tricky. To avoid tilting over, the rider on the inside of the arc had to slow down while the outside driver sped up.[5]

The odd-looking threesome cycled on to Seattle, where they ended their adventure. They had to abandon their plan to continue

Slim Williams and John Logan on their 1939 journey along the Telegraph Trail to promote it as the route for a road to Alaska. After passing through the wilderness, their bikes were joined together at Hazelton for road travel, with a platform for their outfit and husky Blizzard.

to the world's fair in New York, because the summer trip had taken too long. Their primary goal had been accomplished: to focus attention on a highway to Alaska, specifically on the feasibility of the Telegraph Trail Route.

It had been a marvellous experience for both men, especially for the young cheechako John Logan, who years later remembered Slim Williams with affection and perhaps still with a degree of awe.[6] Among other trail skills, he recalled how Slim had taught him to make bannock by dipping water into the flour bag to make dough, and how to live for months on bannock, tea, bacon, beans, and small game.

North to Alaska

In 1938, the American government, in an effort to speed up a decision about the location of the highway, established an International Highway Commission to make a recommendation. The Canadian government, which was less enthusiastic about the project, reluctantly set up its own commission. A year later, when the American commission reported, the representatives of Alaska, British Columbia, and Washington state were all in favour of Route A, the Telegraph Trail Route.[7] Of the several factors involved in the decision, from the American perspective the most important was the route's ability to provide access to communities in the Alaska Panhandle. However, before anything more could be done to promote this route, the Second World War interceded and all decisions were put on hold, dependent upon the needs of the military.

In August 1940 the Canada–United States Joint Board on Defence was created. Canada was already in the war in support of Great Britain; the U.S. was preparing for the defence of Alaska. One of the board's recommendations was to speed development of a flyway from the lower states to Alaska to ensure that personnel and materials could be moved north by air. Called the Northwest Staging Route, it required supporting airfields every 200 miles. In northern Canada, airfields already existed at Fort Nelson and Whitehorse, but they were 400 miles apart. An intermediate field was required, and Watson Lake seemed an ideal location, but there was no access road to move construction equipment and supplies to the work site.

There was one possible route, albeit a difficult one, via the Stikine and Dease rivers. These waterways and the portage between them had been used for eons by Tlingit traders travelling between the coast and the interior settlements, and later by white explorers and fur traders. Wrangell would be the staging depot from which riverboats would transport materials up the Stikine River to Telegraph Creek, reminiscent of the Stikine Trail used 40 years earlier by the stampeders of '98. From Telegraph Creek there was a rough 75-mile tractor road to Dease Lake, followed by a voyage on the often-perilous Dease River to Watson Lake.

During the spring and summer of 1941 the Stikine River saw more traffic than it had since gold-rush days. Boats and barges hauled, pushed, and winched 3,500 tons of cargo up the river to Telegraph Creek. Heavy equipment (trucks, bulldozers, and graders) was given priority so that it could be employed improving

To transport materials to build the wartime airfield at Watson Lake, the Canadian government in 1940–41 improved this cat-train road between Telegraph Creek and Dease Lake.

the portage road to Dease Lake. Construction materials followed, including thousands of 45-gallon barrels of asphalt to surface the airfield's runway. Large pieces of disassembled boats and barges were also hauled over the roadway. Once reassembled at the lake, they were used to move the materials on the third leg of the journey down the Dease River.

Construction materials were stockpiled at Telegraph Creek before being sent over the portage road. Although the bulldozers and graders made improvements to the road, the 75-mile trip still took four to five hours, and after a rain, when the roadbed turned into a mud bog, it could take several days.[8]

By midsummer and despite many difficulties—not least the Dease River's low water and rapids—materials began to arrive at Watson Lake and construction commenced. By September a rough airstrip had been cut out of the bush and levelled. A few months later, when the U.S. entered the war, a string of airfields was available to support the flyway. Their importance was recognized soon after, when the Japanese invaded islands in the Aleutians.

But the primary use of the flyway during the war was to support the Lend-Lease program, which included flying airplanes from the United States to the Soviet Union. The planes were refuelled and serviced at the airfields on their way to Alaska, where Soviet pilots flew them to Siberia. During the war years more than 7,000 airplanes passed over the flyway.[9]

The location of the airfields, particularly the ones at Fort Nelson and Watson Lake, became the determining factor in selecting the route for the road to Alaska. The road's purpose had changed from being a gateway to Alaska to supplying fuel and other materials to the airfields. Consequently, the favoured route was the one that earlier had been considered least likely to be chosen—Route C from Edmonton and Dawson Creek—because it was the most direct route to the airfields. The war had changed everything.

It would seem that all of Slim Williams' and John Logan's efforts had been for naught. There was, however, some compensation in knowing that they were not alone in their contention that the Telegraph Trail was the best route. Among others, the well-known wilderness adventurer R.M. Patterson opined: "Probably better and easier routes west of the Rockies were rejected ... [when] the new airports came into use."[10]

The Telegraph in the War

When the war broke out in the Pacific, the Canadian government expressed interest in rejuvenating the telegraph's land line, because radio transmissions could be intercepted and their contents fall into the wrong hands. Telegraph messages would be more secure. Considering this possibility, the division superintendent of the government's Telegraph Service reported on the condition of the line.

He wrote that the roofs of the abandoned stations between Hazelton and Telegraph Creek had probably caved in and would require extensive rebuilding; however, the Telegraph Creek-to-Atlin section, shut down only a year earlier, was still in fair shape. On both sections, however, many miles of lines would need to be rebuilt. He recommended that this work could best be accomplished by using mechanized army units.

The superintendent also evaluated the original route of the Yukon Telegraph, specifically the section over Nass Summit. He noted the recurring difficulty linemen had experienced keeping it in operation and advised that if the line were rebuilt, this section should be rerouted. He suggested that it be moved away from the mountains and redirected from Fourth Cabin through the river valleys to rejoin the old route near Echo Lake. This would "avoid the sliding glaciers and the high barren summits between Sixth and Eighth Cabins."[11] Nothing came of the scheme to resuscitate the land line; the wilderness section's only contribution to the war effort was that military pilots used its cutline as a directional guide.

The war caused a dramatic increase in the number of messages transmitted over both the remaining land line (north of Atlin and south of Hazelton) and the wireless system of the Yukon Telegraph. In the north, operators were responsible for providing flight and weather information to the Canadian and American pilots. Great demands were placed on the land line at times when the radio channels failed due to atmospheric or other conditions.

To handle the increased war work, a call went out for operators. Since it takes years of experience to produce a good operator, old-timers, earlier considered redundant, were recruited. The stock market crash of 1929 had put thousands of them out of work, or they had been replaced by the advance of technology. Many of the old "brass pounders" answered the call, and women operators, who had left the key for steadier work or to raise families, joined up for the duration.[12] The war provided one last opportunity for the old Morse men and women to exhibit their skills.

The wartime operators worked hard, under less than ideal conditions, often frustrated by the inadequacy of their equipment. As one operator at Hazelton wrote to his member of Parliament:

> We have worked all through the war at unprecedented congestion of traffic ... over one old worn out line between here and Ashcroft, with obsolete radio equipment. [The] only improvement is the ones carried out by one of the staff who ... rebuilt and improved the old junk heap we were using for a transmitter, the same applies to government

telegraph lines north of Atlin into the Yukon. We have had to struggle, and I mean struggle, along over an old line that is made of No. 6 steel wire, unable to send except by hand … which taxes our strength to the utmost. This building [that] has been here for years is drafty, cold and filthy, poorly lighted, poorly heated and keeps us busy killing flies that come through the cracks in the windows and doors. Many stables in the country are warmer and just as clean.[13]

One wonders how the bush operators, who lived in unheated, unlit, draughty, fly- and mosquito-infested cabins, would have responded to the complaints of this latter-day operator. A few of those old-timers were still working on the Yukon Telegraph, but their time was growing short.

CHAPTER 18

Abandoned: 1936–52

The Hazelton–Telegraph Creek section was not the first segment of the Yukon Telegraph to be abandoned. Four years earlier, in 1931, the 95 miles of wire between Dawson City and Boundary, which provided a connection to the Alaska system, had been closed, although a telephone line to Forty Mile was maintained for the use of the RCMP. Earlier, a portion of the Prince Rupert branch had been transferred to the Grand Trunk Pacific Railway (now part of the Canadian National Railway), and sections of the line south of Hazelton had been incorporated into other government divisions or railway systems, or sold to the British Columbia Telephone Company. However, these were all peripheral changes that did not affect the operation of the main line from Dawson City to Ashcroft. With the closing of the Hazelton–Telegraph Creek section, this continuity was severed, as messages to and from the north were thereafter relayed by radio.

Closing the line and abandoning the stations also discouraged travellers from using the Telegraph Trail. Without the convenience and security of the line cabins, and the largesse of the telegraph men, travel became nearly impossible for all but the most experienced and self-sufficient. Even those who employed pack animals, or were skilled at living in the bush, found the journey more difficult and dangerous.

For a while the cabins remained to provide shelter, but eventually, under unrelieved snow loads, the roofs collapsed, allowing decay to set in. The trail, no longer maintained, quickly became overgrown by willow and blocked by blowdowns. Bridges that washed away were not replaced, and the tramlines at the larger rivers fell into disrepair. The telegraph poles rotted or were pulled down by trees falling on the wire, which became entangled in the brush. Hunting outfitters, trappers, and Native peoples who wanted to continue using the trail now had to keep it clear themselves. Little if any thought had been given to the moose and caribou, whose antlers became entangled in the wire, and to other animals, including horses, whose legs could become ensnared.

The telegraph men who found themselves out of work were a mixed lot, but most were older, long-time employees. Dumped into the fickle, depressed economy of the 1930s, their chances for employment were not good. Some drifted away to look elsewhere for work; others retired. It is not clear what government retirement benefits were available. Some years earlier there had been a program for telegraph workers, but it had been discontinued, replaced by a system the retirees could buy into. The cost, however, seems to have been prohibitive for many of the men, and the benefits meagre.

Some of the men who had lived in the bush for years were mentally unprepared for a steady diet of civilization. They were not disposed to enter into town life, choosing instead to continue to live away from people. C.W. Mitchell (whose letter to Louis LeBourdais was quoted in Chapter 12) found a cabin two miles from the nearest neighbour, where he was perfectly content to have as his closest friends the wild birds and animals.

The Department of Public Works continued to operate the remaining wilderness section, but with only two linemen's stations to cover the 220 miles of wire between Telegraph Creek and Atlin. Both stations were located on the old Teslin Trail, one on the Shesley River, 45 miles north of Telegraph Creek, and the other on the Nahlin River about halfway to Atlin. The lineman at Nahlin, in particular, had a great distance of line to patrol and maintain, more than 50 miles. Shesley was staffed by a lineman and his wife;

*Lineman John Sutherland on the roof at Nahlin Station in 1940
shortly before the line to Atlin was shut down.*

Nahlin was occupied by a single lineman, Richard Landry, whom
we have previously met (see Chapter 16).

After Echo Lake, Landry found Nahlin, situated "in a lovely spot"
on the river, much more to his liking, but it was a lonely post. He
could go for months in the winter without seeing another human,
especially after the mail run was discontinued. He did have an
occasional visitor, like Slim Williams in 1933, and again in 1939 with
John Logan on their trip to promote the Alaska Highway.

When Landry was transferred to Nahlin, his replacement at Echo
Lake was John Sutherland. And in the summer of 1940, when he went
on leave, it was John Sutherland who once again appeared at his
cabin door to take over. After Echo Lake was shut down, Sutherland
had spent the intervening five years trapping, with moderate success.
He was only too happy to be rehired by the telegraph.

When Landry returned from his leave, Sutherland was sent to Atlin. On his way out he was instructed to repair a break two miles before the Pike River cabin. A bull moose had managed to get his antlers hooked in the wire, and with his great weight and strength the brute had just kept pulling, taking down three poles and a half-mile of wire, until he was freed when an old splice broke. There does not seem to have been much urgency to repair the line, which by this time was used only to transmit messages to and from Telegraph Creek, and then only when the wireless tower, erected there in 1935, was not functioning for one reason or another.

Sutherland spent the winter of 1940–41 in Atlin. Several years earlier an "emergency radio-telegraph station" had been set up for transmission to Telegraph Creek.[1] Radio operator Ted Smith was in the process of replacing the emergency set-up with a more permanent system, and Sutherland was to assist him. He had to climb the tallest flagpole in town to attach the antenna, and when messages started to come in he served as a "glorified radiogram messenger boy."[2] He also became an enthusiastic participant in town activities, enlisting to take a part in a local theatre production. Like Guy Lawrence, Sutherland genuinely liked to be with people,

John Sutherland appeared in a Globe Theatre play in 1940. He is the tall policeman in the back.

yet he could spend months alone on a trapline or in an isolated lineman's cabin.

In the spring he went with another lineman to check the wire to the north. The two had intended to stay at a refuge cabin 15 miles from town, but they found it occupied by a French-Canadian farmer who had cultivated nearby fields to establish a truck garden. Technically the cabin was the property of the telegraph, but they did not wish to disturb him, so they set up their tent nearby.

The government continued to maintain the line north of Atlin, but there was no point in working on the southern section. It was closed, and the cabins, with all their contents in place, were turned over to the Indian Commission. Landry was transferred to Whitehorse; Sutherland was once again unemployed. Since 1926, when he entered the country by snowshoeing more than 400 miles to Dease Lake, he had spent 15 years either working for the Yukon Telegraph or living in a cabin trapping and hunting. As a sign of the changing times, he left the north on an airplane. He would not return for 30 years.[3]

Trail Travellers in the 1940s

The southern district of the Yukon Telegraph line had been abandoned, but the trail between cabins continued to be used by a few travellers. One whose experiences are worth retelling is Archie Hunter, who was a witness to what was happening around Telegraph Creek during and after the war years.

A career employee of the Hudson's Bay Company (HBC), Hunter was assigned to the company's store at Telegraph Creek in 1941. To get to his new post he sailed with his family on the *Princess Louise* from Vancouver up the Inside Passage to Wrangell. Because of the threat of Japanese submarines, the ship was escorted by Canadian corvettes and then by the U.S. Coast Guard.[4]

At Wrangell the Hunters were joined for the trip up the Stikine by a detachment of 50 U.S. Army engineers, on their way to work on the Alaska Highway. Telegraph Creek still served as a depot for supplies going to the Watson Lake airport and to support construction of the highway.

Wires in the Wilderness

In Vancouver, Hunter had been told that Telegraph Creek was a choice assignment, with a first-rate hotel that featured a toilet with running water. Upon arrival he was introduced to this toilet; the water was provided by a creek that had been diverted through the outside privy.

His initial impression of his new post was not promising. The hotel, built in 1914, was a fire trap, and the waiter presiding over its restaurant managed to get both his thumbs into the soup. The fellow who leased the hotel from the HBC was an occasional prospector who apparently wasn't much of a businessman. Once, when he was hired as a guide at $6 a day, he employed two women to fill in for him while he was gone—at $7 a day each. Hunter was not impressed with Telegraph Creek and did not intend to stay more than two years, but for some reason he changed his mind, stayed for 16 years, "and enjoyed every minute."[5]

The HBC let him set up a big-game hunting and guiding business as long as it did not interfere with his company duties. He used a ranch 18 miles from Telegraph Creek as a base camp, where he kept his string of horses. Although the store remained his main occupation, he occasionally was able to get away for hunting trips or just to camp out. On one occasion he flew to Atlin to fetch a herd of 30 horses that had been brought down the Telegraph Trail from the new Alaska Highway.

The horses were corralled at a mink ranch 15 miles south of town, not far from the old Pike River cabin. From there Hunter and his crew started on the trail for Telegraph Creek. Although the line had been closed for only a few years, the trail was already showing signs of neglect. It was overgrown, and many of the bridges had been washed out. The streams that normally could have been forded were in full flood, transformed into raging torrents, requiring the party to detour upstream to find suitable crossing places. One of the most difficult sections was up and over Nakina Summit, where the horses became mired in belly-deep snow. In all they were forced to travel more than 80 miles farther than anticipated. Hunter and his horses made it to Telegraph Creek, but the trip had been more difficult than expected.

The Hunters became good friends with Agnes and George Ball, operators of the Diamond B Ranch across the river from Glenora. Normally, when the Balls needed new horses they brought them up the river by barge to the ranch. One year they decided to try a different route, bringing in a new batch from Hazelton over the Telegraph Trail. They were in for an unexpected experience.

To help pay the expenses of the trip, the Balls allowed three "dudes" to accompany the six Native wranglers, with the whole outfit under the care of Henry Gleisen, a Tahltan from Telegraph Creek. The three dudes were W.D. Smith, the MLA representing the enormous constituency of Atlin; Miss Jean Davidson; and Janet Patterson, the 16-year-old daughter of R.M. Patterson, the well-known wilderness adventurer who was a friend of the Balls.[6]

The party left Kispiox with 62 horses on July 8. As there were no longer any line cabins to report their progress, nothing was heard about them for weeks. They had estimated that it would take 30 days to cover the 330 miles, so after a month they were considered overdue. Planes were sent to search for them, without success, and headlines began to appear in the Vancouver and Victoria papers: "Party Missing in the Wilds of Northern B.C."

They were having trouble. Information about the trail proved to be misleading and inaccurate, and as the trail was no longer maintained, they lost much time going around blowdowns and other obstructions. The weather was horrid and bridges were out. Horses were lost fording rivers; others fell victim to cliffs and muskegs. The party was not always able to find game, and provisions ran low.

Janet Patterson kept a diary of the trip. She recorded that on July 23 the party reached Fifth Cabin—barely 100 miles travelled in 16 days. From Fifth they left the Telegraph Trail for the Ashcroft Trail, crossing Groundhog Mountain in snow on August 1. By this point they had lost seven horses, so were down to 55. They ascended other passes in freezing rain and fog and had to build a raft to cross the Klappan River. Near the end of the trip, as Janet recorded in her diary, the food supply was getting low:

Sixteen-year-old Janet Patterson in 1946, ready to set off with a party of wranglers driving a herd of horses over the abandoned and overgrown Telegraph Trail from Hazelton to Telegraph Creek.

August 14th—Fed up with everything today—want Daddy.

August 17th—The going is better but we are out of meat again. No more flour or baking powder, and we ate what we called slumgullion: cheese, macaroni and everything all thrown into the same pot.

August 18th—We now have 39 horses. Finished the coffee.

August 19th—No lunches today and only rice for breakfast. Used the last of the sugar ... Had a cheese slumgullion and a bath—a freezing dip in a creek. Ate the last of the bannock.

August 20th—Rice and tea for breakfast. Now nothing in the grub box but barley and a little salt. 12 miles to Telegraph.[7]

Forty-four days instead of 30. Twenty-three horses lost. The Ball party had not met a human, Native or white, during the entire trip. The abandoned telegraph line was now truly a trail through wilderness.

Further evidence of the condition of the trail was provided a few years later by a party of geologists who were out to explore the Groundhog Coalfields. Their route from Hazelton followed the telegraph line to Fifth Cabin, then branched northward over Groundhog Pass, as the Ball party had done. The geologists found that some streams were still spanned by cable cars, but at other crossings all that remained were the abutments of washed-out bridges. The corduroy over boggy places had rotted, and the trail was badly blocked by windfalls and undergrowth. "The condition of the trail has changed so much that information from those who have not travelled it since 1936 may be badly misleading, however familiar they may have been with it previously."[8] The geologists also reported that many of the feed grounds, essential for travel with pack animals, had gone to weed and brush.

New Roads and Reorganization

Decaying, but not forgotten, the old Yukon Telegraph line, now the Telegraph Trail, remained in the minds of some never-say-die entrepreneurs and boards of trade. Even though the Alaska Highway had been completed and was open to commercial and private travel, there were still those who agitated for a route more beneficial to their interests. Occasionally they put forward a plan for a "Coastal Highway," which would follow or run parallel to the Telegraph Trail.

One such proposal was advanced in 1949 by the Associated Boards of Trade of Central British Columbia and the affiliated Chambers of Commerce of southeastern Alaska. They backed a plan to build a highway connecting Hazelton with Fairbanks, arguing that by following the telegraph for much of the way, the road could tie in the coastal towns (Stewart/Hyder, Juneau, etc.) and also provide access to the great Groundhog Coalfields and other rich mining areas. They called attention to "the mild coast temperatures which prevail in winter from Hazelton well toward Atlin, and the comparatively light snowfall." According to them, the route was not only ideal for a road, but also "possessed a grade suitable for railway construction all the way to the Alaska Highway at Jake's Corner and Whitehorse. [There would be] little rock work, few bridges, no swamps and only one major undertaking, that of crossing the 500-foot-wide canyon of the Stikine River."[9]

The reality of the minus 40° Celsius temperatures, the week-long storms, the 10-foot snow packs, and the dozens of streams to be crossed were all swept away in the enthusiasm for what some called "progress." Twenty years would pass before a highway was completed from south to north through British Columbia, and then only about 60 miles parallelled the telegraph line. The Cassiar Highway followed the river valleys to Dease Lake and Watson Lake, rather than the route toward Telegraph Creek and Atlin.

In 1950, in a reorganization of government agencies, the Department of Public Works relinquished administration of the Government Telegraph and Telephone Service to the Department of Transportation. The latter's management of the Yukon Telegraph lasted only a few years, until the remaining line between Atlin and Dawson was abandoned.

Both of these towns and Whitehorse had been connected to radio systems for long-distance transmissions. The Royal Canadian Corps of Signals—yes, the same outfit that tried to put the Yukon Telegraph out of business in 1925—had stations at Whitehorse and Dawson that were connected through Mayo to Edmonton. Atlin was connected to the Canadian National Telegraphs via Hazelton. The only question that remained was whether the settlements between the wireless stations—those along the Yukon River—continued to warrant a telegraph system. Their primary function for at least the past decade had been to service the riverboats: to monitor their progress, report problems, and send telegrams for passengers.

When a road was built connecting Dawson to Whitehorse, the riverboats were no longer needed to transport supplies to Dawson. By the summer of 1952 the major shipper, the White Pass and Yukon Transportation Company, had eliminated most of its boats and was running only one or two trips a week for the tourist business. These boats were equipped with radio phones and no longer relied upon the telegraph to report their progress.

The reduction in river traffic also contributed to a decline in the number of people living along the river. After the riverboats stopped running, only a handful of people remained between Selkirk and Dawson, and the community of Stewart soon lost its Hudson's Bay Company store and the White Pass office.

The amount of revenue generated by all the stations along the river had declined to less than $600 a month, far less than the cost of keeping the line operating. The continuing expense of the operators and linemen could no longer be justified.[10]

In a letter dated February 18, 1952, the Department of Transportation's division superintendent, D.C. Schubert, stated that the two radio systems could absorb the business of the land line. He, therefore, favoured turning the Atlin–Whitehorse section over to the Canadian National Telegraphs so that messages no longer had to be sent to Hazelton. The line from Whitehorse to Dawson would be transferred to the Signal Corps, and the communities in between would be served by radio phones.[11] In short, he was proposing to shut down the remaining land line in favour of a combination of radio stations, telephones, and radio phones.

At about the same time, discussions were underway to get the federal government out of the telegraph business in British Columbia. A study team was sent to examine the government's entire system in the province and to report on its condition and value. The survey included the main line and the branches in central B.C. that had been such an important part of the Yukon Telegraph and that had become positive revenue generators. The study team wasn't much interested in the line in the north, which by that time was a minor part of the system. At the last minute, someone realized the omission and insisted that the Atlin station submit an inventory.[12]

Ottawa agreed to sell portions of the system to the Canadian National Telegraphs and to B.C. Telephone, with each paying $750,000.[13] The line in the Yukon, including the 30-mile B.C. portion between Atlin and the Yukon border, was simply abandoned. The assets were turned over to the Crown Assets Disposal Corporation to be sold as surplus. These assets, described as "approx. 663 miles of galvanized wire … and approx. 15,450 insulators, sideblocks and poles," were sold to the Yukon Telephone Company.[14] Most of the wire, insulators, side blocks, and poles remain in the bush to this day.

Even though the government telegraph system had never made money, it had not cost all that much considering the service it had provided over many years, including free communication for government offices. A list of expenses and revenues of the British Columbia and Yukon land lines from 1899 to 1951 shows that through all those years the difference between costs and revenue was about $5 million, or an average outlay of $100,000 per year. Deduct the $1.5 million received from its sale, and the annual cost is further reduced. The government had built a successful operation in the southern and central parts of the province, and now private companies would reap the profits from it.

The Yukon Telegraph was dead; long live the Telegraph Trail.

CHAPTER 19

The Telegraph Trail after 1952

The Telegraph Trail conveniently breaks down into three distinct sections: the northern "river trail" between Atlin and Dawson City; the central "wilderness trail" between Atlin and Hazelton; and the southern "developed trail" between Hazelton and Ashcroft. I refer to this last section as the "developed trail" because portions have been re-established as hiking trails.

The River Trail

The river trail includes the main line along the Yukon River and Marsh Lake between Tagish and Dawson City, and the branch to Atlin.

North of Tagish the "trail" follows the shoreline of Marsh Lake, which feeds into the Yukon River, its chaperone the rest of the way to Dawson City. This section can hardly be called a trail because travel along the river is mostly by boat, which has precluded the development of a trail along the shore. And by boat is the best way to view the remnants of the telegraph line. Jennifer Voss's *Klondike Trail*, a guide to paddling the river, provides excellent maps that show the location of most of the line.[1] Since river travel by canoe, kayak, and other watercraft is popular, and there are frequent camping spots, it is likely that the portions of line closest to the riverbank have been discovered and the insulators "liberated." There are, however, some cut-offs that deviate a mile or two from the river that warrant further investigation. But please don't remove the insulators.[2]

The Atlin branch goes cross-country from Tagish a short distance and then follows Little Atlin and Atlin lakes. The trail passes through isolated Crown lands, with a few intrusions onto private land and agricultural leases. The sections I have explored are heavily overgrown and show no evidence of recent travel, other than by moose, caribou, and the horses of a local outfitter. There are abundant decrepit poles with hanging wire, and lots of wire along the ground that poses hazards to large animals. Some local people, concerned for the safety of the woodland caribou, have been working to have the wire removed.

The Wilderness Trail

The wilderness between Hazelton and Atlin is the area that has been most associated with the Telegraph Trail. It is further divided into two parts: Hazelton to Telegraph Creek, and Telegraph Creek to Atlin. The trail through the first part, abandoned now for almost 70 years, was little travelled and quickly deteriorated. The Telegraph Creek–Atlin section would have suffered a similar fate had it not been for big-game outfitters and trappers who kept sections cleared, and for Native people who used it to travel between their camps and from one community to another. When a Tlingit man from Atlin married a Tahltan woman, whole families walked the 220-mile trail to get to the ceremony in Telegraph Creek.[3] There was also the occasional recreational or "stunt" traveller.

Stanley Upton, a 30-year-old carpenter from California, set out on horseback in 1958 with three companions on a journey from his home state to Mount McKinley (Denali) in Alaska. The other men dropped out before reaching the Canadian border. Undeterred, Upton rode on alone, reaching Kispiox, where the roadway ended and the Telegraph Trail began. He described what followed as the worst part of his trip: "The trail often dwindling to nothing in swamps, and was barred constantly by deadfalls," through which he had to hack his way. He reported that the trail was so badly overgrown in places that the only way he could find it was to trace the line of the old telegraph wire. Because of the blowdowns, which he had to find a way around, he felt he could have hiked the trail from Hazelton to Telegraph Creek without the horse in a third less time (as a Native woman had done the year before). Of course, he would have had to carry all his camping equipment and food on his back, unless he was adept at living off the land. After 62 days he arrived in Atlin, where he spent the winter before continuing his journey the following June.[4]

Through the 1960s and 1970s there were few reports of activity until the winter of 1978, when a venturesome group of four men from Atlin revved up their skidoos to ride to Telegraph Creek. The trip was possible only after they had spent several weeks of hard work clearing the trail and flying in drums of gasoline to refuel the machines. During their six-day adventure the men camped at some of the old line cabins. At Nakina a trapper hosted them, although it is not clear if he was using the telegraph cabin, and at Nahlin they found the building "in fair shape." The last leg beyond Shesley was difficult because they were running out of snow. The trip was so satisfying, the men said, that someday they might do it by dogsled.[5]

Shesley Free Mike

At about the same time the ski-dooers were on the trail, a man whom most people tried to avoid began roaming the area. Michael Oros, known as Crazy Mike or Shesley Free Mike, was both admired and feared: admired for his exceptional wilderness skills; feared because he was weird and considered dangerous. He was one of the young Americans who had come north to avoid the Vietnam War draft. Initially he settled in Alaska, then sought asylum in Canada, looking for a place where he could pursue an independent lifestyle, one that suited his definition of freedom. He found his refuge in northwestern British Columbia.[6]

He travelled through the area establishing his domain, which he came to believe was his alone. It extended over a large region, from Telegraph Creek to Teslin Lake and westward as far as Atlin. Cutting right through the middle was the Telegraph Trail, which he used frequently to move between his several camps.

In time Oros developed survival skills that even his detractors admired. Seldom had there been a white man who learned to live in the bush for as long as he did during all seasons. But there was a price to be paid for his freedom in the wild, a tragic cost both to himself and to others.

While still in the U.S., Oros had been assessed as suffering from paranoid delusions, and the isolation of the bush intensified his conviction that "they" were out to get him. The "sneak arounds," as he called them, were always hiding, waiting to poison and drug him. He became suspicious of anyone who entered his space and often threatened intruders, which earned him the name "Crazy Mike." He believed that he had the right to defend his freedom by any means, a right that included raiding his neighbours' cabins.

Oros established one of his camps on the Shesley River not far from the site of the old Shesley telegraph station, which accounts for his other name, "Shesley Free Mike." He built an unusual octagonal-shaped cabin less than a mile from the base camp of Fletcher Day, the veteran outfitter whose stepfather had come north seeking gold in 1898. Day had helped Oros get started by employing him around his camp, but Oros later repaid him by trapping beaver out of season on Day's trapline. When Day reported Oros to the

Crazy Mike Oros, who terrorized people along a section of the Telegraph Trail in the 1980s, and trapper Gunter Lishy, whom he murdered.

wardens, he made a lifelong enemy. Crazy Mike threatened to kill him, posting notices of his intention on trees in the area.

Oros occasionally travelled to nearby towns to work for cash. Some people in Atlin remember seeing him on the road hitching a ride; they were happiest when he was heading out of town. Mostly he stayed in his territory and lived off the land by hunting and fishing. He was also suspected of being responsible for plundering several cabins, including Fletcher Day's base camp, but there were never any witnesses or sufficient evidence to lay charges.

In 1981 Oros built another camp at Hutsigola Lake, just south of Teslin Lake. When Gunter Lishy, a trapper from Atlin, moved into the area and started to build a cabin nearby, Crazy Mike's paranoia intensified. He stalked Lishy, shot him in the back, and buried the body near the lake in a shallow grave that he covered with thick moss.

When Lishy did not return to a prearranged pickup point, the pilot alerted the RCMP. The police suspected Crazy Mike, and after a search of his cabin uncovered much of Lishy's gear, he was taken into custody. However, they were unable to find the body, and without a corpse it would have been next to impossible to convict Oros of murder. In order to detain him, the RCMP laid charges for several lesser infractions, and he was remanded for psychological evaluation. Oros was in jail, in hospital, or free on bail for more than five months, until a judge finally decided that he was not guilty and released him to return to his life in the bush. Those who knew Oros, especially the police, were convinced that he had killed Lishy and that it was just a matter of time and circumstance until he killed again.

Three years passed and Shesley Free Mike continued to survive alone in the wilderness and to plunder isolated cabins with impunity, all the while nursing his demons and fear of intruders. His paranoia came to dominate his life. He knew "they" were out there, and he spent most of his days scouring the bush, looking for signs of his tormentors, but never finding any.

He spent part of the winter of 1984–85 living in a vacant vacation cabin south of the village of Teslin, not far from Teslin Lake. After carting off most of the cabin's contents to his camp at Hutsigola

Lake, he used the inside of the building to butcher the game he killed during the winter. When the owners returned in early spring and discovered the devastation, they reported it to the police. Since Oros was the only one who wintered in the area, he was the prime suspect.

The RCMP sent a plane to look for him. The pilot spotted him, but when Oros saw the plane he fired a shot at it. This further convinced the police that he had plundered the cabin and that he had gone off the deep end. They believed he would not surrender without a fight, so they brought in the RCMP's Emergency Response Team to capture Oros. When he was spotted on the Teslin Lake ice, a helicopter went out with two teams of three men. One team was landed ahead of him, the other behind, planning to cut him off before he could get into the deep bush, where he might lead them on a longer and more perilous pursuit.

The teams were not quick enough. Oros was able to get off the lake and into the bush. He circled behind one of the groups and shot officer Michael Buday dead, but when he attempted to shoot a second officer, his bullet misfired and he himself was killed. Thus ended the life of a paranoid loner whose quest for complete freedom had resulted only in his death and the death of two other men. Several months later an RCMP constable stumbled across the grave of Gunter Lishy, thus ending the mystery of his death.

Shesley Free Mike's reign of terror over people who ventured into his domain was finally over, and the dangers of the area he had occupied so ominously, including the Telegraph Trail, reverted to the old hazards of weather and an occasional grizzly. But there are people today who still shudder when they recall the eerie and frightening feeling "that he was watching us from the bush."[7]Others reported their sense of dread when they knew that Oros was about. Christoph Dietzfelbinger and Irene Weiland, two hikers from Germany who were on the trail in the summer of 1984, the year before Crazy Mike was killed, spent some time with Fletcher Day at his Shesley River camp. When asked if they had ventured out to look at Oros's unusual eight-sided cabin, they replied: "Oh, no, we didn't want to go anywhere near his place."[8]

The Forgotten Trail

The German couple is typical of the hikers attracted to the wilderness trail. Young, fit, and adventurous, most are from Europe rather than Canada or the United States. Perhaps North Americans have shown so little interest because there are so many other peopleless places available to them, locations that are more convenient to get to, such as the Pacific Crest Trail in the United States. One exception to the dominance of European hikers was Larry Pynn, a *Vancouver Sun* journalist, who in 1992 set out on the Teslin Trail to gather information for a book, *The Forgotten Trail*.[9] Although he travelled on only a short portion of the Telegraph Trail, he provided a valuable description, and his experience illustrates some of the difficulties of travel in this wilderness area.

Pynn took the usual route by boat from Wrangell up the Stikine River to Telegraph Creek, which he described as a "virtual ghost town [of a] few dozen houses, most of them empty and ramshackle … arranged in a hodgepodge." There he hooked up with Fletcher Day, who was packing supplies to his hunting camps and agreed to take Pynn part of the way.

Day's party took the trail along the Tahltan River that joined the combined Teslin and Telegraph trails at a place called Saloon, where, during the 1898 rush to the gold fields, a fellow sold shots of rum to the thirsty stampeders. Pynn reported that the trail north of Saloon varied greatly, from steep hillsides with rock slides to swampy marshes. The horses were frequently halted by deadfalls, the result of heavy snows during the previous winter.

Fletcher Day's base camp at the Shesley River contained many of the comforts of civilization. It had an "airstrip, generator, cook house and running water," as well as individual cabins for his rich, mostly foreign, trophy hunters. Anticipating these comforts, Day's crew and Pynn found their euphoria abruptly deflated when they discovered that the main lodge had been ravaged by a grizzly. The damage to the interior was beyond the maliciousness of what a gang of vandals could have accomplished. Food was strewn everywhere in the kitchen, a foam mattress had been ripped apart, and the windows were smashed out.

After the cleanup, Pynn ventured on a side trail to the site of Shesley Free Mike's cabin. "Not just any log cabin, mind you," he wrote. "Built as an octagon—hand-peeled logs chinked with moss, the roof an intricate tapestry of interlocking pieces—the cabin is among the most elaborate you could find in the Canadian North." The precision of the work in such a remote area suggested to Pynn the work of a deranged builder, certainly an accurate assessment of Oros.

Continuing north on the Telegraph (Teslin) Trail, the party stopped at one of the old refuge cabins, which was still standing because it had an asphalt roof covering; those with roofs of dirt over logs had long since collapsed. Day reported that the other reminder of the telegraph line, the wire, was a menace for animals, both wild and domestic. It became entangled in his horses' feet and had to be carefully unwound. It also caused problems for moose and caribou, and he added that he had seen a swiftly fleeing grouse cut in half when it hit the wire.

Pynn described the trail as "nothing more than a foot-deep trench engulfed on both sides by head-high willows and dwarf birch." He passed through swampy areas where the corduroy logs were in amazingly good condition, followed by places where the horses sank into mud up to their bellies.

Day and Pynn parted company at the Koskin River crossing, south of where the trail crosses the Nahlin River. Without a horse, Pynn now had to carry his heavy pack. He reported that the trail soon deteriorated even more, clogged with blowdowns that required him to make repeated detours through the brush. Through muskegs he lost the trail entirely, getting back on track only after finding the old telegraph poles and wire. Along the way he "claim[ed] a heavy white porcelain insulator as a souvenir."

At the Nahlin River, Pynn came upon the old telegraph cabin that had been preserved over the years by trappers, and where the current occupants left a room open for travellers. Beyond, he crossed the Nahlin on the old cable platform and shortly thereafter reached the junction where the Telegraph Trail diverges to the northwest. He took the historic Teslin Trail northward toward Teslin Lake and the Klondike.

On his own, Pynn became disillusioned with his adventure within a couple of days and decided that further travel was impossible. He headed back, seeking a way out of the wilderness. At this point, still with sufficient provisions, he might have hiked back to Telegraph Creek or at least to Day's camp at Shesley. Instead, he elected to wait to be rescued. For days he searched the sky for a plane to signal, but was unable to attract the attention of the few that flew over. Discouraged, he activated an Emergency Locator Transmitter (ELT), a device normally used only by downed aircraft. This action set in motion a series of costly and inconvenient rescue operations. Pynn was eventually found and flown out to Atlin. Although he expressed "deep regret," Pynn did not admit any error in setting off the transmitter, nor did he seem overly concerned about his inappropriate action.

Pynn's failure was due in part to his poor preparation and lack of knowledge of the conditions he would face. At the same time that he was having problems, there was another man not far away who was better prepared. Bart deHaas, from the Netherlands, has made numerous hikes in northern British Columbia, solo and as a wilderness guide for small groups. He made his first hike on the Telegraph Trail from Atlin to Telegraph Creek and beyond in 1989. It was not a pleasant introduction to the trail, as he was lost on several occasions, but eventually, after 40 days, he made it to Telegraph Creek. As of 2003 he had hiked this section at least eight times.

DeHaas, describing one of his solo hikes from Atlin, told of easy walking for several days, followed by a nondescript morass of mud and willow thickets. At one place, hanging wire guided his way; at another, nothing was left of the track and he had to use a compass. He came upon a slash in a tree with the inscription "Gunter Lishy, July 8, 1980," which marked a trapline of the man murdered by Mike Oros.

On his hikes he has been helped by the generosity of several of the outfitters who have cabins on the line, and he appreciates their work clearing the trail. He has encountered many animals and carries a rifle he uses for potshooting small game

Dutch hikers ford the icy waters of the Nahlin River on their 25-day adventure from Atlin to Telegraph Creek in 2001.

(grouse and rabbits) to supplement his provisions. On one occasion, however, he used it to try to ward off the advances of a grizzly.

A young adult Grizzly, about three years old, is following me at a distance of 40 to 50 meters (120 feet). Continuously I keep an eye on the bear. Late in the afternoon I have to get rid of him, I cannot pitch my tent with a bear in the neighbourhood. A gunshot in the air doesn't help, imperturbably the bear keeps following me. After some time the bear disappears in the fog. It is time to look for a campsite, it is getting dark. In the pattering rain and whistling storm I pitch my tent and numbed with cold and wet I go into my sleeping bag. Yet once I look through the mosquito netting and look straight into the eyes of the bear. Now I become mad, another gunshot in the air out of my tent, but the bear is not even surprised. I met many bears in my life, but this is the queerest bear I ever met. I forget all the "Bear rules" and start shouting and abusing. My terrifying terms of abuse frighten the bear and he darts off. I didn't sleep well that night.[10]

On another occasion he met two wolves and found himself staring into the yellow eyes of a big black one. Growling, the two advanced on him, but then disappeared into the bush.

DeHaas now operates Taku Adventures, which takes small groups, mostly Dutch adventurers, on trips through the B.C. wilderness. Each year he guides one or two treks from Atlin to Telegraph Creek. Before starting out, the group assembles in Atlin for several days of training in wilderness survival skills: first aid, medicinal and edible herbs, compass and map orienting, animal tracking and bear behaviour, and how to make a fire without matches. The participants are also instructed in the need to respect nature and the art of "leave no trace" hiking.

The trip takes about 24 days, with one resupply midway by floatplane. The Europeans are astonished to find cabins along the way, untouched by anything but time. "It was like going back in history, seeing some of those abandoned log cabins," wrote one participant. "You would see the dog sled standing up against the cabin wall, pots hanging on the walls, the bed still there."[11]

Wilderness travel is a growing part of the region's appeal to tourists. Presently, recreational use of the wilderness portion of the Telegraph Trail is limited to deHaas's groups and to rare independent travellers.

The Telegraph Trail and the Forest Service

In British Columbia, the trail passes through no fewer than eight Forest Service districts. Most have recognized the trail in their management plans, some going so far as to refer to it as a "Heritage Trail." It is not clear what this label signifies, or what protection it provides the trail, if any. Apparently only a *designated* heritage trail is protected, such as the Nuxalk–Carrier Grease Trail (the Alexander Mackenzie Heritage Trail), which intersects the Telegraph Trail north of Quesnel.

Even though some of the management plans note the historic significance of the trail and may call for preserving a 200-metre corridor, the loopholes available to loggers and other business interests are so numerous as to render the requirement little more than wishful thinking. I learned that in one district loggers were told to avoid cutting over the trail "if possible," and to leave a corridor. When I asked who determines the location of the trail that the loggers were being asked to avoid, the answer of one official was: "The loggers." No Forest Service personnel were assigned to flag the route. The danger, of course, is that unregulated logging practices will obliterate the trail to the extent that it will lose its historic identity, making it less appealing for recreational travel. Already sections of the trail have been clear-cut. Nevertheless, some of the Forest Service districts have accumulated valuable information on the location and condition of the trail, which could contribute to developing more comprehensive plans for its preservation.

In 1995, personnel of the Kalum Forest District carried out a helicopter survey of the northern part of their district to locate the physical remains of the Telegraph Trail.[12] The area they inspected comprised the middle third of the Hazelton–Telegraph Creek section, from Damdochax Lake (approximately 120 miles from Hazelton) to Echo Lake (110 miles farther). The survey provides a look at this remote section of line 60 years after it was abandoned.

As they flew over the area, they could clearly see in wooded sections "a narrow cutline through the trees." The trail was difficult to locate only where it had been burned over or where it was above treeline. Landing at Damdochax Lake, the foresters found that the refuge cabin midway between Fifth and Sixth cabins had been restored and was being used by a guide/outfitter to house his guests. "Messages and dates from the time when the telegraph line was in operation are still readable on the walls of the cabin."

From the air, they saw a large cleared area and two collapsed cabins at Sixth Cabin. At the mouth of Muckaboo Creek, the site of the remains of refuge cabin 6½, the foresters found telegraph wire, old bottles and jars, and enamel cooking pots. On a large tree blaze was written in pencil, and still partially legible: "1935, May 12, L. Johnson."

At Seventh Cabin they identified two collapsed cabins and a third smaller building that was still standing. Farther on, the line became more difficult to follow from the air because of the open area approaching Nass Summit. Landing at Eighth Cabin, they found the remains of four buildings, including the main cabin, which had completely collapsed. In addition to the usual detritus, they found old batteries and radio tubes, a rifle stock, and a decorative cast-iron stove door with a patent date of 1893. (A photograph taken 20 years earlier by another helicopter party shows Eighth Cabin's walls upright, but the roof in a state of advanced decay, heralding imminent ruin.[13])

The survey showed that most parts of the trail can still be traced from the air and that there are sufficient physical remains to determine the location of many of the stations and refuges. On the ground there is additional evidence (wire, insulators, decaying poles), as well as artifacts around the stations.

The next station north of the area surveyed is the one at Echo Lake, located just off the Cassiar Highway. The spot is marked by an historic plaque beside the highway. Most of the buildings at Echo Lake collapsed many years ago, victims of the water rising behind a beaver dam.[14]

In 1975 these men landed by helicopter at Eighth Cabin, where they found a box of records from the long-deserted telegraph station.

No portion of the wilderness trail has as yet been preserved for recreational use, although a few years ago an ambitious proposal was put forward. The Dease Lake Chamber of Commerce, reckoning that the Telegraph Trail could attract adventure-traveller dollars, sponsored a study of the section between the Cassiar Highway and Atlin. Initial research was done in 1987 and expanded into a detailed report in 1997.

The result was a plan to create a trail suitable for foot travellers, including designated campsites and shelters. The researchers estimated the cost of brushing out the trail, removing blowdowns, and bridging swampy sections. They also suggested a variety of ways to cross the many streams along the trail. It was an excellent report and plan, but with quite a price tag. The estimated cost of the project was more than $800,000, including the cabins. For the time being it has been put on the back burner.

The Developed Trail

The southern section from Ashcroft to Hazelton, with one notable exception, was originally built along existing roads and trails, or was later overrun by the construction of highways and railways. From Ashcroft to Quesnel the line followed the Cariboo Road, and after the Grand Trunk Pacific Railway was built, more of the line was absorbed into the railway/highway vortex. The only sizeable section that survives to be identified and reclaimed is between Quesnel and Fort Fraser.

This section is notable because it is really three trails in one. Local Natives first used a path through the area. Then the Collins Overland Telegraph generally followed their route when stringing wire in 1866. The Collins route in turn became a guide for the location of the Yukon Telegraph.

When telegraph surveyors are laying out lines, they usually select the most direct route, the one that requires the fewest number of poles and least amount of wire. Portions of this telegraph line are an exception. It follows a more serpentine course along the tops of eskers, flowing with the land. Perhaps this is the area Hamlin Garland had in mind when he rhapsodized about the differences between trails made by Natives and those manufactured by the practical white men. The latter tried to go directly over the mountains and through the swamps; the Natives made trails that undulated, following the natural, rhythmic contours of the earth. This resulted in longer trails, but ones less difficult to travel and less disturbing to the senses.

This section is also unique because it has remained virtually undisturbed. Shortly after the Collins operation was shut down, the Quesnel–Hazelton line was abandoned, but the linemen's trail continued to be used and grew into a wagon road. To this day a portion is called the Telegraph Trail Road. Local lore has it that parts of the old road can still be identified by the ruts gouged by the wagons and by pieces of 130-year-old wire that remain from the Collins Overland. These artifacts can still be found because the wagon road never grew into a major thoroughfare. It was superseded, after the Grand Trunk Pacific Railway was built, by the road between Quesnel and Prince George.

Included in the Quesnel–Fort Fraser section are two marked trails: the Hogsback Lake Trail, and a 60-mile footpath cleared by the Telegraph Trail Preservation Society. The Hogsback Lake Trail, a "designated recreation trail" developed by the Vanderhoof District Forest Service, starts at the Hogsback Lake campground (25 kilometres south of Vanderhoof) off the Blackwater Road and goes 10 kilometres south. It is a good example of a Native trail in that it follows the winding eskers above the lake.

The Telegraph Trail Preservation Society has a more ambitious goal. For two decades this group of volunteers has been working to develop the trail north of Quesnel. With limited resources, they have so far marked the trail from a point 14 kilometres north of Quesnel to Bobtail Lake.

The group maintains that logging is the main threat to the survival and integrity of the trail, and although it tries to work cooperatively with the Forest Service, at times differences occur. In 1988 a particularly contentious skirmish developed over a clear-cut logging operation. The Forest Service argued that the trail would still be there after logging, only in a different form. Dwight Dodge, a lifelong explorer of the trail and a leading spirit in forming the preservation society, objected. He admitted that the trail would

*The Hogsback Lake Trail, a section of the
Telegraph Trail south of Vanderhoof.*

still be there on the ground, "but it's not going to be the Telegraph Trail. You need the path through the mature timber; otherwise it's just going to be a path through a clear-cut. A person might as well walk on the highway."[15]

Other programs have been developed for re-establishing sections of the trail. The Kispiox First Nation and the Iskut First Nation have initiated projects, and a high school group from Smithers has been working on a section of trail north of First Cabin.

Summing up

All of these projects to create new life and purpose for the trail will help to preserve the memory of the role played by the Yukon Telegraph in the history of British Columbia, the Yukon, and the nation. Eventually, as knowledge of the trail increases, additional sections will be considered for development for recreational use. The trail would seem to be a natural for inclusion in the Trans Canada Trail system, which has generated so much interest and pride as a symbol of the country's size and diversity.

And yet I pause in my enthusiasm for development and organization, for the involvement of government and the imposition of regulations. There is something to be said for keeping parts of the trail uncivilized, especially the central wilderness section. There is a place for a trail of hardship and discovery, for mucking around in a swamp looking for it, for wondering if the path one is following is it or just another animal trail. And then you spot it: a piece of wire hanging from a tree; a tilting, rotting pole; wire looping through the willow; or, best of all, a white porcelain insulator still attached to a wire or a tree. (It would be nice if it remained there so the next person who comes along can also experience that thrill).

If pressed to choose, I would look for a compromise: maximum information, minimum development. A marked trail with an informative trail guide, but no designated camping areas or shelters, and no bridges, except perhaps platform trams over the rivers most prone to high flooding.

The Telegraph Trail provides a link to the adventurous spirit of the Klondike gold rush. It evokes, in a time of rapid changes in the speed and breadth of communications networks, the memory of a simpler system of moving words and ideas, one that people could understand. There is also value in remembering a time and place when the rules of nature had to be observed, a world of wild and unpredictable things, of moose and grizzlies, and of seasons and survival under the most horrendous weather conditions. And there is the symbol of determination and dedication epitomized in the image of a solitary lineman setting out from his isolated, snow-covered cabin to repair a break and keep the telegraph line operating. For all these reasons, we should remember and preserve the Yukon Telegraph.

Epilogue

I'm a collector. During the course of my research I have accumulated a quantity of books, articles, photographs, maps, and interviews. I call this collection the Yukon Telegraph (Trail) Archives, and I would like to add to it. Eventually it will be offered to a suitable repository, probably the British Columbia Archives.

Until then, it is an archives-in-progress. Donations are solicited. If you have any stories, photographs, or other materials related to the Yukon Telegraph or Trail, I would like to add them to the collection. I can make copies and return the originals. Contact me c/o Heritage House Publishing Co. Ltd., #108-17665 66A Ave., Surrey, BC, V3S 2A7, or e-mail me at bmiller@atlin.net

Endnotes

Abbreviations:
- NAC   National Archives of Canada
- BCA   British Columbia Archives
- YA   Yukon Archives
- AHS   Archives of the Atlin Historical Society

Chapter 1

1. I have followed the practice of the time, expressing distances in miles and feet, rather than employing the cumbersome process of converting to kilometres.
2. Allen A. Wright, *Prelude to Bonanza: The Discovery and Exploration of the Yukon* (Sidney, B.C.: Gray's Publishing, 1977; reprint, Whitehorse: Studio North, 1992), 256ff.
3. George M. Dawson, *Report on an Exploration in the Yukon District, N.W.T. and Adjacent Northern Portion of British Columbia, 1887* (Montreal: Dawson Brothers, 1888; reprint, Whitehorse: Yukon [Historical] Museum Association, 1987), 183.
4. "Report of Inspector Constantine ..." in *Report of the Commissioner of the North-West Mounted Police, 1895* (Ottawa: King's Printer, 1896), 7.
5. *Dawson Daily News*, August 5, 1899. See also Ken S. Coates and William R. Morrison, *Land of the Midnight Sun: A History of the Yukon* (Edmonton: Hurtig, 1988).
6. Coates and Morrison, *Land of the Midnight Sun*, 99.
7. Ibid., 97.

8. Comptroller of the NWMP to [Minister of Public Works], December 29, 1898, NAC: RG 18, vol. 218, RCMP 1901, #789-814.

9. Robert Craig Brown, *Canada's National Policy 1883–1900: A Study in Canadian–American Relations* (Princeton: Princeton University Press, 1964), 300.

10. *Electric World* magazine, December 4, 1897.

11. David E. Richeson, "Canadian Government Involvement in Telegraphic Communications in Western Canada," *Journal of the West* 23, no. 4 (October 1984).

12. Canadian Telegraphic Historical Newspaper Accounts, January 16, 1899. Author's files.

13. Canada, Order-in-Council No. 405, March 13, 1899, NAC: RG 11, vol. 1269.

Chapter 2

1. [Generally] at the time only initials were used to identify the given names of males. Through scores of references, J.B. Charleson's complete name was never used and was only discovered on his death certificate in the Ontario Registry.

2. Marion Charleson, interview by Gina Smith, Ottawa, August 2001. Author's files.

3. *Dawson Daily News*, September 28, 1899.

4. Distances along the Yukon River are from Jennifer Voss, *Klondike Trail: The Complete Hiking and Paddling Guide* (Whitehorse: Lost Moose Publishing, 2001).

5. Roy Minter, *The White Pass: Gateway to the Klondike* (Toronto: McClelland and Stewart, 1987).

6. Charleson to Gobeil, June 11, 1899, NAC: RG 11, vol. 1297, #206083.

7. Tache to Charleson, May 10, 1899, NAC: RG 11, vol. 1280, #202213.

8. *Dawson Daily News*, September 28, 1899.

9. Charleson to Gobeil, June 11, 1899.

10. *Dawson Daily News*, September 28, 1899.

11. Ibid.

12. Charleson to Tarte, May 25, 1899, NAC: RG 11, vol. 1280, #202091.

13. Charleson to Gobeil, June 11, 1899.
14. Ibid.
15. Edward Spurr, "From the Coast to the Golden Klondike," *Outing Magazine*, September 1897.
16. Charleson to Gobeil, June 11, 1899.
17. *Victoria Colonist*, November 24, 1899.
18. Art Downs, *British Columbia–Yukon Sternwheel Days* (Surrey, B.C.: Heritage House, 1992), 148.
19. *Atlin Claim*, July 1, 1899.
20. There is confusion about the identity of the victim. J.C. Tache was the engineer, not Louis Tache, who may have been confused with Charles Tache, a young Department of Public Works employee assigned to Charleson as a payroll clerk. The newspaper article seems to have raised concern in Ottawa, as Charleson, responding to a query, emphatically states in his report of September 20, 1899, that J.C. Tache is in "perfect health." NAC: RG 11, vol. 1297.
21. *Dawson Daily News*, August 5, 1899.
22. Ricord's death was noted in Charleson's report of September 20, 1899.
23. Voss, *Klondike Trail*, 132.
24. David E. Richeson, "Canadian Government Involvement in Telegraphic Communications in Western Canada," *Journal of the West* 23, no. 4 (October 1984).
25. Charleson's progress report, September 7, 1899, NAC: RG 11, vol. 1294, #205256.
26. *Dawson Daily News*, September 28, 1899.
27. Ibid.
28. Gobeil to Laurier, July 25, 1899, NAC: Laurier Papers #35892. Tarte may have left Ottawa as a way of registering his opposition to the government's growing involvement in the Anglo-Boer War.
29. *Dawson Daily News*, March 9, 1902.
30. Ibid., September 28, 1899.
31. Ian Macdonald and Betty O'Keefe, *The Klondike's "Dear Little Nugget"* (Victoria: Horsdal & Schubart, 1996), in a September 1899 issue of the *Nugget*.
32. *Dawson Daily News*, September 28, 1899.

33. Congdon to Tarte, September 24, 1899, NAC: RG 11, vol. 1416. [Dated four days before completion of the line?]

34. *Atlin Claim*, October 7, 1899.

35. Ibid., March 10, 1900, quoting from Minister Tarte's report to the House of Commons, February 12, 1900.

Chapter 3

1. *Dawson Daily News*, October 2, 1899.

2. The boat sank near Selwyn, 150 miles upriver from Dawson City. The story of moving the stranded passengers and mail to Dawson City by dogsled was reported in the *Dawson Daily News*, October 8 to November 11, 1899.

3. Tom Perera, "History, Theory, and Construction of the Electric Telegraph," http://www.chss.montclair.edu/~pererat/pertel.htm.

4. List of "Provisions used at Big Salmon, November–1901," YA: Federal Government Records Miscellaneous, vol. 1085.

5. Edward Broderick, "The Little Cabin on Bobtail Lake," *Victoria Daily Colonist* "Islander," August 2, 1964.

6. A. Bowen Perry, Superintendent NWMP Yukon Territory to F. White, Comptroller NWMP, September 25, 1899, NAC: RG 18, vol. 218.

7. Ibid.

8. Perry to Officer Commanding NWMP Dawson, October 17, 1899, NAC: RG 18, vol. 218.

9. Z.T. Wood, Superintendent NWMP, to Constable Thorn, Skagway, September 21, 1899, NAC: RG 18, vol. 218.

10. *Atlin Claim*, February 3, 1900.

11. Crean report, December 11, 1899, NAC: RG 11, vol. 1307, #208490.

12. H.J. Woodside to Clifford Sifton, Minister of the Interior, June 18, 1899, NAC: RG 11, vol. 1289, #203948.

13. Telephone or telegraph wire can still be seen, as observed by the author during a hike in August 2000.

14. "Register of listing of interruptions June 1899–May 1900," YA: Federal Government Records Miscellaneous, vol. 1076, Ac. 77/6.

15. Crean to [DPW], January 8, 1900, NAC: RG 11, vol. 1307, #208875.

16. *Dawson Daily News*, October 3, 1899.

17. Ibid., September 22, 1899.

18. *Atlin Claim*, January 27, 1900.

19. The following account is from Allan Curtis, "The Christmas Day Murders," *Canadian West* (Fall 1988). See also "General Synopsis of the O'Brien Murder Case 1899–1901," NAC: RG 18, vol. 254.

20. See Chapter 4 for an account of Wells' journey over the Ashcroft Trail.

21. Hulet M. Wells, "Back Door to the Klondike," *Alaska Sportsman*, April to September 1960, in six parts.

22. Ibid.

23. Guy Lawrence, *40 Years on the Yukon Telegraph* (Vancouver: Mitchell Press, 1965; reprint, Quesnel, B.C.: Caryall Books, 1990).

24. *Alaska–Yukon Magazine* (April 1905).

Chapter 4

1. Adrien G. Morice, *The History of the Northern Interior of British Columbia* (W. Bragg, 1904; reprint, Fairfield, WA: Ye Galleon Press, 1971).

2. Rosemary Neering, *Continental Dash: The Russian–American Telegraph* (Ganges, B.C.: Horsdal & Schubart, 1989), is the source, unless otherwise noted, for the following history of the Collins Overland Telegraph.

3. Douglas Hill, *The Opening of the Canadian West* (London: Heinemann, 1967), 104.

4. S.J. Marsh and Robert Borland, *The Cariboo Trail*, undocumented article, BCA: Louis LeBourdais Collection, Ac. 676, Box 11.

5. Peter C. Newman quote on the cover of Neering's *Continental Dash*.

6. William F. Butler, *The Wild North Land: The Story of a Winter Journey, with Dogs across Northern North America* (Originally published in 1873; reprint, Edmonton: Hurtig, 1968), 333.

7. BCA: Map Collection, CM-B 96.

8. Gerald Chapman, "Exploring for the Telegraph in B.C.," *The Beaver* 66, no. 3 (May 1986), contains a letter from Pope in which he provides more details of his journey.

9. Canada, *Journals of the Senate*, 1898, vol. 33, Appendix 5, "Routes to the Yukon."

10. Hamlin Garland, *The Trail of the Goldseekers: A Record of Travel in Prose and Verse* (London: Macmillan, 1899).

11. Ibid., 100

12. Ibid., 108.

13. Ibid., 166.

14. Ibid., 181.

15. Ibid., 205-206.

16. This is not to say that they did not work from notes and diaries, but when there are discrepancies, Garland's account will be favoured.

17. Hulet M. Wells, "Back Door to the Klondike," *Alaska Sportsman*, [in six parts] April to September 1960.

18. Walter R. Hamilton, *The Yukon Story* (Vancouver: Mitchell Press, 1964), 11.

19. Ibid., 15.

20. Norman Lee, *Klondike Cattle Drive: The Journal of Norman Lee* (Vancouver: Mitchell Press, 1960; reprint, Surrey, B.C.: Heritage House, 1991).

21. Ibid., 16.

22. Ibid., 31

23. Ibid., xxiii.

Chapter 5

1. Robert Craig Brown, *Canada's National Policy 1883–1900: A Study in Canadian–American Relations* (Princeton: Princeton University Press, 1964), 302ff.

2. Glenora is a compound of the Gaelic *glen* (valley) and the Spanish *oro* (gold), meaning Valley of Gold.

3. Brown, *Canada's National Policy*, 308.

4. *Vancouver Province* and *Victoria Daily Colonist*, quoted in Larry Pynn, *The Forgotten Trail* (Toronto: Doubleday, 1996), 123–125.

5. The Chicago Record Company, *Klondike: The Chicago Record's Book for Gold-Seekers* quoted in *Dawson City Nugget*, n.d., 25ff.

6. *British Columbia Mining Record*, January 1898.
7. Selections from George Kirkendale's unpublished diary of his experiences on the Stikine Route in 1898, from R.M. Patterson, *Trail to the Interior* (Toronto: Macmillan, 1966), 93.
8. John W. Dafoe, *Clifford Sifton in Relation to His Times* (Toronto: Macmillan, 1931), 163. See also Ken S. Coates and William R. Morrison, *Land of the Midnight Sun: A History of the Yukon* (Edmonton: Hurtig, 1988), 109ff.
9. Canada, *House of Commons Debates*, 1902, vol. 62, 4860ff.
10. *Glenora News* masthead.
11. Ibid., June 13, 1898.
12. Ibid.
13. Walter N. Sage, ed., "'Record of a Trip to Dawson, 1898': The Diary of John Smith," *B.C. Historical Quarterly* 16, nos. 1 and 2 (1952).
14. John Windsor, "The Yukon Field Force," *British Columbia Digest* 19 (May/June, 1963).
15. Cheryl MacDonald, "From Founding to Frontier: The VON in the Klondike," *The Beaver* 77, no. 5 (October/November 1997), published on the occasion of the 100th anniversary of the VON, which had grown to 7,000 staff members in 71 branches across Canada.
16. Brereton Greenhous, ed., *Guarding the Goldfields: The Story of the Yukon Field Force* (Toronto: Dundurn Press, 1987).
17. Ian McCulloch, "Yukon Field Force 1898–1900," *The Beaver* 77, no. 5 (October/November 1997).
18. Windsor, "The Yukon Field Force."
19. MacDonald, "From Founding to Frontier."
20. Greenhous, *Guarding the Goldfields*, 124-125.
21. Guy Lawrence, *40 Years on the Yukon Telegraph* (Vancouver: Mitchell Press, 1965; reprint, Quesnel, B.C.: Caryall Books, 1990).
22. Ibid., 16.
23. *Glenora News*, July 1, 1898.
24. Ibid., June 17, 1898.
25. George Kirkendale, quoted in Patterson, *Trail to the Interior*, 95–96.

Chapter 6

1. Pierre Berton, *The Klondike Fever* (New York: Knopf, 1958), 164.
2. *Dawson Daily News*, August 5, 1899.
3. Company directors, especially Allan Haley, MP, argued their case in several letters to Minister Tarte and Prime Minister Laurier in April 1899, NAC: RG 11, vol. 1280; Laurier Papers, #32321–32353.
4. Originally incorporated on June 13, 1898, as the Dawson City and Victoria Telegraph Company, in December 1898 the directors reorganized as an English joint stock company. See prospectus in NAC: Laurier Papers, #30854ff.
5. Tarte to Laurier, December 13, 1899, NAC: Laurier Papers, #39800ff.
6. Tarte to Laurier, December 14, 1899, NAC: RG 11, vol. 1308, #208565.
7. Tarte to J. Morris Cotton, NAC: RG 11, vol. 1301, #206868.
8. "Statement of Claims" for compensation from the government, NAC: RG 11, vol. 1308.
9. Memo from R.W. Scott, MP, to [Gobeil], September 6, 1899, NAC: RG 11, vol. 1297.
10. Instruction written on report of Deputy Minister Gobeil, December 18, 1899, NAC: RG 11, vol. 1308, #208565.
11. Gobeil to Tarte, December 18, 1899.
12. Quoted in *Dawson Daily News*, August 17, 1917.
13. Before the branch to Atlin was built, the plan had been to proceed from Whitehorse to Teslin Lake and then to follow the Teslin Trail to Telegraph Creek.
14. Report of J.E. Gobeil, general inspector of the Yukon Telegraph, appended to "Report of the Government Telegraph Service," in Canada, *Sessional Papers*, 1908, No. 19.
15. Peter J. Leech, "The Pioneer Telegraph Survey of British Columbia," *The Mining Record* 5, no. 6 (August 1899).
16. Gobeil to Tarte, December 18, 1899. See also David Richeson, "The Yukon Telegraph: Construction of the Atlin to Quesnel Section 1900–1901," *B.C. Historical News* 15, no. 2 (Winter 1982).

17. Charleson to Gobeil, February 17, 1900, NAC: RG 11, vol. 1318.

18. *Atlin Claim*, March 10, 1900.

19. Ibid., March 10, 17, and 24, 1900.

20. Ibid., March 24, 1900.

21. Ibid., March 31, 1900.

22. Ibid., April 7, 1900. For these and later criticisms, Charleson labelled the *Atlin Claim* a tool of the Conservative Party, and referred to it as a "rag."

23. Ibid., March 31, 1900.

24. Ibid., April, 28 1900.

25. Charleson to Gobeil, June 12, 1900, NAC: RG 11, vol. 1339.

26. Ibid.

27. Report of Charles Adamson to Gobeil, January 19, 1900, NAC: RG 11, vol. 1309, #208961.

28. Charleson to Gobeil, May 13, 1900, NAC: RG 11, vol. 1339.

29. Ibid.

30. In several messages to Gobeil in April 1900, Charleson admonishes Ottawa for sending supplies to the wrong depots against his instructions, NAC: RG 11, vol. 1326.

31. *Victoria Colonist*, October 2, 1900.

32. Ibid.

33. Charleson to Gobeil, October 26, 1900, NAC: RG 11, vol. 1359.

34. Canada, *House of Commons Debates*, May 5, 1902, 4151.

35. Charleson to Gobeil, May 13, 1900.

36. Charleson to Gobeil, October 26, 1900.

37. Canada, *House of Commons Debates*, May 2 and 5, 1901.

38. Ibid.

39. George Woodcock, *Faces from History: Canadian Profiles and Portraits* (Edmonton: Hurtig, 1978).

40. Auditor General to DPW, December 13, 1900, NAC: RG 11, vol. 1364, #220969.

41. Clerk of the Public Accounts Committee to [DPW], March 27, 1901, NAC: RG 11, vol. 1384, #224673.

42. Charleson to DPW, May 13, 1901.

43. Gobeil to Charleson, May 14, 1901, NAC: RG 11, vol. 1394, #226668.

44. *Vancouver Province*, May 13, 1901.
45. Charleson to DPW, May 21, 1901, NAC: RG 11, vol. 1394, #226675.

Chapter 7

1. Charleson to Gobeil, November 22, 1900, NAC: RG 11, vol. 1363, #220658.
2. David Richeson, "The Yukon Telegraph: Construction of the Atlin to Quesnel Section 1900–1901," *B.C. Historical News* 15, no. 2 (Winter 1982). Although Charleson reported that the scheme to use dogsleds was tried, there is no evidence that the intermediate stations were staffed with linemen, which would have been essential to keep the telegraph operating.
3. Charleson to Gobeil, November 22, 1900.
4. "Sketch Map Showing Parts of Quesnelle–Atlin Telegraph Line Constructed and Part Remaining to be Built, To accompany report of J.B. Charleson, November 22, 1900, Prepared by Aurelien Boyer, In Charge of Location of Line," Charleson to Gobeil, November 22, 1900.
5. Charleson to Gobeil, July 17, 1901, NAC: RG 11, vol. 1416, #232029.
6. *Vancouver Province*, May 13, 1901.
7. Ibid.; Charleson to Gobeil, May 20, 1901, NAC: RG 11, vol. 1395, #226861.
8. Charleson to DPW, March 23, 1901, NAC: RG 11, vol. 1384, #224661.
9. *Vancouver Province*, September 14, 1901.
10. Charleson to DPW, May 13, 1901, NAC: RG 11, vol. 1394, #226662.
11. Charleson to DPW, June 14, 1901, NAC: RG 11, vol. 1396, #227157.
12. Charleson to Gobeil, July 17, 1901.
13. Martha W. Boss [O'Neill], "A Tale of Northern British Columbia," BCA: MSS. 771.
14. Ibid.
15. Ibid.
16. Charleson to Gobeil, May 20, 1901.

17. Charleson to Gobeil, July 17, 1901.
18. Charleson to Gobeil, August 29, 1901, NAC: RG 11, vol. 1411, #230934.
19. Diamond Jenness, "The Yukon Telegraph Line," *Canadian Geographical Journal*, December 1930.
20. *Vancouver Province*, September 26, 1901.
21. NAC: Laurier Papers, #59123.
22. Louis LeBourdais, "On the Yukon Telegraph Line," *Maclean's*, October 15, 1932.
23. Canada, *House of Commons Debates*, May 2, 1901.

Chapter 8

1. Canada, *Sessional Papers*, 1905, No. 19, DPW Annual Report.
2. *Vancouver Province*, September 14, 1901.
3. Canada, *House of Commons Debates*, May 5, 1902, 4151–54.
4. At this time telephone technology was not sufficiently developed to replace telegraph and was prone to error. The one-wire grounding system may also have been unsuitable for clear voice transmission.
5. Canada, *Sessional Papers*, 1902, No. 19, DPW Annual Report.
6. Crean to Gobeil, May 5, 1902, NAC: RG 11, vol. 1452, #242034. Subsequent DPW lists of employees in annual reports do not indicate any staff reductions at the three stations.
7. Congdon to Tarte, July 25, 1902, NAC: RG 11, vol. 1464, #245661.
8. Tarte to Congdon, July 29, 1902, NAC: RG 11, vol. 1464, #245663.
9. Tarte to F. White, Comptroller NWMP, August 5, 1902, NAC: RG 11, vol. 1464, #245666.
10. *Dawson Daily News*, September 3, 1902.
11. Ibid., August 9, 1902.
12. *Vancouver Province*, August 21, 1902.
13. Ibid., July 10, 1903.
14. The following details of Gobeil's inspections, unless otherwise noted, are from his reports in the DPW annual reports: Canada, *Sessional Papers*, 1907, 1908, 1909, No. 19.
15. Edward Broderick, "The Little Cabin on Bobtail Lake," *Victoria Daily Colonist* "Islander," August 2, 1964.

16. Years after the line was abandoned, the station was moved to the Vanderhoof Historic Village.

17. G.E. Gooding to Louis LeBourdais, May 7, 1928, BCA: Louis LeBourdais Collection, Ac. 676.

Chapter 9

1. H. Glynn-Ward, *The Glamour of British Columbia* (Toronto: Doubleday, 1932), 113.
2. John Dore to Louis LeBourdais, n.d., BCA: Louis LeBourdais Collection, Ac. 676.
3. Louis LeBourdais, "On the Yukon Telegraph Line," *Maclean's*, October 15, 1932.
4. Ibid.
5. *Vancouver Sun*, March 28, 1942.
6. Crean to DPW, March 27, 1902, NAC: RG 11, vol. 1442, #239527.
7. Account prepared by Louis LeBourdais, based on a letter from an unidentified telegraph man, included in his collection of recollections of life on the Yukon Telegraph, LeBourdais Collection.
8. Ibid.
9. Robert Service, *Ballad of a Cheechako* (Toronto: William Briggs, 1909).
10. Canada, *Sessional Papers*, 1907, No. 19, DPW Annual Report. Charleson's earlier report that the span was 1,600 feet must have been inaccurate.
11. Louis LeBourdais Collection.
12. Martha W. Boss [O'Neill], "A Tale of Northern British Columbia," BCA: MSS 771.
13. Canada, *Sessional Papers*, 1905, No. 19, DPW Annual Report. The inscription on Lanktree's tombstone reads: "Wm S. Lanktree / of Stirling, Ont. / b. May 28, 1876 / Drowned / Rink Rapids / June 9, 1904."
14. Louis LeBourdais, "On The Yukon Telegraph Line."
15. R.G. McKay, letter to the editor of *Maclean's* magazine in response to an earlier article about Heinz's death, n.d., LeBourdais Collection.

16. William Clark to Louis LeBourdais, March 21, 1926, LeBourdais Collection.
17. Guy Lawrence, *40 Years on the Yukon Telegraph* (Vancouver: Mitchell Press, 1965; reprint, Quesnel, B.C.: Caryall Books, 1990), 40.
18. *Vancouver Province* article, n.d., LeBourdais Collection.
19. Ibid.
20. Provincial Constable Sperry Cline's recollections of Cataline during his later years, written in March 1959 and published on the website "Cataline's Packtrail" (http://packtrail.com/index.html).
21. Glynn-Ward, *The Glamour of British Columbia.*

Chapter 10

1. An unidentified source quoted by Louis LeBourdais, BCA: Louis LeBourdais Collection, Ac. 676.
2. Louis LeBourdais, "On the Yukon Telegraph Line," *Maclean's*, October 15, 1932. In *40 Years on the Yukon Telegraph*, Guy Lawrence recalls that the test was conducted in September, but his memory is sometimes suspect.
3. Louis LeBourdais, "On the Yukon Telegraph Line."
4. William John "Wiggs" O'Neill also published books about steamships on the Skeena River.
5. Martha W. Boss [O'Neill], "A Tale of Northern British Columbia," BCA: MSS #771.
6. Guy Lawrence, *40 Years on the Yukon Telegraph* (Vancouver: Mitchell Press, 1965; reprint, Quesnel, B.C.: Caryall Books, 1990), 56.
7. Hugh Bostock, interview by [Yukon Archives], tape, YA: Ac. 88/59R.
8. Verna Carson (née Vernon), interview by Dwight Dodge, in his manuscript history of the Yukon Trail. Author's files.
9. Guy Lawrence, *40 Years*, 112.
10. Ibid., 45
11. Ibid., 49.
12. Ibid., 52ff.
13. Norman Fisher, interview by [Atlin Historical Society], 1976, AHS. Fisher also did the mail run from Carcross Station on

the White Pass to Atlin. Although a much shorter run, it was more dangerous because it went over lake and river ice that could be treacherous. Fisher felt that it was one of the most difficult mail runs in Canada. This bit of postal history has been commemorated every year since 1975 by the 75-mile Carcross to Atlin Mail Dogsled Run, with mushers carrying commemorative envelopes to raise money for charity.

14. Guy Lawrence, *40 Years*, 60.
15. J.J. Dore to Louis LeBourdais, January 8, 1937, LeBourdais Collection.
16. Almost 100 years later, pieces of a meteorite landed on the ice not far from Atlin, gaining worldwide attention.
17. At the time the cabin was actually at Tedideech Creek, half a mile from Nahlin.
18. Guy Lawrence, *40 Years*, 85.
19. Ibid., 86.

Chapter 11

1. David R. Morrison, *The Politics of the Yukon Territory, 1898–1909* (Toronto: University of Toronto Press, 1968), Appendixes A and B. Morrison warns that the numbers for gold production are only approximations, since many of the operators did not report their total outputs to the collectors of royalties. Between 1901 and 1911 the population of the Yukon declined from 27,219 to 8,513. Gold production went from $22.3 million in 1900 to $4.6 million in 1910, and to $1.9 million in 1918. These patterns continued in subsequent years.
2. Guy Lawrence, *40 Years on the Yukon Telegraph* (Vancouver: Mitchell Press, 1965; reprint, Quesnel, B.C.: Caryall Books, 1990), 83.
3. Canada, *Sessional Papers*, 1909, DPW Annual Report.
4. F.A. Talbot, *The New Garden of Canada: By Pack-Horse and Canoe through Undeveloped New British Columbia* (Toronto: Cassell and Co., 1911), 177ff.
5. The identity of the lineman and his station is a mystery. Talbot's description suggests that he lived with his wife somewhere between Burns Lake and Fraser Lake.

6. Canada, *Sessional Papers*, 1910, DPW Annual Report.
7. Ibid., 1912, 1913.
8. Ibid., 1914.
9. The following account of Lawrence's experiences are from Lawrence, *40 Years*.

Chapter 12

1. Hamlin Garland, *The Trail of the Goldseekers: A Record of Travel in Prose and Verse* (New York: Macmillan, 1899), 67.
2. There are several forms of the name, such as Gun-Ah-Noot. Gunanoot is used because it is on family gravestones in the Gitanmaax Cemetery at Hazelton.
3. David Ricardo Williams, *Trapline Outlaw* (Victoria: Sono Nis Press, 1982). See also Don Sawatsky, "Gun-An-Noot," *Yukoner Magazine*, no. 17 (March 2001).
4. Williams, *Trapline Outlaw*, 37.
5. Ibid., 23.
6. Sawatsky, "Gun-An-Noot."
7. Ibid.
8. After the Grand Trunk Pacific (GTP) was built westward through Prince George, a telegraph line was built to connect the growing town. Another effect of the railway was to make a section of the Skeena branch redundant, resulting in a 160-mile section being transferred to the Canadian National Railway (successor to the GTP).
9. Williams, *Trapline Outlaw*, 58.
10. H. Glynn-Ward, *The Glamour of British Columbia* (Toronto: Doubleday, 1932), 119ff.
11. C.W. Mitchell to Louis LeBourdais, December 14, 1929, BCA: Louis LeBourdais Collection, Ac. 676.
12. Guy Lawrence, *40 Years on the Yukon Telegraph* (Vancouver: Mitchell Press, 1965; reprint, Quesnel, B.C.: Caryall Books, 1990).
13. Peter Steele, *Atlin's Gold*, (Prince George, B.C.: Caitlin Press, 1995), 36.
14. LeBourdais Collection.
15. Ibid.
16. Guy Lawrence, *40 Years*, 105.

17. Georgiana Ball, "Telegraph Creek and the 1920 New York to Nome Flight." Author's files.
18. Ibid.
19. Ibid.
20. *Dawson News*, May 12–19, 1925; DPW Annual Report, 1926.
21. *Dawson News*, June 2, 1925.

Chapter 13

1. General Superintendent of Telegraphs to [Minister of Public Works], April 7, 1899, NAC: RG 11, vol. 1271, #200561.
2. M.O. Scott, "Marconi In Canada," *The Canadian Magazine* 18 (1901/1902), 338–340.
3. *Victoria Colonist*, August 23, 1906.
4. Canada, *Sessional Papers*, 1912, No. 19, Report of the Government Telegraph Service.
5. Under-Secretary of State to Commissioner of the Yukon Territory, August 8, 1911, YA: Gov. 2075, f.4, TS 8, vol. 5A.
6. G.P. MacKenzie to J.B. Hunter, September 15, 1921, NAC: RG 11, vol. 2842, #997-4-8.
7. J.E. Banks, "Electronic Limited," *RCMP Quarterly* 28, no. 4 (January 1963).
8. Ibid.
9. Dianne Green, *In Direct Touch with the Wide World: Telecommunications in the North 1865–1992* (Whitehorse: NorthwesTel, 1992), 20ff .
10. Ibid., 22.
11. *Victoria Colonist*, December 2, 1922.
12. *Toronto Daily Star*, March 15, 1924.
13. Gobeil to Hunter, May 13, 1924, and January 20, 1925, NAC: RG 11, vol. 2842, #997-55.
14. Ibid.
15. Hunter to O.S. Finnie, Director Northwest Territories and Yukon, Department of the Interior, January 23, 1925, NAC: RG 11, vol. 2842, #997-55.
16. Finnie to Hunter, February 12, 1925, NAC: RG 11, vol. 2842, #997-55.

17. Editor of *Dawson News* to Superintendent Government Telegraphs, April 4, 1925, NAC: RG 11, vol. 2842, #997-55.
18. J. H. King, Minister of Public Works, to William Sloan, Minister of Mines, June 4, 1925, NAC: RG 11, vol. 2842, #997-55.
19. Gobeil to Hunter, June 4, 1925, NAC: RG 11, vol. 2842, #997-55.
20. Hunter to Gobeil, NAC: RG 11, vol. 2842, #977-55.
21. Telegram from *Dawson News* to DPW, August 20, 1925, NAC: RG 11, vol. 2842, #977-55.
22. Business leaders to DPW, August 20, 1925, NAC: RG 11, vol. 2842, #977-55
23. George Black to King, July 17, 1925; King to Black, August 1, 1925; Black to King, August 26, 1925; King to Black, September 17, 1925, NAC: RG 11, vol. 2842, #977-55.
24. Desbarats to Hunter, September 21, 1925, NAC: RG 11, vol. 2842, #977-55.
25. Hunter to Desbarats, September 30, 1925, NAC: RG 11, vol. 2842, #977-55.
26. Desbarats to Hunter, November 13, 1925 (8 pages); Hunter to Desbarats, March 15, 1926 (9 pages), NAC: RG 11, vol. 2842, #977-55.

Chapter 14

1. Diamond Jenness, "The Yukon Telegraph Line," *Canadian Geographical Journal*, December 1930.
2. The high regard in which Jenness is held in the north is evidenced by places named after him, for example the purple high school in Fort Smith.
3. Jenness, "The Yukon Telegraph Line."
4. Ibid.
5. Edward Hoagland, *Notes From the Century Before: A Journal From British Columbia* (New York: Random House, 1969; reprint, Vancouver: Douglas and McIntyre, 1995), 113ff.
6. From John Sutherland's reminiscences of his life in the north, YA: Sutherland Collection, Ac. 82/200.
7. Caption on Sutherland photo titled "The Communist," Sutherland Collection.
8. Ibid.

9. Richard Morenus, *Alaska Sourdough: The Story of Slim Williams* (New York: Rand McNally, 1956).

Chapter 15

1. This account of Alling's journey is from Diane Solie Smith's pamphlet, *The Legend of Lillian Alling, The Woman Who Walked to Russia* (Atlin: AHS, 1997). Although there is little first-hand information about Alling, she has inspired numerous articles and one book: Cassandra Pybus, *The Woman Who Walked to Russia*.
2. Eric Janze, nephew of Charlie Janze, quoting his uncle, interview by author in the Hazelton Hospital, Hazelton, May 9, 2001. Author's files.
3. Ullman's story is based mostly on R.A. Diespecker's "When Lone B.C. Girl Faced Icy Death: Nurse Ullman, at 19, Cheated the Wilderness of its Prey," *Vancouver Province*, 1932, BCA: Louis LeBourdais Collection, Ac. 676, Box 12. The author, who claims the girl was German, includes extensive quotes attributed to Ullman, although he provides no information about when and where he interviewed her. Call it "creative journalism"?
4. LeBourdais Collection.
5. When Eighth Cabin was shut down in 1935, a clock, dating to the beginning of the telegraph, was brought out. It was inscribed with the names of many of the men who had been stationed there, and also the names of Minny Matheson and Thea Francis, NY, 1932, who were getting "colour for their stories." Thea in her letter does not mention a travelling companion.
6. Quotes in this section from Mary Joyce's obituary, *Southeast Alaska Empire*, July 28, 1976.

Chapter 16

1. Landry's articles appeared in *Alaska Sportsman* (later renamed *Alaska*), Sutherland's in *Alaska* and *The Northwest Digest*. Sutherland's manuscript autobiography is in the Yukon Archives. (See bibliography for lists of their articles.)
2. Richard Landry, "I'm a Wilderness Hermit," *Alaska Sportsman* 7, no. 10 (October 1941).

3. Richard Landry, "The Telegraph Trail," *Alaska*, November 1969.

4. The following accounts, unless otherwise noted, are from Sutherland's memoir, YA: Sutherland Collection, MSS 82/200.

5. The mailman's trail probably joined the telegraph line somewhat sooner along the Little Salmon River.

6. Caption on Sutherland's photo, Sutherland Collection.

Chapter 17

1. DPW Purchasing Agent to Salvage Officer, September 29, 1939, NAC: RG 11, vol. 2842, #997-55.

2. Ken S. Coates, *North to Alaska* (Toronto: McClelland and Stewart, 1992), 25ff.

3. *Anchorage Daily News*, October 10, 1999; video: "Slim and John's Great Adventure." Unless otherwise noted, the following account of their trip is from these two sources.

4. *Atlin News-Miner*, August 26, 1939.

5. Ernie Clifford, interview by author, Whitehorse, April 28, 2001. Author's files.

6. John Logan, interview by author, August 2001. Author's files.

7. Coates, *North to Alaska*, 20.

8. Archie Hunter, *Northern Traders: Caribou Hair in the Stew* (Victoria: Sono Nis Press, 1983), 98ff. Today the Dease Lake–Telegraph Creek road is still a hazardous trip, to be avoided in inclement weather.

9. Bruce McAllister and Peter Corley-Smith in *Wings Over the Alaska Highway* (Boulder: Roundup Press, 2001), lists 5,066 fighters, 1,495 bombers, 711 transports, and 54 training aircraft, 27.

10. R.M. Patterson, *Trail to the Interior* (Toronto: Macmillan, 1966), 231.

11. R. Brserst [*sic*], Division Superintendent, to General Superintendent, February 4, 1942, NAC: RG 11, vol. 2842.

12. *Vancouver Sun*, March 28, 1942, BCA: Louis LeBourdais Collection, Ac. 676.

13. J.E. Panter of Hazelton, September 10, 1945, quoted in Dianne Green, *In Direct Touch with the Wide World: Telecommunications in the North 1865–1992* (Whitehorse: NorthwesTel, 1992), 19.

Chapter 18

1. Canada, *Sessional Papers*, 1938, DPW Annual Report.
2. YA: Sutherland Collection, Ac. 82/200.
3. Sutherland revisited the area in the 1970s, motoring up the new Cassiar Highway and stopping at the site of his first station at Echo Lake. He took photos of the remains of the buildings, which had been flooded by a beaver dam.
4. Archie Hunter, *Northern Traders: Caribou Hair in the Stew* (Victoria: Sono Nis Press, 1983), 96.
5. Ibid., 100.
6. R.M. Patterson, *Trail to the Interior* (Toronto: Macmillan, 1966), 7ff.
7. Ibid., 10.
8. A.F. Buckham and B.A. Latour, "The Groundhog Coalfield, British Columbia," *Department of Mines, Geological Survey of Canada No. 16* (Ottawa: King's Printer, 1950), 75–80.
9. "Proposed Coast Highway to Alaska of Great International Importance," *Cariboo and Northwest Digest* 7, no. 6 (June 1951), reprinted from *Construction World*.
10. D.C. Schubert, Division Superintendent, to Controller of Communications, Department of Transportation, February 18, 1952, NAC: RG 12, vol. 2180, #7282-6.
11. Ibid.
12. "Report on Tour of British Columbia Division, June–July, 1952," and Inventory of Atlin B.C. station, NAC: RG 12, vol. 2180.
13. Canada, "Minutes of Cabinet Meeting," November 4, 1953, NAC: RG 2, vol. 2653.
14. S.A. Armstrong to M. Robertson, Department of Transportation, September 11, 1957, NAC: RG 11, vol. 2180.

Chapter 19

1. Jennifer Voss, *Klondike Trail: The Complete Hiking and Paddling Guide* (Whitehorse: Lost Moose Publishing, 2001).
2. Hikers on the Chilkoot Trail are asked to look but don't touch the numerous artifacts along the trail, and this admonition seems to be working. Similar respect and cooperation is needed to preserve the remains of the Yukon Telegraph.

3. Archie Hunter, *Northern Traders: Caribou Hair in the Stew* (Victoria: Sono Nis Press, 1983).
4. *Vancouver Sun*, September 17, 1958.
5. John Reed, "Atlin to Telegraph Creek," *Atlin Nugget*, January 26, 1979.
6. Vernon Frolick, *Descent Into Madness: The Diary of a Killer* (Surrey, B.C.: Hancock House, 1993). Frolick was a government prosecutor who had access to Oros's diaries, which the title implies this book was based upon. Non-diary events and dramatizations are not documented. Unless otherwise noted, the Oros story is from this source.
7. Linda Reed, interview by author, August 2001. Author's files. Reed spent time in the bush around Nahlin Station at the time Oros was in the area.
8. German hikers, interview by author, May 2001. Author's files.
9. Larry Pynn, *The Forgotten Trail: One Man's Adventure on the Canadian Route to the Klondike* (Toronto: Doubleday, 1996).
10. Bart deHaas, "Summary of an Eight Hundred Kilometre Backpacking Trip through The Northern Wilderness, in 1995." Author's files.
11. *Whitehorse Star*, August 4, 1999.
12. Ken Newman, "The Yukon Telegraph Trail/Line in the Kalum Forest District," report prepared for the Kalum Forest District, August 1995.
13. The helicopter visitors in 1975 were able to salvage some of the station's reports, now preserved in the Bulkley Valley Museum in Smithers.
14. Even so, the author found a pile of side blocks, most so weathered that the threads for the insulators had eroded away.
15. *Quesnel Cariboo Observer*, August 10, 1988. See also the Telegraph Trail Preservation Society Newsletter, www.telegraphtrail.org.

Bibliography

Selected Sources

Anderson, F.H. "Yukon Winter." *Alaska–Yukon Magazine* 1, (April 1905).

Ball, Georgiana. "An Overview of the History of the Stikine/ Cassiar Region up to 1930." Victoria: Planning, Research and Interpretation Division, Heritage Conservation Branch, Ministry of Provincial Secretary and Government Services, 1983.

Banks, J.E. "Electronic Limited." *RCMP Quarterly* 28, no. 4 (January 1963).

Berton, Pierre. *The Klondike Fever*. New York: Knopf, 1958.

Black, Robson. "A Telegraph Line in the Wilderness." *Popular Electricity Magazine* 5, no. 12 (April 1913).

Boss, Martha W. [O'Neill]. "A Tale of Northern British Columbia." BCA; MSS.771.

Broderick, Edward. "The Little Cabin on Bobtail Lake." *Victoria Daily Colonist* "Islander," August 2, 1964.

Bronson, William. *The Last Grand Adventure*. New York: McGraw-Hill, 1977.

Brown, Robert Craig. *Canada's National Policy 1883–1900: A Study in Canadian–American Relations*. Princeton: Princeton University Press, 1964.

Browne, Belmore. "Diary of a Trip up the Stikine River from July–November, 1902." Historical Manuscripts, Alaska State Library, Juneau, Alaska.

Buckham, A.F. and B.A. Latour. "The Groundhog Coalfield, British Columbia." *Department of Mines, Geological Survey of Canada No. 16*. Ottawa: King's Printer, 1950.

Burdick, Andrus Davis. "Diary of Trip up the Stikine River, March–July, 1898." Historical Manuscripts, Alaska State Library, Juneau, Alaska.

Butler, William F. *The Wild North Land: The Story of a Winter Journey, with Dogs Across Northern North America*. London, 1873. Reprint, Edmonton: Hurtig, 1968.

Campbell, Creighton. "The Unexplored Valley." *Alaska Sportsman* 12, no. 12 (December 1946).

Chapman, Gerald. "Exploring for the Telegraph in B.C." *The Beaver* 66, no. 3 (May 1986).

Coates, Ken S. *North to Alaska*. Toronto: McClelland and Stewart, 1992.

Coates, Ken S. and William R. Morrison. *Land of the Midnight Sun: A History of the Yukon*. Edmonton: Hurtig, 1988.

Connelly, Dolly. "The One World of Perry Collins." *The Beaver*, Summer 1971.

Curtis, Allan. "The Christmas Day Murders." *Canadian West*, 13 (Fall 1988).

Dafoe, John W. *Clifford Sifton in Relation to His Times*. Toronto: Macmillan, 1931.

Dawson, George M. *Report on an Exploration in the Yukon District, N.W.T. and Adjacent Northern Portion of British Columbia, 1887*. Montreal: Dawson Brothers, 1888. Reprint, Whitehorse: Yukon [Historical] Museum Association, 1987.

Deppermann, W.H. "Two Cents an Acre." *The North-American Review* 245 (1938).

Dickinson, Christine Frances and Diane Solie Smith. *Atlin: The Story of British Columbia's Last Gold Rush*. Atlin: Atlin Historical Society, 1995.

Disher, Arthur L. "The Long March of the Yukon Field Force." *The Beaver*, Autumn 1962.

Downs, Art. *British Columbia–Yukon Sternwheel Days*. Surrey, B.C.: Heritage House, 1992.

———. "Prince Rupert: Gateway to the Pacific Northwest." *Northwest Digest* 45 (November–December 1954).

———. *Wagon Road North*. Quesnel, B.C.: Northwest Digest, 1960.

Fitzgerald, Kathleen. "Collins Overland Telegraph." *History of the Canadian West* 1 (August 1985).

Fraser Lake and District Historical Society. *Deeper Roots and Greener Valley*. Vanderhoof, B.C..

Frolick, Vernon. *Descent Into Madness*. Surrey, B.C.: Hancock House, 1992.

Galbraith, John S. "Perry McDonough Collins at the Colonial Office." *B.C. Historical Quarterly* 17, nos. 5 and 6 (July and October 1953).

Garland, Hamlin. *The Trail of the Goldseekers: A Record of Travel in Prose and Verse*. London: Macmillan, 1899.

Glynn-Ward, H. *The Glamour of British Columbia*. Toronto: Doubleday, 1932.

Gomery, Percy. "The Side Door to the Klondike." *Journal of the Canadian Bankers' Association*, March 1923.

Green, Dianne. *In Direct Touch with the Wide World: Telecommunications in the North 1865–1992*. Whitehorse: NorthwesTel, 1992.

Greenhous, Brereton, ed. *Guarding the Goldfields: The Story of the Yukon Field Force*. Toronto: Dundurn Press, 1987.

Hamilton, Walter R. *The Yukon Story*. Vancouver: Mitchell Press, 1964.

Hancock, Lynn, ed. *Vanderhoof: "The Town That Wouldn't Wait."* Vanderhoof, B.C.: Nechako Valley Historical Society, 1979.

Hill, Douglas. *The Opening of the Canadian West*. London: Heinemann, 1967.

Hoagland, Edward. *Notes From the Century Before: A Journal From British Columbia*. New York: Random House, 1969. Reprint, Vancouver: Douglas and McIntyre, 1995.

Hunter, Archie. *Northern Traders: Caribou Hair in the Stew*. Victoria: Sono Nis Press, 1983.

Jenness, Diamond. "The Yukon Telegraph Line." *Canadian Geographical Journal*, December 1930.

Jennings, W.T. *Report on Routes to the Yukon*. Ottawa: S.E. Dawson, 1898.

Knowles, W.J. "Man Who Could Not Hang." *Shoulder Strap* [Journal of the British Columbia Provincial Police], Winter 1940.

Landry, Richard. "I'm a Wilderness Hermit." *Alaska Sportsman* 7, no. 10 (October 1941).

———. "Deep in the Cassiars." *Alaska Sportsman*, May 1943.

———. "The Telegraph Trail." *Alaska*, November 1969 and January 1970.

Lawrence, Guy. *40 Years on the Yukon Telegraph.* Vancouver: Mitchell Press, 1965. Reprint, Quesnel, B.C.: Caryall Books, 1990.

———. "And Some Are Still Looking." *Alaska Sportsman* 9, no. 4 (April 1943).

———. "Lost Bonanza." *Alaska Sportsman*, November 1955.

———. "Forty Years on the Yukon Telegraph." *Northwest Digest*, December 1960. Photos by John Sutherland.

———. "The Stikine Trail." *British Columbia Digest* 20, no. 6 (December 1964) and 21, no. 1 (February 1965).

———. "130 Pounds of Fighting?? Policeman." In *Off Patrol: Memories of British Columbia Provincial Policemen.* Surrey, B.C.: Heritage House, 1991.

LeBourdais, Louis. "On the Yukon Telegraph Line." *Maclean's*, October 15, 1932.

———. Louis LeBourdais Collection. BCA: Ac. 676.

Lee, Norman. *Klondike Cattle Drive: The Journal of Norman Lee.* Vancouver: Mitchell Press, 1960; reprint, Surrey, B.C.: Heritage House, 1991.

Leech, Peter J. "The Pioneer Telegraph Survey of British Columbia." *The Mining Record* 5, no. 6 (August 1899).

Leonard, John W. *The Gold Fields of the Klondike.* London: T. Fisher Unwin, 1897. Reprint, Whitehorse: Clairedge, 1994.

Lienweber, Martin. "Stumbling Stampeders." *Alaska Sportsman* 10, no. 3 (March 1944).

———. "Years on the Yukon." *Alaska Sportsman* 10, no. 4 (April 1944).

MacBride, W.D. "From Montana to the Klondyke." *Cariboo and Northwest Digest* 7, no. 4 (April 1951).

MacDonald, Cheryl. "From Founding to Frontier: The VON in the Klondike." *The Beaver* 77, no. 5 (October/November 1997).

Macdonald, Ian and Betty O'Keefe. *The Klondike's "Dear Little Nugget."* Victoria: Horsdal & Schubart, 1996.

MacDonald, Norbert. "Seattle, Vancouver and the Klondike." *Canadian Historical Review* 49, no. 3 (September 1968).

Mackay, Corday. "The Collins Overland Telegraph." *B.C. Historical Quarterly* 10, no. 3 (July 1946).

Malcolm, Murray J. *Murder in the Yukon: The Case Against George O'Brien*. Saskatoon: Western Producer Prairie Books, 1982.

McAllister, Bruce and Peter Corley-Smith. *Wings Over the Alaska Highway*. Boulder: Roundup Press, 2001.

McCulloch, Ian. "Yukon Field Force 1898–1900." *The Beaver* 77, no. 5 (October/November 1997).

Minter, Roy. *The White Pass: Gateway to the Klondike*. Toronto: McClelland and Stewart, 1987.

Money, Anton, with Ben East. *This Was the North*. New York: Crown, 1975.

Morenus, Richard. *Alaska Sourdough: The Story of Slim Williams*. New York: Rand McNally, 1956.

Morice, Adrien G. *The History of the Northern Interior of British Columbia*. W. Bragg, 1904. Reprint, Fairfield, WA: Ye Galleon Press, 1971.

Morrison, David R. *The Politics of the Yukon Territory, 1898–1909*. Toronto: University of Toronto Press, 1968.

Morrison, William R. *Showing the Flag: The Mounted Police and Canadian Sovereignty in the North, 1894–1925*. Vancouver: UBC Press, 1985.

Neering, Rosemary. *Continental Dash: The Russian–American Telegraph*. Ganges, B.C.: Horsdal & Schubart, 1989.

———. "The Line to Nowhere That Made a Difference." *Beautiful British Columbia* 32, no. 2 (Summer 1990).

Newell, Dianne. "The Importance of Information and Misinformation in the Making of the Klondike Gold Rush." *Journal of Canadian Studies* 21, no. 4 (Winter 1986/87).

Patterson, R.M. *Trail to the Interior*. Toronto: Macmillan, 1966.

Pynn, Larry. *The Forgotten Trail: One Man's Adventure on the Canadian Route to the Klondike*. Toronto: Doubleday, 1996.

Remley, David A. *Crooked Road: The Story of the Alaska Highway*. Toronto: McGraw-Hill, 1976.

Richardson, Bert. "Wilderness Trek." *Alaska Sportsman* 9, no. 8 (August 1943).

Richeson, David E. "The Yukon Telegraph: Construction of the Atlin to Quesnel Section 1900–1901." *B.C. Historical News* 15, no. 2 (Winter 1982).

———. "Canadian Government Involvement in Telegraphic Communications in Western Canada." *Journal of the West* 23, no. 4 (October 1984).

Sage, Walter N., ed. "'Record of a Trip to Dawson, 1898': The Diary of John Smith." *B.C. Historical Quarterly* 16, nos. 1 and 2 (1952).

Sawatsky, Don. "Gun-An-Noot." *Yukoner Magazine*, no. 17 (March 2001).

Scidmore, Eliza R. "Stikine River in 1898." *National Geographic Magazine* 10, no. 1 (January 1899).

Scott, M.O. "Marconi in Canada." *The Canadian Magazine*, 18 (1901/1902).

Service, Robert. *Ballad of a Cheechako*. Toronto: William Briggs, 1909.

Smith, Diane Solie. *The Legend of Lillian Alling, The Woman Who Walked to Russia*. Atlin: Atlin Historical Society, 1997.

Spurr, Edward. "From the Coast to the Golden Klondike." *Outing Magazine*, September 1897.

Steele, Peter. *Atlin's Gold*. Prince George, B.C.: Caitlin Press, 1995.

Stewart, Robert. *Sam Steele: Lion of the Frontier*. Toronto: Doubleday, 1979.

Sutherland, John. "The Snowshoe Horse." *Northwest Digest*, October 1957.

Talbot, F.A. *The New Garden of Canada: By Pack-Horse and Canoe through Undeveloped New British Columbia*. Toronto: Cassell and Co., 1911.

Turton, M. Conway. *Cassiar*. Toronto: Macmillan, 1934.

Voss, Jennifer. *Stikine River: A Guide to Paddling "The Great River."* Calgary: Rocky Mountain Books, 1998.

———. *Klondike Trail: The Complete Hiking and Paddling Guide*. Whitehorse: Lost Moose Publishing, 2001.

Wallace, Jim. *Forty Mile to Bonanza: The North-West Mounted Police in the Klondike Gold Rush*. Calgary: Bunker to Bunker, 2000.

Wells, Hulet M. "Back Door to the Klondike." *Alaska Sportsman*, in six parts, April to September 1960.

Williams, David Ricardo. *Trapline Outlaw*. Victoria: Sono Nis Press, 1982.

Windsor, John. "The Yukon Field Force." *British Columbia Digest* 19 (May/June 1963).

Woodcock, George. *Faces from History: Canadian Profiles and Portraits*. Edmonton: Hurtig, 1978.

Wright, Allen A. *Prelude To Bonanza: The Discovery and Exploration of the Yukon*. Sidney, B.C.: Gray's Publishing, 1977. Reprint, Whitehorse: Studio North, 1992.

Government Records
National Archives of Canada:
RG 2 Privy Council Office Records
RG 11 Department of Public Works
RG 12 Department of Transportation
RG 18 RCMP Records
MG-26G Laurier Papers
House of Commons Debates, 1901–1903
Journals of the Senate, 1898
Annual Report of the Department of Public Works, *Sessional Papers*, No.19, 1899–1941
Yukon Archives: Federal Government Records Miscellaneous.

Newspapers
Atlin Claim, 1899-1900
Dawson Daily News, 1899-1917
Glenora News, 1898
Quesnel Cariboo Observer, 1988
Toronto Daily Star, 1924
Vancouver Province, 1899-1902
Vancouver Sun, 1942, 1958
Victoria Colonist, 1899-1922
Whitehorse Star, 1999

Photo and Map Credits

Alaska Historical Library p. 233 (PCA 67-24B)

Atlin Historical Society Archives pp. 96 (P-1711), 161 (P-2685), 164 (P-2129), 212 (P-2692), 223 (Marie Murphy), 229 (P-767), 230 (Marie Murphy), 242 (P-274), 244 (P-283), 268 (P-372)

BC Archives pp. 24 (F-3352), 26 (F-3353), 37 (F-03366), 43 (F-3390), 78 top (D-09027), 83 (D-06932), 98 (I-76424), 117 top (I-61616) bottom (F-3379), 132 (D-00450), 140 (I-51525), 148 (I-61625), 150 (F-03374), 153 (I-51525), 171 (G-09469), 176 (G-06434), 184 (A-07788), 192 (C-08538), 194 (I-61619), 261 (H-06842), 272 (I-67706)

Bulkley Valley Museum pp. 173, 289

Downs, Art *Wagon Road North* p. 58

Frolick, Vernon *Descent into Madness* p. 280

Glenbow Archives pp. 17 (NA-1052-3.1), 78 bottom (NA-1052-20)

Hamilton, Walter *The Yukon Story* p. 70

Harvey, R.G. *Carving the Western Path* p. 69

Hazelton Pioneer Museum pp. 205, 225

Lee, Norman *Klondike Cattle Drive* pp. 71, 73

Logan. John p. 259

Miami University (Ohio) Library p. 64

Miller, Bill pp. 60, 286, 292

National Archives of Canada pp. 13 (PA-027977), 40 (C-018641), 53 (RG 18, Vol. 254, f. 318), 80 (PA-209377), 84 (PA-206928), 110 (RG11, Vol. 1363), 135 (PA-95734)

Northwest Digest, November/December 1954 p. 169

Nova Scotia Museum p. 197

Remley, David *Crooked Road, The Story of the Alaska Highway* p. 255

Royal Canadian Regiment Archives p. 18

Vancouver Public Library p. 100 (316 Lance Burdon)

Yukon Archives pp. 29 (2484), 158 (3862), 193 (9411), 218 (Sutherland Collection 82/200, #364), 220 (R.C. Coutts Collection, #237, 78/69), 247 (Sutherland Collection 82/200, #240), 267 (Sutherland Collection 82/200, #277)

Index

Index

O'Neill, Martha Washington Boss (operator) 114-16, 145-46, 158-59
O'Neill, Wiggs (operator) 159
Ogilvie, Scottie (operator) 224-25
Ogilvie Island 36 195
Olsen, Lawrence (lineman) 52-54
150 Mile House, B.C. 124, 177
Operators and linemen 41-47, 125, 139; conditions of work 115-16, 125-26, 139-41, 145-51, 159, 161-62, 188-90; 1902 strike 125-29; retirement 266
Order of the Midnight Sun 16
Order of Pioneers of Alaska 234
Oros, Michael (Shesley Free Mike) 279-82, 284
Outfitters, big game hunting 228, 270, 280-81, 283-84, 285
Packers and pack trains 62, 81, 102, 149-55; provisioning stations 45-46, 149-51, 188-89, 207
Paddy Lake 242
Patronage 24-25, 104
Patterson, Janet 271-72
Patterson, R.M. 262
Pavillion, B.C. 125
Perry, A. Bowen (NWMP superintendent) 48
Phelan, John T. (YT division superintendent) 114, 144-45, 156-58, 160, 166-67, 169, 175-76, 181, 189, 191, 208-9
Philippon, Armel 216-17
Pike River 97
Pinkerton Detective Agency 186
Pioneer Cemetery (Whitehorse) 146
Poems: "Yukon Winter" by F.H. Anderson 55; "The Goldseekers" by Hamlin Garland 66; "The Telegraph Operator" by Robert Service 143
Poison Mountain 134
Poles, number of 133, 135-36
Pope, Franklin 60, 94
Port Essington 113
Port Simpson Branch 112-17, 123-24, 158, 177. See also Prince Rupert Branch
Portland Canal 112, 177
Powell, Georgina (nurse) 84-85
Prince George, B.C. 169-70, 181
Prince Rupert, B.C. 169
Prince Rupert branch 124, 172, 174-77, 265
Privy Council 19-20
Public Accounts Committee, House of Commons 106-8

Public Works, department of 21, 91, 101, 122, 141, 253, 274; annual reports, 144-45, 159; wireless service 251
Pynn, Larry The Forgotten Trail, 283-85
Quesnel, B.C. 38, 59, 62, 93, 95, 100, 124, 130, 179
Quesnel Forks branch. See Horsefly branch
Radio. See wireless
Railways, proposed: Glenora-Teslin Lake 76, 79; Cassiar Central 86; to Alaska 273-74
Raspberry Pass 94
Reed, Harper 189, 243
Refuge cabins 47, 130, 243, 249
Reid, James 62-63, 73
Relfe, Linn (or Lynn) 52-54
Richardson, J.F. (construction supervisor) 23
Ricord, Frank (construction foreman) 34
Rink Rapids 20, 34, 146
Rochester, J.Y. (construction superintendent) 97-98, 101, 105, 108, 110-11, 116, 118, 129
Royal Canadian Corps of Signals (RCCS) 200-210, 274-75
Royal Canadian Mounted Police (RCMP) 265, 281, 282
Royal North-West Mounted Police 185, 199
"Russian Communist, The" 218-19
Ryan, Corporal Patrick 52
Salmon Lake Indian Reserve 243-44
Saloon (camp on Teslin Trail) 283
Schubert, D.C. (DOT division superintendent) 275
Scows, Construction (barges) 26-28, 30
Selwyn 35, 41
Senate 63, 79
Service, Robert 143
Seybold Company of Great Britain 95
Shesley River 81, 280
Shields, J.C. (contractor) 124
Simon River 111
Six Mile River 20, 26-28
Skagway, AK 15-16, 18-19, 23, 28, 38, 48, 80, 88, 95
Skeena Mountains 61
Skeena River 59, 61, 65, 94, 112-16, 145-46, 169, 174-76, 188
Smith, George 188-89
Smith, Hackley 230, 233

Bill Miller lives with his wife, Nancy Lee, in the old gold-rush town of Atlin in northern British Columbia. He became intrigued by the historic Yukon Telegraph when he learned that it passed through the area. He has worked as a civil engineer and a history teacher, most recently as a university archivist. Now retired, he welcomes the opportunity to explore his own historical studies.